A Criminal Power

A Criminal Power

James Baldwin and the Law

D. Quentin Miller

THE OHIO STATE UNIVERSITY PRESS | COLUMBUS

Library of Congress Cataloging-in-Publication Data

Miller, D. Quentin (Daniel Quentin), 1967–
A criminal power : James Baldwin and the law / D. Quentin Miller.
    p. cm.
Includes bibliographical references and index.
ISBN-13: 978-0-8142-1175-5 (cloth : alk. paper)
ISBN-10: 0-8142-1175-5 (cloth : alk. paper)
ISBN-13: 978-0-8142-9276-1 (cd-rom)
1. Baldwin, James, 1924–1987—Criticism and interpretation. 2. Race discrimination in
literature. 3. Law enforcement in literature. 4. Law in literature. I. Title.
PS3552.A45Z826 2012
818'.5409—dc23
                                2011025165

This book is available in the following editions:
Cloth (ISBN 978-0-8142-1175-5)
CD-ROM (ISBN 978-0-8142-9276-1)

Cover design by James A. Baumann
Type set in Adobe Sabon

∞ The paper used in this publication meets the minimum requirements of the American
National Standard for Information Sciences—Permanence of Paper for Printed Library Mate-
rials. ANSI Z39.48–1992.

9 8 7 6 5 4 3 2 1

CONTENTS

ACKNOWLEDGMENTS

No book, scholarly or otherwise, is written in solitude. I would like to thank some of the many people who have kept me company as I wrote *A Criminal Power*. David Leeming must be at the top of this list. As the man who introduced me to Baldwin's work some two decades ago, David has been instrumental in helping me understand Baldwin. He has also been incredibly generous answering my questions and pointing me in the direction of valuable sources of information over the years. Second on the list is Stavroula (Voula) Venetis, a graduate of Suffolk University who excelled as my dedicated research assistant during her senior year.

I also wish to acknowledge and thank a growing cadre of Baldwin scholars who have given me valuable feedback as I presented pieces of this work as conference papers over the years, and who are themselves doing excellent work on Baldwin. Cora Kaplan and Bill Schwartz of Queen Mary University, London, started a great tradition in 2007 when they organized a conference dedicated to Baldwin's work. This spectacular gathering of scholars inspired me to host a similar conference in Boston in 2009, and I am grateful to Dean Kenneth Greenberg for his support of the conference at Suffolk University. The tireless duo Rich Blint of New York University and Douglas Field of Staffordshire University followed with yet another splendid conference in New York in 2011. This is a very abbreviated list, but the following colleagues are recurrent voices at these conferences who have helped my project along in one way or another: Alliyah Abdur-Raman, Kevin Birmingham, Nigel de Juan Hatton, Lovalerie King,

Emily Lordi, Dwight McBride, Brian Norman, Lynn Orilla Scott, Richard Schur, Hortense Spillers, Çigdem Üsekes, Cheryl Wall, and Magdalena Zaborowska.

In addition to the three conferences on Baldwin, I have presented versions of this work at the Modern Language Association convention and at the American Studies Association convention and as invited talks at Western Connecticut State University and Michigan State University. I would also like to acknowledge the Schomburg Center in New York City for making available the Baldwin material in their collection. "The Fire Reignited" is an altered and expanded version of an essay titled "The Fire Next Time and the Law," which appeared originally in *African American Culture and Legal Discourse,* edited by Lovalerie King and Richard Schur (2009), reproduced with permission of Palgrave Macmillan. "Return to Exile" contains an altered version of the essay "'On the Outside Looking In': White Readers of Nonwhite Prison Narratives," which originally appeared in *Prose and Cons: Essays on Prison Literature in the United States* © 2005 Edited by D. Quentin Miller by permission of McFarland & Company, Inc., Box 611, Jefferson NC 28640. "No Room of One's Own" builds on an essay published in a collection entitled *James Baldwin: America and Beyond,* edited by Bill Schwarz and Cora Kaplan, University of Michigan Press, 2012.

At The Ohio State University Press, Sandy Crooms, Eugene O'Connor, and Louise Seiler have been superb and efficient editors who have streamlined the process.

Finally, for her ongoing support as my first reader and best critic, I'd like to thank my wife, Julie Nash, whose willingness to listen, to encourage, and to inspire makes all of my writing possible.

ABBREVIATIONS OF BALDWIN TITLES

AC—Another Country
Amen—The Amen Corner
BMC—Blues for Mister Charlie
CR—The Cross of Redemption: Uncollected Writings
D—A Dialogue (with Nikki Giovanni)
DFW—The Devil Finds Work
E—Evidence of Things Not Seen
FNT—The Fire Next Time
GM—Going to Meet the Man
GR—Giovanni's Room
GTI—Go Tell It on the Mountain
IBS—If Beale Street Could Talk
JB—Jimmy's Blues
LM—Little Man, Little Man
Nobody—Nobody Knows My Name
NN—No Name in the Street
NNS—Notes of a Native Son
NP—Nothing Personal
OD—One Day, When I Was Lost
PT—The Price of the Ticket
RR—A Rap on Race (With Margaret Mead)
TM—Tell Me How Long the Train's Been Gone

"A Criminal Power"

James Baldwin and the Law

IT IS DECEMBER 27, 1949. James Baldwin, just released from a French prison, stands on a chair. He is sweating as he holds a sheet in his hand, and he twists it, with bitterness and desperation, into a rope. He has left his home, his church, and his country in order to discover himself. He has published a short story, a dozen reviews, and a pair of essays. He is twenty-five years old. He has spent the past eight days in jail because an acquaintance brought a stolen sheet into his room.

The water pipe above his head is as revolting as everything else in this fleabag hotel. As in the house of John Grimes, the protagonist of the novel he is working on, there is dirt everywhere; dust rising all around him; no end to it. Even the City of Lights offers no hiding place from the world's dirt, from the chaotic complexity of human consciousness. Aware that black American men have been dying with nooses around their necks for centuries now, Baldwin fashions his own hanging rope with bitterness, with tears in his eyes. The young, black, bisexual, expatriate writer destined to become famous, to appear on the cover of *Time* magazine, to be known as the spokesman for his race in its crucial hour, to be regarded as a prophet, a witness, a transcendent spirit, tosses the twisted sheet over the rusty pipe, secures it around his neck, and jumps.

When the water pipe breaks in the Grand Hôtel du Bac that day, Baldwin is saved, even "rebaptized by the flood," as biographer David Leeming says.[1] The incident that caused Baldwin to spend over a week in jail before being laughed out of the French courts becomes the subject of an

1

early essay called "Equal in Paris," and his early suicide attempt is deeply buried beneath an impressive mountain of work.[2] His career flourishes for nearly four decades, reaching a high point in the early 1960s. His death in 1987, though premature, becomes an occasion for celebration of the life rescued from what could have been the truly premature death in 1949 that would have rendered his life a tragedy. A tragedy like Richard's death in *Go Tell It on the Mountain,* like Rufus's death in *Another Country,* like Giovanni's death in *Giovanni's Room,* like Richard's death in *Blues for Mister Charlie.* These characters, not coincidentally, have all served time in jail and/or have been systematically scrutinized and monitored by the police. Like Baldwin, they have all felt the terrifying effects of the law's power first-hand. Artists are somehow able to survive in Baldwin's fiction, to get a second chance on life after prison as Baldwin did when the water pipe broke, like Sonny in "Sonny's Blues," or like Fonny in *If Beale Street Could Talk.*

Art may act as the most enduring form of salvation for characters in Baldwin's work, but for every black artist who survives the humiliation and degradation of police brutality, unfair legal trials, and wrongful imprisonment, there are many more black non-artists who do not, some of whom live in a bitter or damaged state, others of whom commit suicide. Baldwin's prison experience brings into focus a theme that flourishes throughout his career. These eight days in Paris clarified for him the reality of the law's power to subjugate individuals and to preserve societal hierarchies. Baldwin's life work becomes a thorough interrogation of the law's power and the way it affects the lives of people like him. His early essay "Many Thousands Gone," which advances his aesthetic through a critique of Richard Wright's *Native Son,* speaks of the necessity of combating stereotypical images of African American life and pursuing instead a deeper understanding. Wright's Bigger Thomas, in Baldwin's mind, had no agency, and was not rendered subtly or with sufficient human complexity in Wright's novel. Baldwin perhaps experienced such terror in Paris because he felt trapped and without agency, like Bigger, and he was determined to render his characters in as much human depth as he was capable of, not only to redirect the trajectory of African American literature, but to combat the capacities of the legal, judicial, and penal systems to define black men. In fact, Baldwin's entire career can be seen as an attempt to revise *Native Son,* a novel of crime and punishment, filled with sensational courtroom drama yet devoid of any real articulation by the accused criminal of the forces that have shaped him, or of his own role in shaping his own identity. Bigger's emotional experience essentially never develops beyond fear; Baldwin's response to the law and to the forces that shape it is a lifelong journey that develops from fear to outrage, and ultimately into a sense of autonomy, transcendence above the law's force, and empowerment through the development of a voice that blends the sensibility of a literary artist with the authoritative rhetoric of a lawyer.

In Baldwin's work, the dehumanizing effects of incarceration can only be fought through a lifelong commitment to writing about the lives of the incarcerated, and not "solely in social terms" (*NNS* 33), as he says of Wright's novel. As his thinking evolves, Baldwin looks at the law not only in terms of incarceration, but in terms of the way the division symbolized by incarceration is replicated in society and regulated in the courts. Wright's novel, a blunt test case for the intersection of law and literature, emphasizes Bigger's crime and his trial, during which he is virtually mute, and deemphasizes his period of incarceration. In contrast to Baldwin, Bigger's awareness of his place in society does not fully come to life in prison. Part of Baldwin's purpose in his lifelong commitment to this subject is to illuminate the feelings of powerlessness associated with incarceration as a way of departing from Bigger, who experiences a fatalistic sense of relief when he is caught and put in jail. Initially, Baldwin's time in jail aligns him with the "victims" H. Bruce Franklin describes in *The Victim as Criminal and Artist*: "Their art expresses the experience of being legally kidnapped, plundered, raped, beaten, chained, and caged—and the understanding that results."[3] It is this understanding that provides Baldwin with keen insight into the legal system and into the social power structure that serves as its foundation.

In this book I will examine Baldwin's life and virtually all of his works in the context of the law. I am defining "the law" broadly to include two of its main connotations: (1) jurisprudence, or the official history of policies and legal decisions that comprise the American legal system, and (2) the common perception of the law as a potentially menacing regulatory force represented by police, corrections officers, juries, and prisons. Both of these facets of the law represent for Baldwin the potential for those in power to sustain their position of privilege while oppressing those who do not have it: the poor, the black, the immigrant, the homosexual, the artist, the drug addict—in short, the hero-victims of Baldwin's work. These figures, whether real or fictional, illustrate the principle that the law's power is far from abstract. Over the course of his career Baldwin demonstrates how first-hand experience with incarceration and police brutality constitutes one dimension of the law's power, and that these physical forces can be transcended through a thorough understanding of the way they interact with the law's rhetorical and theoretical manifestations, such as courtroom trials and Supreme Court decisions.

In a number of important ways, Baldwin anticipates the rhetoric of the leftist legal movement known as Critical Legal Studies (CLS) and its close relative, Critical Race Theory (CRT). James Boyle, in his introduction to his edited collection *Critical Legal Studies*, admits that the proponents of this movement "are a diverse group," but that "they are generally marked by a commitment to a more egalitarian society and a dissatisfaction with current legal scholarship."[4] In general, CLS, a movement that developed in the late 1970s and flourished in the 1980s and 1990s, is committed to merging progressive ideologies with legal studies both in theory and in practice. Robert W. Gordon distinguishes CLS from Marxist lawyers and other left-wing legal thinkers such as the National Lawyers Guild; he writes, "For [adherents of CLS], law is neither a ruling class game plan nor a repository of noble if perverted principles. It is a plastic medium of discourse that subtly conditions how we experience social life."[5] According to Gordon's summary, CLS is built upon a few basic beliefs: (1) that legal discourses are discourses of power, (2) that legal discourses rationalize and justify the existing social order, and (3) that legal discourses have the power to legitimate because they posit visions of an ideal society even as they uphold the status quo of an actual, imperfect society.[6] From this perspective, the law is commonly idealized and not scrutinized deeply enough by the average citizen; legal scholar David Kairys writes, "The idealized model, the notion of technical expertise, and the notion of the law as neutral, objective, and quasi-scientific lend legitimacy to the judicial process, which in turn lends a broader legitimacy to the social and power relations and ideology that are reflected, articulated, and enforced by the courts."[7] The essential impulse of CLS is akin to the theoretical fields of deconstruction and New Historicism in literary studies: that is, to expose the contradictions in established institutions and to reveal the power dynamics under the surface of these institutions. Insofar as these theoretical movements are used to critique society, Baldwin anticipates them in his writing throughout his career, viewing the law from perspectives that range from the intensely personal to the broadly sociological, and rendering his critiques with his trademark intelligence, passion, and clarity.

One important article that helps to map Baldwin's gradual shift in thinking from a powerless, alienated individual to a powerful, sophisticated thinker on the subject of the law is "Building Power and Breaking Images: Critical Legal Theory and the Practice of Law" by Peter Gabel and Paul Harris. Gabel and Harris argue "that the legal system is an important public arena through which the State attempts—through manipulation of symbols, images, and ideas—to legitimize a social order that most people find alienating and inhumane. Our objective is to show the way that the legal system works at many different levels to shape popular consciousness toward accepting the political legitimacy of the status quo, and to outline the ways that lawyers can effectively resist these efforts in building a movement for fundamental social change."[8] Although Baldwin was obviously not a lawyer, his ultimate role in "building a movement for fundamental social change" through writing was clear by the end of his career. Without the benefit of a law degree, or any degree, Baldwin had to learn the lessons advanced in Gabel's and Harris's theory first-hand, through experience and observation. The efforts of creative writers and lawyers can co-exist comfortably and productively; as Barry Schaller writes, "Our national literature represents a living history and analysis of the universal legal themes of order and disorder, individual and community, liberty and responsibility, and their changes. The writers of imaginative literature, deeply engaged in perceiving, compressing, analyzing, and reformulating the forces at work in our society, have presented us with blueprints for our task of preserving, reconstituting, and revitalizing a free, civil, and humane society."[9]

Gabel's and Harris's theory, exemplary of CLS, has its parallel in literary studies in neo-Marxist or New Historicist theories such as those inspired by the writings of Michel Foucault. Just as Baldwin rejects strains of naturalism and Marxism in *Native Son,* the CLS movement eyes with suspicion Marxism's tendencies to view individuals primarily through social forces. Gabel and Harris describe their perspective this way: "A central feature of this strand of radical thought has been a shift of focus away from the tendency of classical Marxism to explain all aspects of social life as resulting from 'underlying' economic factors, such as ownership and control of the means of production. While not disregarding the importance of economic factors, neo-Marxist theory places much greater emphasis on social alienation in shaping the contours of social life and argues for a theory of politics that makes the overcoming of alienation a central political objective."[10] In Baldwin's experience, overcoming the alienation he felt as a victim of the law's power in Paris was a painstaking and lifelong process. For him, it was not necessarily a "political objective" so much as a personal struggle, yet the result is the same: the strengthening of his convictions over time led to empowerment with regard to the law, and the characters, fictional or real, who people his later works are a far cry from the terrified young man who fashioned his own hanging rope after being released from jail. The transformation is explained less by the triumphs of the Civil Rights movement of the 1950s and 1960s than by a fundamental shift in Baldwin's thinking.

CLS, like Foucault's work, focuses on power rather than the more traditional legal emphasis on rights. This change in emphasis gradually helped to catalyze CRT, a more radical and specifically racialized outgrowth of CLS. Cornel West writes of how Critical Race Theorists "confronted the relative silence of legal radicals—namely critical legal studies writers—who 'deconstructed' liberalism, yet seldom addressed the role of deep-seated racism in American life."[11] The "liberalism" West refers to is the legacy of the Civil Rights movement itself, which CRT scholars regard with "deep dissatisfaction" even as they acknowledge its groundbreaking necessity.[12] Critical Race Theorists felt that the well-intentioned aims of CLS scholars were too focused on changing the conservative culture of law schools and not focused enough on changing the culture of American society more generally. CRT pushed CLS scholars to scrutinize the way power is manifested in institutions that shape lives, especially in terms of the way the law not only reflects but produces racial power, sometimes referred to as "white supremacy" in their rhetoric.[13] Patricia J. Williams, in her essay "The Pain of Word Bondage," uses an anecdote about a shared experience she had with Peter Gabel as an opportunity to meditate on what she sees as the shortcomings of CLS, particularly in the way it moves away from rights; she writes, "while the goals of CLS and of the direct victims of racism may be much the same, what is too often missing is acknowledgment that our experiences of the same circumstances may be very different; the same symbol may mean different things to each of us. At this level, the insistence of certain scholars that the 'needs' of the oppressed should be emphasized rather than their 'rights' amounts to no more than a word game."[14] She goes on to say that "rights rhetoric has been and continues to be an effective form of discourse for blacks" and identifies "the battle" for black people as "not deconstructing rights, in a world of no rights; nor of constructing statements of need, in a world of abundantly apparent need. Rather the goal is to find a political mechanism that can confront the denial of need. The argument that rights are disutile, even harmful, trivializes this aspect of black experience specifically."[15] Williams ultimately places her faith in arguments about the need for the disenfranchised to develop a voice, which is a key facet of Baldwin's aesthetic.

Baldwin's work in fact anticipates both the intellectual methodology of CLS and the righteous insistence on self-definition of CRT. Despite their differences in emphasis, the goals of both movements are essentially consistent with one another and with Baldwin's recognition of a grave crisis in his nation's movement toward racial harmony in his lifetime. General liberal principles and even Supreme Court legislation was ultimately not enough, from Baldwin's perspective, and the challenges of appreciating Baldwin's later work may be related to his feeling that racial progress during his lifetime had only been made on the surface of American society. Baldwin's anger and emotional turmoil toward the end of his career struck some readers as the anachronistic rhetoric of black militancy, but it can more productively be seen as his frustration with societal complacency, a frustration certainly shared by CRT scholars who "desire not merely to understand the vexed bond between law and racial power but to *change* it."[16]

Powerlessness that results in alienation is reflected, according to Gabel and Harris, in *hierarchy,* a concept that Baldwin felt deeply throughout his life and represented consistently in his writings; Gabel and Harris write, "The source of alienation in capitalist societies (although by no means only capitalist societies) is to be found in the prevalence of hierarchy as the dominant form of social organization. The nature of this alienation is best described as the inability of people to achieve the genuine power and freedom that can only come from the sustained experience of authentic and egalitarian social connection."[17] The trajectory of Baldwin's writings clearly illustrates the struggle of one alienated individual toward the "authentic and egalitarian social connection" the authors describe here. The strength and defiance of his characters in late novels and the strength of his own lawyer-like rhetoric in his final book, *The Evidence of Things Not Seen,* illustrate the success of this transformation. Baldwin eventually came to recognize what Gabel and Harris describe in their article: "The principal role of the legal system . . . is to create a political culture that can persuade people to accept both the legitimacy and the apparent inevitability of the existing hierarchical arrangement."[18] They go on to describe circumstances that relate even more specifically to Baldwin's life: "Blacks can demand legal equality with whites, but they cannot demand the elimination of the societal conditions that produce institutional racism. In other words, the conservative power of legal thought is not to be found in legal outcomes which resolve conflicts in favor of dominant groups, but in the reification of the very categories through which the nature of social conflict is defined. . . . Like religion in previous historical periods, the law becomes an object of belief which shapes popular consciousness toward a passive acquiescence or obedience to the status quo."[19] Just as Baldwin famously works through the hypocrisy of religion and rejects its authority in early works such as *Go Tell It on the Mountain, The Amen Corner,* and *The Fire Next Time,* so does he reject the legitimacy of the law once he realizes its essential impulses to uphold the status quo. The difference is that Baldwin ultimately regarded the power of the law as more pervasive than religion, and thus it took him much longer to transform his feelings of powerlessness into expressions of power than it took him to reject the church's authority over the individual.

In his study *Whispered Consolations*, Jon-Christian Suggs has broken important ground on the subject of African American literature and the law; he argues that "African American literature is universally grounded in law; in fact, all African American fiction carries the question of the legal status of blacks as its subtext."[20] Yet Suggs's study focuses on "a classical African American narrative whose chronological boundaries are roughly 1820 to 1954,"[21] stopping virtually at the beginning of Baldwin's career (Baldwin's first book was published in 1953). Suggs's epilogue does account for the period that comprises Baldwin's life, but only as a way of demonstrating how the trajectory of African American literature has been away from the law as the central "lens through which to view the lives of African Americans,"[22] at least insofar as the law has been thoroughly demythologized in expressions of popular culture. Gregg D. Crane's 2002 study *Race, Citizenship, and Law in American Literature* similarly focuses on nineteenth- and early-twentieth-century American literature.[23] Other recent studies have usefully considered literature alongside race and prison, such as Peter Caster's *Prisons, Race, and Masculinity* or Joy James's *The New Abolitionists,* but Baldwin does not figure into their analysis. Some scholars have begun to look at Baldwin and the law, notably Lawrie Balfour, Lovalerie King, Richard Schur, and Deak Nabers, but until now no one has undertaken a thorough study of Baldwin's writings—fiction, nonfiction, drama, and poetry—in this context.

Because of the prominence of the law in his writings, and because he defines the law from a broad range of perspectives, Baldwin is a crucial figure to focus on when extending the scope of such studies as those by Suggs, Crane, Caster, and James. Virtually all of Baldwin's novels and plays have at their core a narrative of imprisonment, or police brutality, or police intimidation, or a rigged trial. These topics also pervade his nonfiction, where he meditates on the law's other dimensions as well, considering Supreme Court decisions and legal history alongside police brutality. Prison is at the center of this web of associations connecting "the law." Imprisonment becomes for Baldwin the central metaphor not only of the

African American experience, but of the broader restrictions that threaten to suffocate or alienate the disempowered individual, which is precisely the effect (if not always the intent) of imprisonment. Prison, like slavery, like legal decisions, like the police, exists for Baldwin as a means for society to compartmentalize, divide, control, and oppress. The law, in brief, is not a benevolent force, in Baldwin's eyes, but a way to exercise what he calls "a criminal power" (*FNT* 23).

There are a variety of possible responses to the recognition that the law represents, for Baldwin and for other black people, a criminal power. Baldwin's career is especially important in this context because he displays the full range of these responses. His life work can be viewed as a journey that follows a trajectory that leads from fear to engagement, to public outrage, to alienation, and finally to autonomy, mastery, and a sense of community. Baldwin's maturity as a thinker can be directly linked to his response to the law. His identity as a writer represents a transformation discussed in general terms by Robert Cover in his influential article "Nomos and Narrative":

> The transformation of interpretation into legal meaning begins when someone accepts the demands of interpretation and, through the personal act of commitment, affirms the position taken. . . . Creating legal meaning, however, requires not only the movement of dedication and commitment, but also the objectification of that to which one is committed. . . . Creation of legal meaning entails, then, subjective commitment to an objectified understanding of a demand. It entails the disengagement of the self from the "object" of law, and at the same time requires an engagement to that object as faithful "other." The metaphor of separation permits the allegory of dedication. This objectification of the norms to which one is committed frequently, perhaps always, entails a narrative—a story of how the law, now object, came to be, and more importantly, how it came to be one's own.[24]

In Baldwin's case, the "narrative" Cover speaks of is a life's work of narratives which, taken together, represent Baldwin's gradual and sometimes painful transformation from regarding himself as an object of the law to regarding the law itself as an object. By interrogating the law on all levels, he eventually takes control of it (making it "his own," in Cover's terms), transforming his powerlessness to power *through* narrative. Initially taking his cue from *Native Son* and from his own intense fear in prison, the young Baldwin believed the law to be fixed—an instrument of relentless power against which he had no recourse and over which he had no control. Over the course of his career, through projecting variations on his own story and on Bigger Thomas's, Baldwin grows to understand the law as a more flexible force that can certainly intimidate young black men, but that must not be allowed to destroy their hope for a better future.

The motif I have selected—Baldwin's perception of the criminal justice system and its impact on society's power relations—runs through nearly all of his work, and is thus a fitting context for unifying and making sense of Baldwin's complete oeuvre. It has been noted by critics and biographers to varying degrees, but has never been used to assess his legacy or to synthesize his entire career, a career that began virtually at the moment of the landmark *Brown vs. Board of Education* case (1954) and that reached its high-water mark, in terms of notoriety, virtually at the moment of the Civil Rights Act and Voting Rights Act of 1964 and 1965, respectively. In terms of the law as context, my aim is to help to broaden the by now well-established field of literature and the law by combining it with the developing field of prison literature. The law and literature movement, as it is often termed, has its origins in the work of James Boyd White in the 1970s, but flourished in earnest in the 1980s and 1990s through the work of Richard Posner, Ian Ward, Brook Thomas, and others. The study of incarceration and literature has developed sporadically since the English translation of Foucault's *Discipline and Punish* in 1977. The work of H. Bruce Franklin, particularly his 1978 study *The Victim as Criminal and Artist,* laid the foundation for studies of the intersection of incarceration and literature, especially in American literature.

These two movements do not necessarily mesh ideologically: the law and literature movement tends to be conservative, from a literary scholar's point of view, and the literature of incarceration movement tends toward the progressive or even radical (though CLS and CRT tend to be progressive or radical). This somewhat diffuse mixture of approaches creates an especially useful methodology to examine a figure like Baldwin, whose body of literature resists easy classification and monolithic ideology. By foregrounding the importance of incarceration, I am hoping to extend the scope of the law/literature movement through this study of Baldwin, a writer who is conscious of the law on many levels: historical, cultural, dramatic, and personal.

The "criminal power" that is the title of my study refers to the law's power to label criminals as such, but also to act criminally without legal repercussion, according to Baldwin. This perspective is anticipated by law and literature scholars such as Posner who writes, "The frequent discontinuity between the spirit and letter of the law, or between its general aim and its concrete application, is one reason why law so often strikes laymen as arbitrary. And law's apparently arbitrary and undeniably coercive character, combined with the inevitable errors of fact and law in the administration of justice and the resulting miscarriages of justice, and with law's 'otherness' . . . makes law a superb metaphor for the random, coercive, and 'unfair' light in which the human condition—'life'—appears to us in some moods."[25] The law, paradoxically, contains its own transgression: in Baldwin's work, individuals who operate "above the law" are almost always representatives of the law. As a mechanism of order in society, then, the law is a flawed instrument that reinforces social hierarchy more than it promotes justice.

This is not to say that the law is completely malevolent or uniformly misguided in Baldwin's work, though. Baldwin did not render complex concepts that simply. The characters who people Baldwin's writing have served time in prison, but they are not all "innocent." Giovanni, Sonny, and Wayne Williams (if only partially, in Baldwin's argument), for instance, commit the crimes they are accused of committing, but other incarcerated figures, such as Richard, Fonny, Tony Maynard, and Baldwin himself, do not. The idea that resurfaces in Baldwin's work is not simply one of powerless victimization—that black men or poor men are frequently imprisoned for crimes they did not commit and that racist institutions exist to keep disenfranchised groups down, although that is certainly a large part of the idea. Rather, Baldwin's writing, across the span of his entire career, testifies to the way power is abused under the pretext of the law, resulting in a hypocrisy much deeper even than that exhibited by religious hypocrites such as Gabriel in *Go Tell It on the Mountain,* or Sister Margaret in *The Amen Corner.* This response to the law, more than anything else, unifies Baldwin's career and situates it in a way that explains his appeal beyond the turbulent circumstances of his life or his lifetime. Baldwin's unique contribution to American thought and American literature is his analysis of the way power has manifested itself throughout history, disguised as a fair and equitable legal, judicial, and penal system, and how this power has converged on him and on his literary imagination. What kept Baldwin alive is the exact thing that nearly killed him in Paris in 1949: a sense of righteous indignation in response to injustice. Whether his subject was homosexuality or race, whether writing fiction or nonfiction, whether observing himself or others, America or Europe, women or men, this response to injustice is constant. Without it, we would have no Baldwin.

One of the major American writers of the twentieth century, Baldwin has been the subject of a substantial body of literary criticism. However, the only book-length studies to address Baldwin's *entire* career are the two most thorough of his five biographies. Fern Eckman's biography *The Furious Passage of James Baldwin* was published in 1966, so it covers only half of Baldwin's career.[26] W. J. Weatherby's biography *The Artist on Fire* (1989) is, by his own admission, a "portrait" of the artist, not a traditional literary biography with thorough literary analysis.[27] Herb Boyd's *Baldwin's Harlem* (2008) is delimited by geography.[28] Only Campbell's *Talking at the Gates* (1991) and Leeming's *James Baldwin* (1994) address Baldwin's entire career and analyze the body of his work, albeit from a biographer's point of view.[29] Biographers aside, critics have thus far shied away from discussing Baldwin's work as a whole. The tendency has always been to regard Baldwin piece by piece, or to select his works that support a certain argument, or that were written in a certain time period. Unable to reconcile the tremendous variety of Baldwin's work, Baldwin scholars tend to concentrate on only part of his oeuvre, such as his early essays, his later fiction, his work on race, or his inquiries into bisexuality. The titles or subtitles alone of some of the recent major studies on Baldwin indicate this tendency: *Black Women in the Fiction of James Baldwin, New Essays on Go Tell It on the Mountain, James Baldwin's Later Fiction, James Baldwin's Turkish Decade.*[30] The result is that Baldwin scholarship as a whole resembles a half-finished jigsaw puzzle rather than a completed portrait. All of these studies are valuable and excellent at accomplishing their various critical goals, but none has taken on the complete Baldwin.

Baldwin's critics have reconciled themselves to the idea that Baldwin is, as C. W. E. Bigsby put it, "a writer who has always been drawn in two apparently mutually incompatible directions,"[31] though they have defined those directions differently. Take your pick: Baldwin is either an essayist or a fiction writer; Baldwin either writes about racial injustice or homosexuality; Baldwin's early works are clearly superior to his later works. The influential Robert A. Bone, in *The Negro Novel in America,* describes Baldwin in one breath as "The most important Negro writer to emerge during the last decade" and in the next calls him "an uneven writer . . . strongest as an essayist, weakest as a playwright, and successful in the novel form on only one occasion."[32] Although the oeuvres of many prolific and important writers have been similarly subdivided, few have suffered Baldwin's fate of never enjoying a single coherent critical study. Because his critics have tended to divide up his career, Baldwin's place in American literary history has suffered. Baldwin himself spoke of his resistance "to make myself fit in . . . to wash myself clean for the American literary academy."[33] It is not as though Baldwin is absent from college curricula—most students read "Sonny's Blues" in one anthology or another, and literature majors might encounter *Go Tell It on the Mountain* or *The Fire Next Time* in certain contexts—but the richness, complexity, and struggles of this author have not been adequately synthesized. In *Stealing the Fire,* one of the first major nonbiographical studies of Baldwin, Horace Porter codifies this trend, without explanation: "except by implication and in brief allusions, I do not go beyond *The Fire Next Time* (1963)."[34] Porter participates in what has become nearly a cliché in Baldwin studies: that the author stopped writing well after 1963 or so. Even Baldwin's biographer James Campbell speaks of "an actual decline in the quality of his work"[35] beginning in 1965. Baldwin's reviewers and critics in his lifetime initiated this trend of dismissing Baldwin's later work: Eldridge Cleaver's *Soul on Ice* (1968) contains, as Baldwin scholars know, a vicious, homophobic attack that denigrates all of Baldwin's work from *Giovanni's Room* on. That same year, Mario Puzo wrote a scathing review of *Tell Me How Long the Train's Been Gone,* which he described as "a simpleminded, one-dimensional novel with mostly cardboard characters, a polemical rather than narrative tone, weak invention, and poor selection of incident."[36] Darryl Pinckney describes Baldwin as "weary" in his final novel, *Just Above My Head.*[37] Bigsby summarizes this trend in his 1980 essay "The Divided Mind of James Baldwin" this way: "His more recent novels have failed to spark the popular or critical interest of his earlier work."[38] This trend of praising Baldwin's early work and denigrating his later work has only grown: many critics nearly refuse to accept the idea that the same man wrote the early masterpiece *Notes of a Native Son* and a challenging, passionate, though perhaps aesthetically imperfect work at the end of his career like *The Evidence of Things Not Seen.* The tendency to regard Baldwin as someone who lost his artistic powers in the mid-1960s is shopworn, to put it kindly, and it is time to move beyond it.

Some recent work on Baldwin is meant to act as a corrective to this trend, notably Lynn Orilla Scott's *James Baldwin's Later Fiction* (2002). Scott's co-edited collection with Lovalerie King, *James Baldwin and Toni Morrison: Comparative Critical and Theoretical Essays* (2006), is another admirable effort to reconsider Baldwin in a new light.[39] Lawrie Balfour's *The Evidence of Things Not Said* (2001) reads Baldwin's nonfiction through the lens of theories of democracy. Magdalena Zaborowska's *James Baldwin's Turkish Decade: Erotics of Exile* (2009) and Douglas Field's *Oxford Historical Companion to James Baldwin* (2009) deepen the trend of reevaluation that has revived critical interest in Baldwin. Most recently, Randall Kenan edited *The Cross of Redemption—Uncollected Writings* (2010), a collection that makes available Baldwin's previously neglected or hard-to-find publications. These books continue the resurgence in Baldwin criticism beginning with critical collections edited by Dwight McBride (*James Baldwin Now*) and my own *Re-Viewing James Baldwin* in 1999 and 2000, respectively.[40] There have been panels devoted to Baldwin at major conferences such as the Modern Language Association and the American Studies Association over the past half-dozen years, as well as conferences devoted entirely to Baldwin at Howard University in 2000, Queen Mary's College in London in 2007, Suffolk University in Boston in 2009, and New York University in 2011. Clearly the time is right for a comprehensive study of Baldwin's entire career.

My study, which reads the majority of Baldwin's texts in the context of the American legal, judicial, and penal systems, is organized thematically, but also follows Baldwin's career in roughly chronological order. Chapter 1, "No Room of One's Own," focuses on Baldwin's first collection of essays *Notes of a Native Son,* his first story "Previous Condition," his first novel *Go Tell It on the Mountain,* and finally his expatriate novel *Giovanni's Room,* to consider Baldwin's failed attempts to escape or avoid society's persecution in the form of a corrupt police force and penal system. Chapter 2, "Other Countries, Hidden Laws," demonstrates Baldwin's reluctant return to the strife of the early Civil Rights movement, especially the aftermath of the *Brown vs. Board of Education* anti-segregation case (1954), including his essays in *Nobody Knows My Name,* his novel *Another Country,* and his play *Blues for Mister Charlie.* Chapter 3, "A Criminal Power," reveals the maturing of Baldwin's thought with regard to this subject, especially from the point of view of Civil Rights legislation. The law becomes a way to compartmentalize society in the aftermath of the *Brown* decision, prompting Americans to discover nonlegal means to address their society's ills. The primary texts here are the "southern essays" in *Nobody Knows My Name,* his landmark essays in *The Fire Next Time,* and the stories collected in *Going to Meet the Man.* Chapter 4, "Return To Exile," shows Baldwin's anxiety as a public figure regarding the law as he seeks to redefine the criminal/artist in his novel *Tell Me How Long the Train's Been Gone;* his experimental book-length essay *No Name in the Street* in which he meditates on the assassinations of Medgar Evers, Martin Luther King, and Malcolm X, but also on the imprisonment of his friend Tony Maynard; and his film scenario *One Day When I Was Lost* about the life of Malcolm X. Chapter 5, "The Fire Reignited," demonstrates Baldwin's resurgence as a public figure, more like a lawyer than a preacher, railing against post-1960s complacency in his final works: his meditation on film *The Devil Finds Work,* his final novels *If Beale Street Could Talk* and *Just Above My Head,* and his book-length essay *The Evidence of Things Not Seen.* In this final stage Baldwin reveals how, after a long and difficult journey, he has learned to access the power of the law rather than to allow it to oppress him.

At the end of "Equal in Paris" Baldwin is not comforted by the laughter he hears at his trial; indeed, he is "chilled" by it because, "This laughter is the laughter of those who consider themselves to be at a safe remove from all the wretched, for whom the pain of the living is not real" (*NNS* 158). That "safe remove" is made manifest in the walls of the prison, described in great detail in the essay. In prison, Baldwin discovers a metaphor that is to become for him *the* metaphor that will develop throughout his career: prison itself. Carolyn Sylvander notes, "Sometimes in his speeches, Baldwin uses the prison analogy—he is imprisoned in the ghetto, but the man keeping him there, the warden, is to be found in the prison, too, and the prisoner knows the warden better than vice versa."[41] The male body becomes, in one essay, "The Male Prison." The narrow, dirty rooms of John Grimes's home in *Go Tell It on the Mountain* are reminiscent of prison. Giovanni's room in his next novel is similarly dirty and confining, but it operates as a psychosocial space from which the narrator David longs to escape. And yet, as Peter Caster argues, "Something is lost when imprisonment becomes primarily a metaphor . . . any such challenge to definitions of criminality and practices of imprisonment must be grounded in the specificity of material, cultural, and historical conditions."[42] For Baldwin, metaphorical prisons are joined by actual prisons surrounded by real streets with very real cops patrolling them: outside these confining incarcerating spaces are the killing streets that will claim Giovanni, Rufus in *Another Country,* and Fonny's father in *If Beale Street Could Talk.* Laws are created and enforced to keep society safe, but for Baldwin they operate to imperil the individual, to alienate the "wretched" who are often innocent, and to destroy anyone who is bewildered by the massive, mysterious power of the legal system. The prison is for Baldwin the enduring institution, more than a metaphor, that explains the way power operates in the contemporary world. Judges and lawmakers put that power into place, the police enforce it, and the lone victim shuffles around, as Baldwin described himself doing in "Equal in Paris," like a rag-doll, robbed of his shoelaces and belt so he can't hang himself, feeling vulnerable and dehumanized.

Wrongful imprisonment is a phenomenon Baldwin uses to meditate on the failures of American society, but his inquiry into the law goes well beyond imprisonment. According to Baldwin, we cannot attribute America's failure to some isolated bad cops, or racist judges, or accusers who claim that all young black men look alike despite the fact that these three types surface repeatedly in his fiction. His works travel from the courtroom to the streets, and to even more private spaces, in order to examine the threats faced by the powerless, especially African Americans. The nervous expatriate arrested for "receiving stolen goods" in a Paris hotel emerged as the most prominent African American writer of his lifetime, whose final book cast him in the role of a lawyer, trying his nation's conscience. In the nearly four decades between these moments, he produced a body of literature that is rich, complex, perhaps uneven, but far more coherent than critics have believed it to be.

CHAPTER 1

No Room of One's Own

W̲HAT I̲S̲ the primary power of the law? This question is not as straightforward as it may seem, and the answer obviously changes with context and perspective. From the perspective of the "average, law-abiding" citizen, the law has the power to protect the populace, or to productively separate the innocent from the guilty. Such a perspective may seem naive to anyone who has been wrongfully convicted, though, or who is aware that the scales of justice are not equally balanced. The belief in the law as a neutral, objective, regulatory force is as much a fixture of romanticized American ideology as are the belief in unfettered class mobility, or the dream of the melting pot, or the fantasy of American exceptionalism. The law certainly has the effect of preserving the prevailing social order, whether or not that is its explicit intent. One of the ways it does so is by reifying popular associations between minority groups and criminal or illegal behavior. Michael Hames-Garcia summarizes a subfield of Critical Legal Studies known as "deviancy theory" which argues "that certain acts become 'criminal' in a process whose ultimate outcome is the criminalization of whole groups and subcultures. From a critical criminological perspective, the process of manufacturing deviancy becomes, through penalization, a method for separating members of disenfranchised or disfavored groups from the larger society."[1] Regardless of how deeply one wants to look for explanations, a simple fact exists in American society: the nation's jails are disproportionately filled with young black men. To say that black men commit more crimes than other demographic groups is simplistic, if not patently false. To say that they are more likely to be convicted of crimes is to approach the subject more subtly, and more accurately. The societal effect of this fact is that jails are associated with the black and brown people who fill them, and thus that criminality itself is associated with the black and brown people who are not in jail. Hollywood and television further distort this unfortunate and socially destructive perception, but they are not fully responsible for creating it.

One would like to think that the law itself does not cause racism, but to absolve the law of its complicity in perpetuating racism is to ignore reality, and American history. Slavery was upheld by law, even by the Supreme Court in the years immediately preceding the Civil War, and segregation persisted through so-called Jim Crow laws for nearly a century thereafter. As Ian Haney-López details in his book *White by Law*, U.S. citizenship was linked to whiteness from the late-eighteenth century through 1952.[2] He notes how the courts enlisted social scientists to help define whiteness in legal terms in the early twentieth century, then abandoned scientific definitions of race in favor of "common knowledge," or social definitions of race.[3] He argues, "to say race is socially constructed is to conclude that race is at least partially legally produced. Put most starkly, law constructs race. Of course, it does so within the larger context of society, and so law is only one of many institutions and forces implicated in the formation of races. Moreover, as a complex set of institutions and ideas, 'law' intersects and interacts with the social knowledge about race in convoluted, unpredictable, sometimes self-contradictory ways."[4] In her recent book *What Blood Won't Tell*, Ariela Gross concurs; taking the case of a slave who argued for her whiteness as a paradigm, she traces a similar history to the one Haney-López describes: "race may not be objectively observed. Instead it is a powerful ideology which came into being and changed forms at particular moments in history,"[5] moments that she chronicles as a series of challenges to legal wisdom which culminate in her observation, "Fundamental to race is a hierarchy of power."[6] Haney-López similarly concludes, "The operation of law does far more than merely legalize race; it defines as well the spectrum of domination and subordination that constitutes race relations."[7]

The "convoluted, unpredictable, and self-contradictory" intersections of law and society that Hames-Garcia describes are myriad and often invisible. In Baldwin's work, and in late-twentieth-century America generally, they frequently take the form of imbalanced rates of arrest and severity of sentencing based on racial identity. I am referring to the law again in a wide range of its dimensions, from high court decisions through the behavior of police and corrections officers whose duty it is to enforce such decisions. Racial profiling by law enforcement officers, though not legal, is certainly a familiar and egregious dimension of the way the law can be used to "separat[e] members of disenfranchised groups from the larger society." In recent decades, African Americans have wryly noted the tendency to be arrested or at least intimidated on the charge of DWB ("driving while black").[8] Others have noted a disparity in illegal drug sentencing between blacks and whites: possession of crack cocaine, for instance, which is more common among black drug users, carries a much stiffer sentence in most states than possession of powdered cocaine, more common among white drug users. What the law has the power to do in such cases is to construct figurative and literal barriers between racial groups while simultaneously reinforcing the stereotypical assumption that racial minorities are either criminals or potential criminals.

Imprisoned black authors in Baldwin's lifetime occasionally represented their period of incarceration as positive, even when the circumstances of their arrest were unjust, or unjustified. Prison gave Malcolm X the opportunity to reform himself and to read and study in a way he would not have otherwise done; as he writes in *The Autobiography of Malcolm X*, "I don't think anybody ever got more out of going to prison than I did. In fact, prison enabled me to study far more intensively than I would have if my life had gone differently and I had attended some college."[9] For Martin Luther King, writing from prison was a way to raise the political consciousness of his readers and to demonstrate his political solidarity with other members of the oppressed black community.[10] George Jackson, in *Soledad Brother* (1970), also emphasizes the solidarity of the black community in prison, and Eldridge Cleaver in *Soul on Ice* (1968) uses the jail cell as a kind of platform to reinforce the connection between black militancy and the prison complex. Baldwin, however, never depicted incarceration in terms that could be considered even remotely positive, and even if he later regarded it as an opportunity to raise the public's political consciousness or to create solidarity among African Americans, he never would have declared it worthwhile to serve time in order to do so. If there are important reasons for being arrested such as those Martin Luther King details in "Letter from Birmingham Jail" (1963) ("in order to arouse the conscience of the community"),[11] they are outside the Baldwin oeuvre. Prison for Baldwin was always the most depraved space in human existence, and his characters' consistent fear of it, and despondency if they are unfortunate enough to experience it, is consistent throughout his career, but especially prominent in his first decade as a professional writer when his own fear and despondency were most evident.

Baldwin is generally excluded from studies of prison literature, though the field includes two of his own oft-cited nineteenth-century predecessors, Dickens and Dostoyevsky. Definitions of twentieth-century prison literature have expanded to accommodate writers who imagine prison from an outside perspective as well as those who developed as writers in prison, such as Jimmy Santiago Baca or Edward Bunker. In his foundational study *The Victim as Criminal and Artist,* H. Bruce Franklin emphasizes that his work examines "'common criminals' whose understanding of their own situation developed as a direct consequence of their crime and punishment" as opposed to "those who were professional writers before they became convicts."[12] This definition of prison literature has persisted, but the field of prison literature has grown to include professional writers such as Norman Mailer, John Cheever, and John Edgar Wideman who have written about prison through close contact with prisoners, as well as "uncommon criminals"—that is, incarcerated writers such as Leonard Peltier, Mumia Abu-Jamal, and Kathy Boudin—whose writing careers grew out of highly publicized cases. Since Baldwin's time in prison was brief and since it occurred just as he was becoming a professional writer, he fits into both of Franklin's categories, and thus neither. He definitely does not fit into the political reform mode in which the author has been imprisoned "for an act many readers would commend,"[13] yet we can see in his early work the nascent development of a certain political attitude that will flourish in his later works: when incarceration is based on racial profiling, it should inspire outrage rather than despair so it can lead to political action and legal empowerment. In his 1963 essay "We Can Change the Country," for instance, Baldwin writes, "I ask all of you to ask yourselves what would happen if Harlem refused to pay the rent for a month," and adds, in italics for emphasis, "*Some laws should not be obeyed*" (CR 50). In his writings of the 1940s and 1950s, though, he has not yet formed this confidence, and the keynote is despair.

Baldwin's initial engagement with the law was deeply personal and related to two facets of his early life in Harlem and his first period of exile in Paris: namely, the presence of the police on the streets of Harlem and the devastating effects of incarceration. Biographer David Leeming talks of two events in particular from Baldwin's childhood that led to his life-long fear of the police: one was being roughed up at the age of ten and the other was being "scared shitless" by policemen on horses at a May Day parade at the age of thirteen.[14] As a way to escape the dangers of the street—dangers represented by the cops as much as the criminals—Baldwin searches for personal spaces of refuge. His early works are dominated by the motif of the need to find a room of one's own—a space where one can discover the self away from the threats of society, specifically the threat of being labeled a criminal, and assigned to the space that makes this label, as it were, concrete. Thus we see Peter in "Previous Condition" (1948), John in *Go Tell It on the Mountain* (1953), Baldwin himself in "Equal in Paris" (1955), and David and Giovanni in *Giovanni's Room* (1956) discussing in detail their own dingy private spaces. Peter is evicted from his room by a landlady who threatens to call the police; Baldwin is removed from his hotel room by Paris police and taken to jail; Richard (John's biological father) in *Go Tell It on the Mountain* is arrested for a crime he did not commit; and Giovanni is placed in jail and is on the verge of being executed at the novel's conclusion. Baldwin's early works implicitly argue that there is *no* safe haven, *no* room of one's own that can shelter one from the law. The complex intersection of themes related to racism, persecution of homosexuality, poverty, the abandonment of religion, and the need for exile in Baldwin's early works can be focused through a study of the law's power as it intrudes upon the individual's pursuit of self-improvement.

Baldwin scholars and biographers tend to point to three formative moments to define the origin of Baldwin's story, three epiphanies that sketch out the portrait of this artist as a young man: (1) his violent conversion on the threshing floor of his church followed by his decision to leave the church, described in *Go Tell It on the Mountain, The Amen Corner,* and *The Fire Next Time*; (2) the incident in which he throws a water glass at a waitress in a New Jersey restaurant who refuses to serve him because he is black (discussed in "Notes of a Native Son" and reworked in many other works); and (3) his decision to leave New York for Paris, discussed in *No Name in the Street* and in numerous interviews. In his study *Exiled in Paris* James Campbell notes Baldwin's claim for his own origin story, quoted from "Equal in Paris," that his "life . . . began that year in Paris," but Campbell uses the quotation to illustrate Baldwin's promiscuity and profligacy; flanking the quotation are observations about how Baldwin brought a parade of "young French boyfriends" to his room as a way of breaking free from the morality of the church "with extreme fervor," and observations about how Baldwin's "motto" was "Go for broke."[15] To someone unfamiliar with Baldwin's work, it might sound from this description like Paris was a joyful, bacchanalian expatriate experience for the young author, that he had accessed the myths of Hemingway, of

Richard Wright, and of other American models who had gone to Paris to flourish as American literary artists, and to live life with an expatriate's abandon. Although these features were certainly part of Baldwin's experience, it is crucial to return this quotation from "Equal in Paris" to its proper context: his observation that his life began that year comes as a direct result of a vision change he experiences in prison. Paris is merely the location: the setting is jail. This self-described beginning of life as detailed in "Equal in Paris" is born of fear, despair, and bewilderment, not revelry.

In style and tone, "Equal in Paris" stands apart from the other so-called Paris essays in *Notes of a Native Son* for two main reasons. First and most striking is Baldwin's use of the first-person singular pronoun. The other two Paris essays ("Encounter on the Seine: Black Meets Brown" and "A Question of Identity") are characterized by broad generalizations about American expatriates and Parisians, and Baldwin relies heavily on his distancing trademark pronoun "one" in those essays. The other feature separating "Equal in Paris" from its companions is its raw emotion, contrasted with the emotionally neutral reportage that characterizes the other two essays. The personal nature and development of voice in this essay connect it to two of the strongest and most famous essays in *Notes*—the title essay and "Stranger in the Village"—and these features clear the path for his later, more ambitious attempts to master and reinvent the essay genre in *Nobody Knows My Name, The Fire Next Time, No Name in the Street,* and *The Evidence of Things Not Seen.* "Equal in Paris" has not received as much critical attention as other essays in the collection, but it marks an important shift in trajectory that results in the development of Baldwin's voice and provides a paradigm for a theme that unifies his career. To quote fully the final line of "Equal in Paris": "In some deep, black, stony, and liberating way, my life, in my own eyes, began during that first year in Paris" (*NNS* 158). It is deeply ironic, but fitting to my study, that the liberation of Baldwin's voice occurs as a direct result of an eight-day stint in prison. The word "liberating" in this sentence cannot counterbalance the adjectives "deep" and "stony," which strongly connote prison, and the other adjective, "black," is the word that truly troubles Baldwin in this essay. The word "black" is situated within the imprisoning adjectives, buried rather than confronted.

Baldwin attempts to describe the central incident, nearly an anecdote, of "Equal in Paris," in comic terms; he even refers to it as a "comic-opera" (*NNS* 139), and James Campbell refers to the essay as Baldwin's "funniest piece," although he acknowledges that its humor does not obscure its fundamental serious purpose.[16] On December 19, 1949, Baldwin was arrested and held in a French prison after a friend, evicted from a hotel, left a stolen sheet in his room. The police officers assured him that the incident was of minor or no importance, but they held him regardless. The essay chronicles Baldwin's bewilderment: minutes turn into hours, and hours turn into days as he awaits a trial that seems like it will never arrive. Baldwin slows the pace of his essay nearly to a standstill in order to reveal his growing despondency, fear, and alienation from self. His attempts to write an essay reflecting the comic absurdity of the situation fail: his bitterness and anger swell under the surface of the essay. These burgeoning forces are so strong that they propel his entire writing career thereafter.

What Baldwin does not tell us in "Equal in Paris" is that the experience in a Paris jail, far from being the catalyst for his writing life, nearly killed him. As detailed in my introduction, Baldwin attempted to hang himself with a sheet, but the water pipe over which he threw his makeshift noose broke. Having lived through this suicide attempt, Baldwin omits it from his essay, but does give us some indication of his state of mind when he writes, "there was a real question in my mind as to which would end soonest, the Great Adventure or me" (*NNS* 141). The other element Baldwin omits from his essay is an overt connection between the force that kept him in a Paris jail cell for eight days and racism. The essay's comic notes indicate Baldwin's desperate attempts to write off the incident as a case of bad luck, of being in the wrong place at the wrong time, but the humiliation he experiences lays the foundation for the outrage that typifies the rest of his career, an outrage more frequently related to race than to poverty or to foreignness. In exile from America following his first-hand experience with racism, Baldwin is reluctant to admit that racism is not unique to America, and that prison is one means through which racism can be legally reinforced even in the famously liberal City of Lights. Baldwin takes pains in the essay to avoid ascribing his arrest to race; he writes, "That evening in the commissariat I was not a despised black man. . . . For them I was an American" (*NNS* 146). Yet Baldwin published this essay in 1955, and in June of 1954 he and his friend Themistocles Hoetis had also been arrested for no reason, this time in New York. On this occasion, according to Hoetis, Baldwin "*screamed*. All night long. . . . 'I'm a *nigger*, they picked me up because I'm black.'"[17] This screaming voice is muffled in "Equal in Paris."

Notes of a Native Son contains many instances of Baldwin's struggle with racial discrimination, so its apparent absence from "Equal in Paris" is curious, especially given the fact that he made the connection between racism and wrongful arrest so vociferously in New York the year before he published "Equal in Paris," and because other versions of wrongful arrest in Baldwin's early work are so clearly linked to racism: Richard in *Go Tell It on the Mountain* kills himself after he is the victim of racial profiling, for instance. Perhaps Baldwin was eager to place this incident in the broadest possible context; as he insists in his introduction to *Nobody Knows My Name,* "In America, the color of my skin had stood between myself and me; in Europe, that barrier was down" (*Nobody* 11). He clearly wanted to see Paris as a place of integration, where no barriers divide the self. And yet there is a nagging sense under the surface of "Equal in Paris" that racism is one of the factors, if not the main factor, that contributed to Baldwin's feelings of powerlessness. The absence of race from the essay might indicate that Baldwin felt it would do no good to draw attention to it as a relevant factor. Motivated only by fear, he had not yet developed outrage at the law's power to discriminate, and this surprising faltering of Baldwin's conviction can be interpreted by what Cornel West deems "the nihilism that increasingly pervades black communities. *Nihilism is to be understood here not as a philosophic doctrine that there are no rational grounds for legitimate standards or authority; it is, far more, the lived experience of coping with a life of horrifying meaninglessness, hopelessness, and (most important) lovelessness.* The frightening result is a numbing detachment from others and a self-destructive disposition toward the world" (italics West's).[18] Baldwin, having thoroughly rejected religion as hope and having not yet established his belief in the saving power of either art or love to the point that they could prevent despair, does indeed reflect the nihilism West identifies as pervasive. He was young, he was a foreigner, he had little money, and he hadn't mastered the French language. These four factors *combined* with his race led Baldwin to be thrust into a rift he confronts throughout the Paris essays: namely, the black American's tenuous connection to his ancestral African past.

In the face of being judged as just another poor American drifter as opposed to an ambitious author, Baldwin is forced to confront his status as a Westerner of African descent. The question is one of identity, but also of a delicately evoked history. Led deeper and deeper into the hellish bowels of the French prison system, he feels a victim of the extraordinary way in which society enforces its power structure through its legal, judicial, and penal systems. Incarceration forces Baldwin to begin to understand this power and his own powerlessness in the face of it. In prison he observes:

> I was handcuffed again and led out of the Préfecture into the streets—
> it was dark now, it was still raining—and before the steps of the Pré-

fecture stood the great police wagon, doors facing me, wide open. The handcuffs were taken off, I entered the wagon, which was peculiarly constructed. It was divided by a narrow aisle, and on each side of the aisle was a series of narrow doors. These doors opened on a narrow cubicle, beyond which was a door which opened onto another narrow cubicle: three or four cubicles, each private, with a locking door. I was placed in one of them; I remember there was a small vent just above my head which let in a little light. The door of my cubicle was locked from the outside. I had no idea where this wagon was taking me and, as it began to move, I began to cry. (*NNS* 150)

This passage is sure to elicit the vision of an African slave taken from his native land, being put in an absurdly narrow vehicle, taken from a home he would not see again, and led, against his will, he knows not where. Baldwin's response to the French prison testifies to what Foucault observes about prison construction in *Discipline and Punish* ("enclosed, segmented space, observed at every point, in which the individuals are inserted in a fixed place")[19] and anticipates a broader theme even than slavery: the related theme of legal power reinforcing social hierarchy. His arrest and prolonged imprisonment in Paris did not occur simply because he happened to be friends with a petty thief, but rather because of what might be called his "previous condition," or the factors he cannot control, from society's perspective: his race, his poverty, and his nationhood. The essay is about the lack of control over one's destiny. To be "equal" is to be equally powerless wherever one goes.

In "Equal in Paris" Baldwin interprets his powerlessness most evidently in terms of poverty: he believes he is seen in terms of "the familiar poverty and disorder of that precarious group of people of whatever age, race, country, calling, or intention which Paris recognizes as *les étudiants* and sometimes, more ironically and precisely, as *les nonconformistes*" (*NNS* 142–43). It is the presence of the policemen that causes Baldwin to see himself as mainstream Parisians must see him, not as an intellectual and an aspiring writer, but as an outcast who does not belong, and who must be re-placed: as he is marched out of the hotel room with his friend, he imagines the scene from the point of view of the hotel proprietor: "And so we passed through the lobby, four of us, two of us very clearly criminal" (*NNS* 143). The very existence of police uniforms causes Baldwin and his friend to be labeled this way: the police presence immediately and irrevocably alters Baldwin's identity. Having been labeled "criminal," his fate is no longer in his control, and he contemplates his vulnerability in the context of incarceration: "I am not speaking now of legality which, like most of the poor, I had never for an instant trusted, but of the temperament of the people with whom I had to deal" (*NNS* 144)—that is, the jailers, judges, and police officers who held power over him. He observes, "It was quite clear to me that the Frenchmen in whose hands I found myself were no better or worse than their American counterparts. Certainly their uniforms frightened me quite as much, and their impersonality, and the threat, always very keenly felt by the poor, of violence, was as present in that commissariat as it had ever been for me in any police station" (*NNS* 145). This observation adds another layer of meaning to the essay's title, "Equal in Paris"—that is, the poor are treated equally poorly wherever they go—and it also reiterates the Baldwin theme that expatriation does not amount to escape: there is "no hiding place." At the same time, he has understood what it means to be disenfranchised—due to poverty, race, and foreignness—and the experience compromises his view of himself as a confident social and literary critic, advanced in the early essays of *Notes,* and as an honest man and a good writer, advanced in the preface to the volume and in the central essays.

The law, in the form of police officers acting according to the least rational interpretation of criminality, makes Baldwin keenly aware of the fear at the core of his being. Baldwin is frightened not only by the police officers but, in the alienating world of the prison cell, also afraid of his fellow prisoners: North Africans to whom he "could not make any gesture simply because they frightened [him]" (*NNS* 153) and other cellmates who warned him that he might mistakenly face the guillotine; he writes, "The best way of putting my reaction to this is to say that, though I knew they were teasing me, it was simply not possible for me to totally *dis*believe them. As far as I was concerned, once in the hands of the law in France, anything could happen" (*NNS* 154). The law, intended to be the most rational force holding together any society, becomes for Baldwin at this moment the most irrational force within society, one that would murder without remorse. His bewilderment and victimization not halfway into his eight-day detention are only to develop and to cause him to change the way he views not only the law in France, but in Western society more broadly, and the ultimate powerlessness of individuals in response to it.

Baldwin is left with a fatalistic vision of humanity, in marked contrast to the cheerful optimism of the "Autobiographical Notes" at the beginning of the collection where he states, "I want to be an honest man and a good writer" (*NNS* 8). When he finally reaches the courtroom this phrase echoes hollowly; he observes that all the people who were sentenced that day had made, or clearly were going to make, crime their career. This seemed to be the opinion of the judge, who scarcely looked at the prisoners or listened to them; it seemed to be the opinion of the prisoners, who scarcely bothered to speak in their own behalf; it seemed to be the opinion of the lawyers, state lawyers for the most part, who were defending them. The great impulse of the courtroom seemed to be to put these people where they could not be seen—and not because they were offended at the crimes, unless, indeed, they were offended that the crimes were so petty, but because they did not wish to know that their society could be counted on to produce, probably in greater and greater numbers, a whole body of people for whom crime was the only possible career. Any society inevitably produces its criminals, but a society at once rigid and unstable can do nothing whatever to alleviate the poverty of its lowest members, cannot present to the hypothetical young man at the crucial moment that so-well-advertised right path." (*NNS* 155)

The fact that Baldwin has already chosen his own right path—honest man, good writer—seems irrelevant as he becomes aware of the immense and irrational power of the law to incarcerate the innocent, and to assign a preordained criminal identity to the poor, to the immigrants, and to the racial minorities. As Peter Caster writes, "Criminalization is . . . a jurisprudential process, not coincident with the commission of the crime but, rather, an effect of conviction. . . . Criminalization is thus a matter of interpellation, of being named."[20] Baldwin's interest in naming, evident from the titles of his books *Nobody Knows My Name* and *No Name in the Street,* stems from the namelessness he experiences at this moment when the state has taken responsibility for his identity.

Baldwin's perspective on prison and on the law in general as a society's most invidious way to enforce its power structure in terms of race and class was just beginning to develop in "Equal in Paris," though we can see evidence of it elsewhere in *Notes of a Native Son.* The first two essays in the collection—"Everybody's Protest Novel" and "Many Thousands Gone," about the artistic shortcomings of protest novels by Harriet Beecher Stowe and Richard Wright, respectively—are the essays in the collection that initially gained the most attention, and they continue to absorb Baldwin's critics. Both *Uncle Tom's Cabin* and *Native Son* are about the consequences of African Americans breaking the law. As Jon-Christian Suggs reminds us, "The very premise of the escaped slave's tale is that she or he has broken the law,"[21] and Stowe's novel is built on the genre of the slave narrative. Gregg D. Crane argues that "Stowe's images of good-hearted and law-abiding Northerners confronted by weary and shivering fugitives in *Uncle Tom's Cabin* were intended to and did bring home for many of her readers the momentous contest between conscience and law created by the Fugitive Slave Law."[22] In converting the slave narrative genre into the genre of the protest novel, according to Baldwin, Stowe fails to inspire true understanding in the reader, focusing instead on sentimentality and guilt. What is interesting about Baldwin's language in the essay is the prominence of prison metaphors in describing the human and American conditions. Protest novels, according to Baldwin, "emerge for what they are: a mirror of our confusion, dishonesty, panic trapped and immobilized in the sunlit prison of the American dream" (*NNS* 19). He also speaks of the "cage of reality" (*NNS* 20, 21) that determines the fate of individuals deemed inferior by society. Protest novels are not the keys to unlock these prisons and cages, according to Baldwin; in fact, these novels are partially responsible for constructing the cages because they fail to bring us closer to the crucial concept of truth: "truth, as used here, is meant to imply a devotion to the human being, his freedom and fulfillment; freedom which cannot be legislated, fulfillment which cannot be charted" (*NNS* 15). Baldwin is reaching for a lofty, abstract notion of freedom here and elsewhere in his early work. In doing so, he refuses to equate freedom with something granted by law, something "legislated." Part of this perspective is optimism: he wants to think of freedom as something that is above the law. His prison experience, of course, weighs on this idea with heavy irony.

Baldwin's criticism of Wright's *Native Son* is even more focused in terms of the law, for Bigger Thomas, Wright's antihero, is an undisputed criminal whose trial occupies a considerable portion of the novel. In "Many Thousands Gone" Baldwin begins to develop his theory that the fate of black Americans and the fate of white Americans are intertwined, and that to separate them through such means as incarceration is to use legal power to deny the truth and basis of American race relations. Wright's main flaw, in Baldwin's estimation, is that he approaches Bigger as a sociologist would rather than a novelist should. Bigger is not allowed to develop his voice, particularly in the legal arena of the courtroom; Baldwin writes, "It is useless to say to the courtroom in which this heathen sits on trial that he is [the white Americans'] responsibility, their creation, and his crimes are theirs; and that they ought, therefore, to allow him to live, to make articulate to himself behind the walls of prison the meaning of his existence. . . . Moreover, the courtroom, judge, jury, witnesses and spectators, recognize immediately that Bigger is their creation and they recognize this not only with hatred and fear and guilt and the resulting fury of self-righteousness but also with that morbid fullness of pride mixed with horror with which one regards the extent and power of one's wickedness" (*NNS* 43). This observation links Baldwin's critique of *Native Son* to his own experience in the French prison: in both cases, he understands how courtrooms and prisons function to manufacture a scapegoat who can serve to preserve society's power structure. In "Equal in Paris" he feels a victim of the notion that "any society inevitably produces its criminals" (*NNS* 155), and he sees the same idea in *Native Son*. In both cases there is no possibility for self-determination. Like Bigger, he is denied the opportunity to speak on his own behalf in the French courtroom, and he observes the way judges, juries, and witnesses condemn the accused anyway. If criminals are nothing more or less than criminals, in literature as well as in life, then there is no hope that their humanity can be fully developed. Baldwin believes that literature should be the realm where the accused, whether guilty or innocent, should have the opportunity to become human. His reaction to Wright's novel may not only have been a statement of his own aesthetic, but an enraged solidarity with Bigger Thomas born of Baldwin's experience in a French prison: unable to speak, both Baldwin and Bigger are rendered powerless by the massive grinding wheels of the justice system. And yet he wants desperately to distance himself from Bigger, a "heathen" whose very real and absolutely sickening crime repulses Baldwin, as it does all readers. If "receiving stolen goods" lands a black man in jail just as rape and murder do, then the law is a racist, dehumanizing force that puts Baldwin and Bigger in the same cell. Baldwin and Bigger are thus "equal" in Paris, and everywhere else in the Western world. Baldwin's individually created identity is destroyed in favor of a racial identity that labels him a criminal.

If he has any power in the aftermath of his humiliating prison incident, it is the power to rewrite his experience in a voice less naturalistic than Wright's, if no less passionate. Baldwin's early fiction also reveals his fear of the law enforcement officer's power to destroy the individual. Even before his arrest in Paris—which he implies was not his first encounter with the police[23]—Baldwin demonstrated how seemingly confident and angry characters like Peter in "Previous Condition" and Richard in *Go Tell It on the Mountain* are driven to despair when they confront the police. Both Peter and Richard resemble Baldwin in that they are trying to forge a respectable identity by engaging with the artistic creations associated with the finest aspects of white culture. They also resemble two potential outcomes of Baldwin's experience in the Paris prison. Peter retreats to the world from which he has tried to escape and ends his identity quest by giving up, telling a Harlem barfly, "I got no story" (*GM* 100). Richard commits suicide, ending his hopeful identity quest, but somehow passing along his legacy to the novel's protagonist John Grimes. John, in this sense, is the side of Baldwin that lived while Richard represents the side that would have died if the water pipe in the Grand Hôtel du Bac had not burst. Peter inhabits a paralyzed limbo between these two outcomes.

"Previous Condition" was published before the incident described in "Equal in Paris," but it reveals Baldwin's awareness of the power of the law even before he arrived in Paris. Baldwin's first published work of fiction clearly derives from the incident he describes in "Notes of a Native Son" and elsewhere throughout his career when he threw a water glass at a waitress who refused to serve him in a segregated New Jersey restaurant. In "Previous Condition" the waitress is recast as a landlady. Peter illustrates Baldwin's assertion from "Many Thousands Gone"—that "no American Negro exists who does not have his private Bigger Thomas living in the skull" (*NNS* 42). He defines this condition further, strongly echoing Du Bois's definition of double consciousness advanced in *The Souls of Black Folk*:

> no Negro living in America who has not felt, briefly or for long periods, with anguish sharp or dull, in varying degrees and to varying effect, simple, naked and unanswerable hatred; who has not wanted to smash any white face he may encounter in a day, to violate, out of motives of the cruelest vengeance, their women, to break the bodies of all white people and bring them low, as low as that dust into which he himself has been and is being trampled; no Negro, finally, who has not had to make his own precarious adjustment to the 'nigger' who surrounds him and to the 'nigger' in himself. (*NNS* 38)

This rage, in response to racial oppression, is clearly at play when Baldwin throws the glass at the New Jersey waitress, stating, in the film documentary *The Price of the Ticket*, "I wanted to kill her, but I couldn't get close enough." It is also at play when Peter, confronting the racist landlady who wants to evict him, says twice, "I wanted to kill her" (*GM* 91) and elaborates: "I wanted to take a club, a hatchet, and bring it down with all my weight, splitting her skull down the middle where she parted her iron-grey hair" (*GM* 91). We see in Peter's speech not only an echo of Bigger Thomas (whose murder of Mary Dalton is compounded by decapitation), but a foreshadowing of Baldwin's later characters such as Richard in *Blues for Mister Charlie* or Rufus in *Another Country* whose anti-white hostility eventually leads to their own deaths. Peter doesn't act on his rage, though, partly because he has made the "precarious adjustment" Baldwin speaks of in "Many Thousands Gone," but also largely because the landlady threatens him with the most effective weapon she has: "'If you don't get out,' she said, 'I'll get a policeman to put you out'" (*GM* 92).

Peter reveals that his life has been undergoing this "precarious adjustment" for some time, and part of that adjustment involves finding an outlet for his rage that will not land him in prison. Like his earnest expatriate creator who wants to become an honest man and a good writer, Peter has committed himself to acting; yet this acting is a dubious stab at identity formation, especially since he is so often typecast in stereotypical black roles, including "a kind of intellectual Uncle Tom" (*GM* 83) and "the lead in *Native Son*" (*GM* 95), allusions to the two protest novels Baldwin scorns in the first two essays in *Notes*. Peter's acting is also parallel to adjustments he must make so that he is not typecast by the police; he admits,

> I'd learned to get by. I'd learned never to be belligerent with policemen, for instance. No matter who was right, I was certain to be wrong. What might be accepted as just good old American independence in someone else would be insufferable arrogance in me. After the first few times I realized that I had to play smart, to act out the role I was expected to play. I only had one head and it was too easy to get it broken. When I faced a policeman I acted like I didn't know a thing. I let my jaw drop and I let my eyes get big. I didn't give him any smart answers, none of the crap about my rights. I figured out what answers he wanted and I gave them to him. I never let him think he wasn't king. If it was more than routine, if I was picked up on suspicion of robbery or murder in the neighborhood, I looked as humble as I could and kept my mouth shut and prayed. I took a couple of beatings, but I stayed out of prison and I stayed off chain gangs. (*GM* 89)

Peter's survival depends upon this conviction that police power supersedes legal power: he knows better than to talk about his rights, which amount to "crap." His admission shows that he is practical, but also that his ability to act, to "play smart, to act out the role [he] was expected to play," is a form of equivocation or dissembling. His girlfriend Ida responds offhandedly to his strategy for keeping out of prison and off chain gangs, and

Peter's response is, "You mean you think I'm a coward?" (*GM* 89). He is afraid that he has compromised his identity, his place in the world, by conceding to police power and refusing to advocate for his rights.

In fact, he does have the legal right to rent any apartment in the United States: according to the Civil Rights Act of 1866, property owners cannot discriminate against renters or buyers based on race. However, it was common practice to discriminate against renters based on their race or ethnicity before the Supreme Court decision of 1968 known as *Jones vs. Alfred H. Mayer Co.* in which the court decided that the second section of the Thirteenth Amendment could be used in such cases to give Congress the power to enforce this law. In the period between these years, race-based discrimination in property law was made possible through a series of "restrictive covenants" which were originally determined by states, but which later could be applied to cities, even to blocks within cities or to individual buildings. Restrictive covenants proliferated from 1926 (following the Supreme Court decision in *Corrigan v. Buckley*) through 1948, the year Baldwin published "Previous Condition," until the U.S. Supreme Court reversed a decision by the Missouri Supreme Court known as *Shelley v. Kraemer;* according to David Delaney, "The gist of the opinion was that judicial enforcement of the racist contracts counted as 'state action' and therefore violated constitutional rights of equal protection. Restrictive covenants were thereby invalidated as legal techniques for shaping geographies of race and racism."[24] Delaney dubs the period between 1926 and 1948 as "the era of changed conditions,"[25] so named because the most common way to legitimate restrictive covenants was through the line of argument known as "changed conditions"—a slippery term that allowed small courts to argue that local circumstances related to the change in the racial makeup of a neighborhood constituted special cases. The phrase "changed conditions" is a way to interpret the title of "Previous Condition."

Peter, in the late 1940s when the debate over restrictive covenants was reaching a boiling point, understands that he might be able to argue for his legal right to live in this room, but also that the case would be long and costly. He exclaims to his friend Jules, "Can't I get a place to sleep without dragging it through the courts?" (*GM* 93). To Ida's suggestion about Peter's landlady, "We can sue her," Peter replies, "Forget it. I'll end up with lawsuits in every state in the union" (*GM* 96). The courtroom clearly offers no salvation for someone like Peter even if he has the means to hire a lawyer. (Ida claims they can "waste some of [her] husband's money" (*GM* 96) on the suit). Courtroom trials are not an arena he knows; the police, though, are a clear enough symbol of power. When he returns to Harlem at the end of the story, he observes, "There were white mounted policemen in the streets. On every block there was another policeman on foot. I saw a black cop" (*GM* 99). The absolute power of policemen is enough to deflate this enraged young man's budding identity: after the landlady threatens to call them, Peter attempts to keep up his show of bravado, but fails: "I tried to take as long as possible but I cut myself while shaving because I was afraid she would come back upstairs with a policeman" (*GM* 92). This self-inflicted wound, born of fear of policemen and prisons, prefigures Baldwin's suicide attempt under the same circumstances a year after the publication of this story: in both cases, the act of harming oneself is born of an instinctive, desperate desire to escape the law's power.

"Previous Condition" showcases Peter's attempt to find refuge from the streets where there are policemen "on every block." The story's first sentence shows him waking up, "alone in my room," and it is a room described as "dirty" (*GM* 84), "heavy ceilinged, perfectly square, with walls the color of chipped dry blood . . . hideous . . . the kind of room that defeated you" (*GM* 84). And yet it is at least initially a private space where he can smoke cigarettes and listen to Beethoven. The threatened invasion of the room by the police makes sense of Peter's dream at the beginning of the story: in that dream he is running because there is no hiding place, no room of his own. Though confining, the room is paradoxically a space of freedom or protection, or rather it is intended to be. As such, it is a metaphor for Peter's identity quest: his hope that he can determine his own fate is compromised by his nation's prejudices just as his hope that he can dwell in a private room is compromised by the power of the police to evict him, even if he is right, or has rights. He tries to convince himself that this circumstance is not a tragedy; he tells himself, "What's the worst thing that can happen? You won't have a room. The world's full of rooms" (*GM* 91). This bravado is deflated by the fact that he has no room at the end of the story, and moreover, by his own admission in the story's haunting final line, he's got no story. The survival skill he has cultivated to acquiesce to or run from the police has its price.

Yet Peter is alive at the end of his story, and he can cling to the belief that there are other rooms for him in the world. John Grimes's quest in *Go Tell It on the Mountain* is also to forge an identity in the white world apart from the dangerous streets of his youth. His father's house is clearly not the safe space he seeks, nor is the church, the Temple of the Fire Baptized, due to its associations with his father and its restrictive prohibitions of the material world John desires. The church is, of course, more rule-bound than the world in general is. In one of the novel's early scenes Elisha is essentially sentenced in front of the entire church because he has been accused of "walking disorderly" with another church youth, Ella Mae (*GTI* 16). This is one of the reasons John may feel that he and the other youths are "oppressed by their elders" (*GTI* 14) who preside over them according to the absolute authority of their interpretation of the church's laws. C. W. E. Bigsby notes, "'Rejection of God is a natural extension of rebellion against the power of the state,'"[26] but the relationship is actually reversed here: John must first reject the power of the church before he even becomes aware that the state has power. At the beginning of the novel he is only aware of the pleasures of the world outside his father's church, not of its legal power structure: "there awaited him, one day, a house like his father's house, and a church like his father's, and a job like his father's, where he would grow old and black with hunger and toil. The way of the cross had given him a belly filled with wind and had bent his mother's back; they had never worn fine clothes, but here [on Broadway], where the buildings contested God's power and where the men and women did not fear God, here he might eat and drink to his heart's content and clothe his body with wondrous fabrics, rich to the eye and pleasing to the touch" (*GTI* 34). The narrowness and filth of his house contrasts with the glories of midtown Manhattan, and John clearly seeks a private space in the latter; yet he does not know how to access such a space. At the end of the novel he announces, "I'm ready . . . I'm coming. I'm on my way" (*GTI* 221), but that is the extent of his plan.

Two clear alternatives to forming a life outside of the filthy rooms of his youth are represented in the early sections of the book by his father and his brother Roy, both of whom are angry at the white world in general. His father's belligerence manifests itself in abusing his family. Roy takes his anger to the streets: his mother warns him that he is headed "right on down to hell where it looks like you is just determined to go anyhow! Right on, Mister Man, till somebody puts a knife in you, or takes you off to jail!" (*GTI* 24). Roy responds, "I ain't looking to go to no *jail*. You think that's all that's in the world is jails and churches? You ought to know better than that, Ma" (*GTI* 25). The alternative to prison Elizabeth had posited, though, is not church, but the prophecy that someone would stab Roy with a knife, which happens just a few hours later. (This was also the fate of Gabriel's first son through his affair with Esther, also named Royal.) Peter in "Previous Condition" only wanted to avoid prison and chain gangs; John in *Go Tell It* seeks to avoid his brother's destiny (stabbing) and his stepfather's destiny (church). Yet his mother's admonition that jail offers a third alternative to be avoided is represented in her "prayer," the section of the novel devoted to her past, specifically to her connection to John's biological father, Richard.

Though it comprises a relatively small space in the novel, the narrative of Richard's life, often bypassed by critics in favor of John's or Gabriel's narratives, is crucial. From Elizabeth's perspective, the interlude of her life involving Richard represents God's punishment: "being forced to choose between Richard and God, she could only, even with weeping, have turned away from God. And this was why God had taken him from her. It was for all of this that she was paying now, and it was this pride, hatred, bitterness, lust—this folly, this corruption—of which her son was heir" (*GTI* 158). Like John, Elizabeth was compelled to choose between God and between the "sinful" alternative, the godless lover who at one point says of Jesus, "You can tell that puking bastard to kiss my big black ass" (*GTI* 163). Yet her fatalistic interpretation of Richard's death seems less attributable to God than to a corrupt justice system in which racist cops and biased accusers conspire to destroy the soul of a poor, uneducated black man who is trying desperately to access the cultural institutions of the white world. Elizabeth blames herself repeatedly, especially in the following sentences: "What was coming would surely come; nothing could stop it. She had tried, once, to protect someone and had only hurled him into prison" (*GTI* 175). The implication of the second sentence is that *she* was directly responsible for Richard's tragic imprisonment, but an objective observer can clearly see the fault in the broken justice system that is indifferent to Elizabeth's actions.

The love affair between Elizabeth and Richard is the purest in the book, the only one that highlights mutual respect and unselfish devotion. Elizabeth ironically describes love itself as a kind of prison in contrast to the material prisons that surround her: "She sensed that what her aunt spoke of as love was something else—a bribe, a threat, an indecent will to power. She knew that the kind of imprisonment that love might impose was also, mysteriously, a freedom for the soul and spirit, was water in the dry place, and had nothing to do with the prisons, churches, laws, rewards, and punishments that so positively cluttered the landscape of her aunt's mind" (*GTI* 158). If Elizabeth believes that love is a kind of salvation expressed as "imprisonment," Richard's fate is cynical indeed, and the author's cynicism in the creation and suicide of this character is certainly born of his own experience in prison that led to the deepest despair he ever felt.

Richard resembles Baldwin on a number of levels: both are prickly intellectuals, impressed with the art and artifacts of the white world, angry at the fact that they must work to gain access to this art, and ambitious to build on their anger in order to achieve respect; Richard says, "I just decided me one day that I was going to get to know everything them white bastards knew, and I was going to get to know it better than them, so could no white son-of-a-bitch *nowhere* never talk *me* down, and never make me feel like *I* was dirt, when I could read him the alphabet, back, front, and sideways" (*GTI* 167). His knowledge coupled with this bravado makes Richard seem like a survivor. Yet the event that reduces his confident façade to rubble is his arrest and imprisonment for a crime he did not commit.

In the scene surrounding Richard's arrest, we see a direct echo of the anger Peter from "Previous Condition" felt toward the white landlady who threatened to call the cops to evict him, but here the anger is transferred from the victim (Richard) to his loved one (Elizabeth). Sexually harassed by the white police officers who arrested Richard, Elizabeth meditates on their (phallic) symbols of power, then is consumed by virtually the same revenge fantasies Peter expressed: "She found herself fascinated by the gun in his holster, the club at his side. She wanted to take that pistol and empty it into his round, red face; to take that club and strike with all her strength against the base of his skull where his cap ended, until the ugly, silky, white man's hair was matted with blood and brains" (*GTI* 169). This graphic fantasy of violence directed at a white authority figure proves how deeply Baldwin linked racism to wrongful arrest. Here he overcomes the impulse in "Equal in Paris" to leave race out of the power dynamic: Richard is arrested because he is black, and the police and the accuser make no secret about this fact. When Elizabeth asks the police officer why Richard has been arrested, he responds, "For robbing a white man's store, black girl" (*GTI* 169) and when Richard tells the accuser that he wasn't at the scene of the crime, the accuser responds, "You black bastards . . . you're all the same" (*GTI* 171). Baldwin also adds a sexual dimension to this power dynamic: as the policemen repeatedly make suggestive comments to Elizabeth, she becomes aware of the way she must respond: "She knew that there was nothing to be gained by talking to them any more. She was entirely in their power; she would have to think faster than they could think; she would have to contain her fear and her hatred, and find out what could be done" (*GTI* 170). Her response is similar to Peter's understanding that silence is his only recourse when faced with the law's power.

If Elizabeth and Peter represent the fast-thinking, shrewd side of Baldwin when facing the police, Richard represents his fearful, despairing side. As if the psychological torment of being arrested isn't enough, Richard has been physically brutalized when Elizabeth visits him in prison (prefiguring the fate of Tony Maynard in *No Name in the Street*): "He had been beaten, he whispered to her, and he could hardly walk. His body, she later discovered, bore almost no bruises, but was full of strange, painful swellings, and there was a welt above one eye" (*GTI* 170). We later learn that he had been beaten because he refused to sign a confession for a crime he did not commit. The addition of a physical element to the psychological torment of wrongful imprisonment makes the experience of incarceration more immediate to the reader. The fact that Richard's wounds are nearly invisible demonstrates how efficient the police are at exercising their criminal power: even if justice is served and the accused is found innocent, the damage has been done.

Compounding the actual damage done is Richard's realization that all of this would happen: as soon as he sees white men chasing black men in the subway just prior to his arrest, "he knew that whatever the trouble was, it was now his trouble also; for these white men would make no distinction between him and the three boys they were after" (*GTI* 171). The perpetrators of the crime do not initially rush to Richard's defense because "they probably also felt that it would be useless to speak" (*GTI* 171). Like Elizabeth, their only recourse when talking to the arresting officers is silence; even when they speak for Richard's innocence in the station, "they were not believed" (*GTI* 171). Race may be the reason Richard is arrested, but poverty is the reason he will not receive a fair trial. Realizing this, Elizabeth "sat before him, going over in her mind all the things she might do to raise money, even to going on the streets" (*GTI* 172). Illegal behavior is the only viable way to combat the criminal power that Elizabeth and Richard are confronted with, but it seems futile. The power of the courts, in Richard's thoroughly jaundiced view, is even greater than the power of God; he sarcastically suggests, "'Maybe you ought to pray to that Jesus of yours and get Him to come down and tell these white men something.' He looked at her a long, dying moment. 'Because I don't know nothing *else* to do'" (*GTI* 172). Richard's realization that he has no viable options echoes in Elizabeth's mind on the same page, and she, like Peter, is thrust out onto the streets away from any safe domestic space: "In the streets she did not know what to do. . . . She looked out into the quiet, sunny streets, and for the first time in her life, she hated it all—the white city, the white world" (*GTI* 172–173).

Richard is released from prison due to lack of evidence, and like Baldwin in Paris, the legal world seems either indifferent to or sadistic about his plight: "The courtroom seemed to feel, with some complacency and some disappointment, that it was his great good luck to be let off so easily" (*GTI* 173). Hoping for a safe space away from the jail cell and the streets, Elizabeth and Richard "went immediately to his room" (*GTI* 173), but its safety and sanctity have been destroyed by the police and the courts. Richard weeps in despair and when Elizabeth touches him she discovers that "his body was like iron" (*GTI* 174), demonstrating how thoroughly the prison has gotten into his system. The experience overwhelms him as it did Baldwin: "That night he cut his wrists with his razor and he was found in the morning by his landlady, his eyes staring upward with no light, dead among the scarlet sheets" (*GTI* 173). In Richard's bloody, tragic end, the image of the sheet is once again associated with death, and a landlady looms over the scene, a haunting reminder of the landlady who substituted for the police in "Previous Condition." Perhaps the most defiant rendition of this character we have seen yet, Richard is brought lower than the others here, and his suicide against the backdrop of a sheet confirms that, because of the law's invasive power, no room is safe.

Baldwin explores the metaphorical dimensions of rooms in great detail in *Giovanni's Room,* his novel that pays the least attention to race relations. In keeping with *Giovanni's Room*'s emphasis on interiority, the law in this novel is initially reflected inside the protagonist David who declares, "My crime, in some odd way, is in being a man" (*GR* 95), an idea Baldwin earlier develops in the essay "The Male Prison" (1954). David's statement is incomplete, though, just as his confession throughout *Giovanni's Room* is never fully formed: his crime is not in being a man, but in failing to admit his homosexuality in a culture that adheres to heterosexist definitions of manhood. The other dimension of David's halting admission of criminality, though, is that homosexuality was indeed criminal behavior in 1956 when the novel was published. Most states had anti-sodomy laws on the books, though many were not enforced. These laws were not deemed unconstitutional until 2002 in the Supreme Court case *Lawrence et al. vs. Texas.* When Giovanni says to David, "We have not committed any crime," the guilty American lover replies, "it *is* a crime—in my country and, after all, I didn't grow up here, I grew up *there*" (*GR* 107). Giovanni responds, "If your countrymen think that privacy is a crime, so much the worse for your country" (*GR* 107–8). His interpretation that the law criminalizes privacy rather than homosexuality is telling: David has absorbed the message of his country's laws and transferred them to his own set of beliefs, which means that, for him, privacy and the possibility for homosexual love are simultaneously forbidden. Public judgment and criminal activity become synonymous for David, and the word "guilt" amounts to his admission of sin and crime.

We can see in *Giovanni's Room* Baldwin reworking his Paris jail experience in another way. Richard in *Go Tell It on the Mountain* represents the suicide outcome, but Baldwin had begun to imagine the redemptive power of love as another outcome. In two reworkings of "Equal in Paris" unpublished in Baldwin's lifetime—the television play *Dark Runner* and a short story entitled "Equal in Paris," both co-written with Sol Stein and recently published in *Native Sons* (2005)—Baldwin added a female love interest to the story. Both of these fictionalized scenarios end, rather improbably, with the protagonist, just released from prison, reuniting with a young woman named Siddy whose love presumably will help erase the pain of wrongful imprisonment. As Baldwin translates his experience into fiction, imprisonment has two outcomes: suicidal despair or the hopefulness of love. In *Giovanni's Room* both of these elements are present, but Baldwin varies and rearranges the formula in order to explore the theme in detail: the rejection of love leads to despair, which manifests itself in Giovanni's imprisonment and death sentence, a form of suicide. As David realizes, "Perhaps he wanted to die. He pleaded guilty" (*GR* 208). David allows the French justice system to absolve him of his own guilt with one clean drop of the guillotine's blade, but the novel is in fact a study in how false such a resolution is.

David's situation in Paris initially echoes Baldwin's experience in overt ways: emphasizing his own poverty repeatedly, David tells Giovanni during their initial meeting, "My hotel wants to throw me out" (*GR* 62). Giovanni later invites him back to his room, arguing, "There is certainly no point in going home now, to face an ugly concierge and then go to sleep in that room all by yourself and then wake up later with a terrible stomach and a sour mouth, wanting to commit suicide" (*GR* 85). David later provides an admission that explains Baldwin's own rationalization about his suicide attempt: "I had thought of suicide when I was much younger, as, possibly, we all have, but then it would have been for revenge, it would have been my way of informing the world how awfully it had made me suffer" (*GR* 136). The skeleton of the "Equal in Paris" story in place, with a poor young American being thrown out of a hotel and contemplating suicide, Baldwin then develops the interrelationship of the criminal power of the state and the failure of the individual to act courageously.

If "Equal in Paris," "Previous Condition," and Richard's narrative in *Go Tell It* are the stories of how the individual's sense of safety is violated by the law's power, *Giovanni's Room* is the story of how that sense of safety is and always has been an illusion. Public safety is ostensibly the main goal of the law as it is represented by police on the street, and David uses that public safety as an excuse to validate his own need for personal safety, the safe choice of rejecting the love that his countrymen have criminalized. In a telling paragraph he reveals that the reason he loves Paris "so much" is because of its walls, the barriers that separate the private world of the French middle class from the public world of the streets: "Those walls, those shuttered windows held them in and protected them against the darkness and the long moan of this long night. Ten years hence, little Jean Pierre or Marie might find themselves out here beside the river and wonder, like me, how they had fallen out of the web of safety" (*GR* 137). We see this same imagery when David is wrestling with his personal demons as Giovanni is about to be executed: "Walls, windows, mirrors, water, the night outside—they are everywhere. I might call—as Giovanni, at this moment lying in his cell, might call. But no one will hear. I might try to explain. Giovanni tried to explain. I might ask to be forgiven—if I could name and face my crime, if there were anything or anybody anywhere with the power to forgive" (*GR* 148). The wall imagery that pervades the latter half of the novel represents the division between the public and the private, but also the division between the criminal and the free. At this moment David fully realizes his complicity in Giovanni's crime and feels as though he is in the same jail cell.

This feeling of empathy leads David, who has struggled to lead an upright life in the eyes of society, into a meditation on prison that further develops the image of the wall:

> I walk up and down this house—up and down this house. I think of prison. Long ago, before I had ever met Giovanni, I met a man at a party at Jacques' house who was celebrated because he had spent half his life in prison. He had then written a book about it which displeased the prison authorities and won a literary prize. But this man's life was over. He was fond of saying that, since to be in prison was simply not to live, the death penalty was the only merciful verdict any jury could deliver. I remember thinking that, in effect, he had never left prison. Prison was all that was real to him; he could speak of nothing else. All his movements, even to the lighting of a cigarette, were stealthy, wherever his eyes focused one saw a wall rise up. His face, the color of his face brought to mind darkness and dampness, I felt that if one cut him,

his flesh would be the flesh of mushrooms. And he described to us in avid, nostalgic detail the barred windows, the barred doors, the judas, the guards standing at far ends of corridors, under the light. It is three tiers high inside the prison and everything is the color of gunmetal. Everything is dark and cold, except for those patches of light, where authority stands. (GR 149)

The passage, which continues to contemplate the prison cell, is striking for its tactile and visual detail, especially coming from David who is generally adept at distancing himself from unpleasantness. As Kathleen Drowne points out, "For the most part, the physical places described in *Giovanni's Room* are dark and dirty and close; virtually every indoor scene is characterized by a feeling of airlessness, and the characters often seem on the verge of suffocation."[27] Giovanni accuses David of sharing the American trait of wanting everything to be clean, orderly, and light (GR 187), which is why David rejects Giovanni's disorderly and filthy room. In fact, this meditation on prison leads David back to a contemplation of the room: "I wonder about the size of Giovanni's cell. I wonder if it is bigger than his room" (GR 150). The private space that contained their love affair is here directly linked to the alienated space of incarceration in David's mind, and presumably in Giovanni's experience: "Whether he is with others or not, he is certainly alone. I try to see him, his back to me, standing at the window of his cell. From where he is perhaps he can only see the opposite wing of the prison; perhaps, by straining a little, just over the high wall, a patch of the street outside" (GR 150–51). David is attempting here to peer over the walls of the prison, and even to imagine himself inside Giovanni's cell with him. But he is also aware of his participation in building the walls that separate them. This connection and separation between Giovanni and David is the central theme of the novel as it is manifested in the room as metaphor. The penal system has evolved an elaborate mechanism for what Foucault calls "the principle of elementary location or partitioning. Each individual has his own place; and each place its individual. . . . Disciplinary space tends to be divided into as many sections as there are bodies or elements to be distributed."[28] Having largely subscribed to the values of his society that disciplines prisoners this way, it is no surprise that David translates the logic of the prison to his relationship with Giovanni: most notably, it is *Giovanni's room,* in David's mind and in the novel's title, and it never becomes a shared space.

The walls that David helps to build are in fact related to the walls of the prison. As Giovanni tells David, homosexuality is not a crime in Paris; however, the law has a way of displaying public distaste for homosexuality even though it is not illegal. We learn early on in the novel of one of Jacques' favorite bars, "Every once in a while it was raided by the police" (*GR* 37), an act that is explained after Giovanni has apparently murdered Guillaume: "Plainclothes policemen descended on the quarter, asking to see everyone's papers, and the bars were emptied of *tapettes* [derogatory term for homosexual men]. . . . Most of the men picked up in connection with this crime [Guillaume's murder] were not picked up on suspicion of murder. They were picked up on suspicion of having what the French, with a delicacy I take to be sardonic, call *les gouts particuliers*. These 'tastes,' which do not constitute a crime in France, are nevertheless regarded with extreme disapprobation by the bulk of the populace" (*GR* 197–98). If one homosexual allegedly killed another homosexual, the effect of the police raid is not only to find and arrest the murderer, but to "out" the men who frequent this bar who might otherwise be considered respectable hetero- sexuals: "Fathers of families, sons of great houses, and itching adventurers from Belleville were all desperately anxious that the case be closed, so that things might, in effect, go back to normal and the dreadful whiplash of public morality not fall on their backs" (*GR* 198). This passage empha- sizes the connection between law enforcement and public approval or dis- approval.

The law is ostensibly based on public approval or disapproval, and Baldwin reveals an understanding of the way the general public and law enforcement officers participate in the same processes of vigilance. When David observes that "it was astonishing that in so small and policed a city [Giovanni] should prove so hard to find" (*GR* 201), the "policing" he speaks of involves the community as well as the actual police. David's initial fantasy that France offers complete privacy and a lack of surveil- lance proves as self-deceptive as his belief in emotional safety; he says near the beginning of his narrative, "these nights were being acted out under a foreign sky, with no one to watch, no penalties attached" (*GR* 9–10), but he gradually reveals a public watchfulness that exists under this for- eign sky just as it did back home. He expresses fear at the feeling of being watched when he first encounters Giovanni: "And then I watched their faces, watching him. And then I was afraid. I knew that they were watch- ing, had been watching both of us. They knew that they had witnessed a beginning and now they would not cease to watch until they saw the end. It had taken some time but the tables had been turned; now I was in the zoo and they were watching" (*GR* 53). The privacy and sanctity of an individual's room is fully exposed as illusory here: David is in a cage, being watched, yet unable to escape, and the analogy to being imprisoned is all but explicit. The surveillance that invades the private space of love is also omnipresent on the Parisian streets: "it was a fireman who, seeing [Giovanni] crawl back into hiding with a loaf of bread one night, tipped off the police" (*GR* 101). David's guilt, caused by his upbringing in a nation where homosexuality is criminalized, is exacerbated by this very real sensation that he is always being watched, observed, and judged. Giovanni may be literally imprisoned, but psychologically, nothing separates him from David.

David is eager to ally himself with the general heterosexual population, which is why he is reluctant to reveal his homosexuality to either his father or to Hella, and in fact perpetuates the pretense that he is going to marry Hella in order to please both of them. But his refuge in heterosexual mores is probably born more of fear than of the will to please anyone. He expresses this fear in terms of one of his failures of willpower: in trying to repress his homosexual desires, he declares, "I had decided to allow *no room* in the universe for something which shamed and frightened me" (*GR* 30; emphasis mine), yet he admits to a number of "drops," which he describes "like an airplane hitting an air pocket. And there were a number of those, all drunken, all sordid, one very frightening such drop while I was in the Army which involved a fairy who was later court-martialed out. The panic his punishment caused in me was as close as I ever came to facing in myself the terrors I sometimes saw clouding another man's eyes" (*GR* 31). Here his adoption not only of heterosexual mores, but of heterosexist stereotypes ("fairy") is linked directly to crime and punishment.

David's solution to his complex problem of wanting both homosexual love and heterosexual approval is to join forces with the upholders of the law and of public taste: the police. He realizes how powerless he is, especially after Giovanni narrates an episode in which Guillaume threatens to have him arrested; Giovanni says, "[Guillaume] began saying that I was a *tapette* and a thief and told me to leave at once or he would call the police and have me put behind bars. . . . Everybody knew that Guillaume was right and I was wrong, that I had done something awful. . . . I hated to walk away but I knew if anything more happened, the police would come and Guillaume would have me put in jail" (*GR* 143, 144, 145). David becomes the only character in a Baldwin novel to attempt to make friends with the police: "There was a policeman standing there, his blue hood, weighted, hanging down behind, his white club gleaming. He looked at me and smiled and cried, '*Ça va?*'

'*Oui, merci.* And you?'

'*Toujours.* It's a nice day, no?'" (*GR* 193).

Their small talk continues, and David seems desperate to keep his attention, but the officer begins bantering with a middle class housewife. After briefly fantasizing about her life, David hopes that he can continue his substanceless conversation with the officer, but he is disappointed: "The bus came and the policeman and I, the only people waiting, got on— he stood on the platform, far from me. The policeman was not young, either, but he had a gusto which I admired" (*GR* 193). Tellingly, the last time he encountered a policeman was when he and Hella had just met upon her return to Paris, and David describes the officer in exactly the same way: "Hella looked about delightedly at all of it, the cafés, the self-contained people, the violent snarl of traffic, the blue-caped traffic police-man and his white, gleaming club" (*GR* 160). Clearly the policeman, especially the details of his uniform (blue cape, white, gleaming club) are associated in David's mind with both safety and with heterosexuality. In cozying up to the policeman at the bus stop, he is trying to avoid the fate of Giovanni: the poor, homosexual street kid who is initially criminalized through the accusations of his wealthy social superior, Guillaume. Even though David succeeds in distancing himself from Giovanni, the price he pays is eternal torment.

One factor that unites all of Baldwin's protagonists discussed in this chapter is their roomlessness, a metaphor for isolation. This isolation is not merely a condition of a disenfranchised young man trying to find his place in the world in the absence of traditionally stable cultural institutions like family, religion, and higher education. It is a direct function of the realization of the law's monolithic power; as Foucault says of the first logical principle of the prison, "Isolation provides an intimate exchange between the convict and the power that is exercised over him."[29] In his early creative imagination, Baldwin interprets the criminal power of the law in terms of the way it exercises its influence unevenly due to differ-ences in economic worth, race, and sexuality. Race is perhaps surprisingly underemphasized in "Equal in Paris" and in *Giovanni's Room,* but his ren-ditions of the incident in "Previous Condition" and *Go Tell It* demonstrate the shape of things to come: in future writings, the law will most often manifest its criminal power in terms of race. But sexuality and poverty are not unimportant in this formulation, and the three together provide an example of what Critical Race Theorists describe as intersectionality, or the combination of social circumstances that lead to criminalization. The law has the ability to aid in the persecution of anyone who is relatively powerless in society's eyes. The only rooms available to the persecuted are jail cells, and these are rooms that belong to the state, not to the self.

CHAPTER 2

Other Countries, Hidden Laws

T HE CONCEPT of interest convergence, a cornerstone of Critical Race
   Theory, argues that some of the most progressive-seeming acts of
legislation with regard to race may actually exist not because of moral
imperatives, but because there is a certain social advantage for majority
groups to pass legislation that supposedly benefits minorities. In this way,
racial hierarchies can be sustained even when the passing of such legislation would seem to indicate a move toward equality. As Baldwin began to
emerge from his cocoon of fear of incarceration, he was able to develop a
nascent recognition that the law operates in sometimes invisible ways, and
even when it was not persecuting him directly, it certainly did not exist to
prevent his persecution. As the Civil Rights Movement entered its heyday
and progress seemed within reach, Baldwin reserved a suspicion that any
legal progress he observed was not designed with his interests in mind.

The earliest phase of Baldwin's career, from the mid-1940s through
the late 1950s, involved exile and the need to discover and define his role
as an artist. The next phase, from the late 1950s through the mid-1960s,
involved a return to his homeland, both in his life and in his writings, in
order to discover the meaning of his troubled citizenship. The title of the
first essay in his second essay collection, "The Discovery of What It Means
to Be an American," announces this quest, and the subtitle of the collection, *Nobody Knows My Name: More Notes of a Native Son,* signals his
need to preserve his early identity, but also to refine or augment it. In this
second phase of Baldwin's career his personal life is still primary, but the

lives of others take a more prominent position in his writings. He was poised to emerge from the rooms and cells that had confined him in his early years.

In "The Discovery of What it Means to Be an American," Baldwin writes, "Every society is really governed by hidden laws, by unspoken but profound assumptions on the part of the people, and ours is no exception. It is up to the American writer to find out what these laws and assumptions are" (*Nobody* 23). Baldwin defines the role of the writer in terms of nationhood here, and he also reveals a tension between the laws we can see and "hidden laws" which "really govern" society. The essay was published in 1959, five years after the landmark *Brown vs. Board of Education* case outlawing segregation in public schools, and the implication of Baldwin's observation is that the "laws" we cannot see are capable of undermining the actual laws we have ratified. If it is officially illegal to segregate our nation based on race, then why does racial discrimination persist? The "hidden laws" that provide the answer to that question involve all of the social forces that actually weaken or even negate the official laws that define a nation.

In the essay "Princes and Powers," a work of reportage about the 1956 Conference of Negro-African Writers and Artists, Baldwin contemplates the unique status of the African American artist that becomes evident when he is compared to his African counterparts. The very definition of a "Negro" is intertwined for Baldwin with American legal definitions; in "Down at the Cross," the longer essay in *The Fire Next Time,* he writes, "Negroes do not, strictly or legally speaking, exist in any other [country]" than the United States (*FNT* 25). In "Princes and Powers" he similarly observes, "The chief of the delegation, John Davis, was to be asked just *why* he considered himself a Negro—he was to be told that he certainly didn't look like one. He *is* a Negro, of course, from the remarkable legal point of view which obtains in the United States" (*Nobody* 28–29). In his use of the word "legal" in these two quotations, Baldwin is undoubtedly referring to the so-called "one-drop" acts defining any American with more than one drop of black blood—that is to say, with any trace of ancestry originating in sub-Saharan Africa.[1] The first of these acts was passed in Tennessee in 1910; by 1925, the majority of states had followed suit, or had adapted the law by specifying that certain fractions of African ancestry defined one's race.[2] In 1924, the year of Baldwin's birth, the commonwealth of Virginia passed its infamous Racial Integrity Act that not only defined racial minorities according to the "one drop" rule, but also forbade intermarriage between anyone in this category and anyone considered white. This act was not overturned until the *Loving* decision of 1967. When Baldwin wrote "Princes and Powers," then, the "remarkable legal point of view" he alludes to was firm and discriminatory. It had the capacity to define citizenship as well as to control and restrict behavior. Moreover, as Ian Haney-López argues, the "many laws that discriminated on the basis of race more often than not defined, and thus helped to create, the categories they claimed only to elucidate."[3] In other words, the law was responsible not only for defining what it means to be black or white, but for arguing why these categories matter.

National identity and racial identity are tied together in Baldwin's formulation, and they are bound inextricably by legal definitions. Baldwin wonders, as he did in his earlier essay "Encounter on the Seine: Black meets Brown," what connects black people across the globe; in "Princes and Powers" he writes, "For what, beyond the fact that all black men at one time or another left Africa, or have remained there, do they really have in common?" (*Nobody* 35). He concludes, "What they held in common was their precarious, their unutterably painful relation to the white world" (*Nobody* 35). Summarizing Aimé Césaire's speech at the conference, Baldwin goes on to describe how this relationship has historically amounted to an exercise of power and to a system of oppression designed to deny legal agency to black men and women: "Europeans never had the remotest intention of raising Africans to the Western level, or sharing with them the instruments of physical, political, or economic power" (*Nobody* 38). Baldwin describes Césaire's speech as "brilliantly delivered" (*Nobody* 40), yet he reserves some skepticism because, in addition to oppression, European colonialism also created "men like himself" (*Nobody* 41)— that is, Césaire, but also Baldwin. In other words, Baldwin bristles at the notion that colonial power, manifested in legal power, can prevent artists and intellectuals from flourishing. This attitude amounts to a repudiation of the law's immense power, born of his need to believe in his own potential to escape it. Baldwin's belief in his ability to thrive as an artist is, after all, what kept him alive after his wrongful imprisonment in Paris.

However, he does accept the general premise that law is a blunt instrument used to preserve hierarchies. He registers a speech from a Sudanese leader in great detail:

> M. Wahal, from the Sudan, spoke in the afternoon on the role of the law in culture, using as an illustration the role the law had played in the history of the American Negro. He spoke at length on the role of French law in Africa, pointing out that French law is simply not equipped to

deal with the complexity of the African situation. And what is even worse, of course, is that it makes virtually no attempt to do so. The result is that French law, in Africa, is simply a legal means of administering injustice. It is not a solution, either, simply to revert to African tribal custom, which is also helpless before the complexities of present-day African life. Wahal spoke with a quiet matter-of-fact-ness, which lent great force to the ugly story he was telling, and he concluded by saying that the question was ultimately a political one and that there was no hope of solving it within the framework of the present colonial system. (*Nobody* 43–44)

Unlike Césaire's speech, which Baldwin sees as a commentary on the fragility of artists and spokespeople like himself, Wahal's speech is for Baldwin a general truth about colonial power, and he doesn't challenge it. He is impressed by the raw truth of the "ugly" story and by the understated way it is conveyed.

French law was the force that had brought him so low in Paris in 1955. In Wahal's speech French law is untranslatable, and thus dangerous, in an African context, but Baldwin points out that the speech began by considering African American history and the law. The trajectory of Baldwin's career at this time, soon after the publication of *Giovanni's Room,* led him to return to the United States, both in his life and in his writings, to test in his home country the lessons he had learned about the tension between European law and African subjugation. In fact, Baldwin's awareness of this tension was one of the reasons he ended this first long period of exile; according to David Leeming, Baldwin originally wanted to return to Paris from Corsica, where the end of a love affair had left him depressed, but "Jimmy's Paris had changed. The race problems there had been complicated by the French colonial wars, and they reminded him constantly of his need to get home."[4] In July of 1957 Baldwin sailed from France to New York in order to complete a number of writing projects, but also because he felt a strong pull to apply the lessons he had learned in Europe to his native land.

The essay immediately following "Princes and Powers" in *Nobody Knows My Name,* "Fifth Avenue, Uptown: A Letter from Harlem," is the most important one in the collection with regard to Baldwin's evolving understanding of and concern with the law. Originally published in *Esquire* in July 1960, this essay is one of Baldwin's first considerations of Harlem itself as a kind of prison; he writes of the "so many, for so long, struggling in the . . . barbed wire, of this avenue" (*Nobody* 55).

He describes the clear boundaries that delineate his old neighborhood, and indicates that these boundaries are contiguous with actual prisons, for most of the young people he observes are "on the way to prison or just coming out" (*Nobody* 57). He is also aware that police brutality has removed some others, "those who, by . . . a policeman's gun or billy . . . are dead" (*Nobody* 56). Still others are faced with the prospect of working "in the white man's world all day and com[ing] home in the evening to this fetid block" (*Nobody* 57). Because he is describing an area much larger than a city block, the evocation of a "cell block" is evident in this phrase, and Baldwin implies that Harlemites are convicts "whose only crime is color" (*Nobody* 58). The world of the Harlem housing projects he describes is bleak, with poverty and racial discrimination combining to form the very portrait of hopelessness. The connection between what would seem like socioeconomic realities and the law and its means of criminalizing the poor is finally explicit in Baldwin's essay: "The projects are hideous, of course, there being a law, apparently respected through the world, that popular housing shall be as cheerless as a prison" (*Nobody* 60). Although he is being facetious in the way he uses "the law" in this sentence, it is clear that Baldwin sees this phenomenon as sanctioned by society—one of its "hidden laws"—and far from coincidental. Society mirrors the partitions and hierarchies of the prison world, even on the outside.

If Harlem and its housing projects are comparable to prisons in Baldwin's interpretation, the police are similarly analogous to corrections officers. The police are also metonyms for prisons, if we follow Baldwin's comparison; he writes, "The projects in Harlem are hated. They are hated almost as much as policemen, and this is saying a great deal. And they are hated for the same reason: both reveal, unbearably, the real attitude of the white world, no matter how many liberal speeches are made, no matter how many lofty editorials are written, no matter how many civil-rights commissions are set up" (*Nobody* 60). The police and the prison-like projects are, for Baldwin, yet more evidence of the hidden laws he speaks of in "The Discovery of What it Means to Be an American." The ubiquity of the police and the evident similarities between Harlem projects and prison strongly connote a lack of freedom, a constant demonstration of scrutiny, and a will to confinement that collectively, in Baldwin's eyes, amount to the "real attitude of the white world" toward the black world.

In this essay Baldwin calls for nothing less than the abolition of ghettos, knowing that they can only make worse the divide between the poor and the wealthy, which largely overlaps with the divide between nonwhite and white at this moment in history. While ghettos exist, economic opportunity and class mobility are prevented, and "law enforcement" only serves to uphold this principle; as Baldwin writes, "the only way to police a ghetto is to be oppressive." He goes on to analyze the police presence in Harlem in such a detailed way that it is worth quoting at length:

> None of the Police Commissioner's men, even with the best will in the world, have any way of understanding the lives led by the people they swagger about in twos and threes controlling. Their very presence is an insult, and it would be even if they spend their entire day feeding gum-drops to children. They represent the force of the white world, and that world's real intentions are, simply, for that world's criminal profit and ease, to keep the black man *corralled up here, in his place.* The badge, the gun in the holster, and the swinging club make vivid what will happen should his rebellion become overt. Rare, indeed, is the Harlem citizen, from the most circumspect church member to the most shiftless adolescent, who does not have a long tale to tell of police incompetence, injustice, or brutality. I myself have witnessed and endured it more than once. (*Nobody* 62; emphasis mine)

A few words are striking in this quotation: "controlling," "force," "corralled," and "rebellion." These words do not describe the official vocation of the police ("to protect and to serve") so much as they describe what might happen in an actual prison. These are terms of what Foucault describes as discipline; for instance, Foucault writes, "Discipline sometimes requires *enclosure,* the specification of a place heterogeneous to all others and closed in upon itself."[5] Baldwin describes the Harlemite as "corralled, in his place" by the police force. Foucault goes on to interpret in detail "the control of activity" and "the composition of forces,"[6] using the same words as Baldwin (control and force) to describe the most efficient way to discipline what he calls "docile bodies." Baldwin's evocation of "rebellion" contains the hope that the bodies of oppressed Harlemites will not remain docile. Perhaps most striking in Baldwin's observation is his explanation of the presence of these police officers: they exist for the white "world's criminal profit and ease." This ease is made possible by the poverty and suffering of the black world whose presupposed criminal status is indicated by the policemen and the prison-like ghetto they patrol.

And yet Baldwin takes pains not to blame the officers themselves, lest the reader forget that they exist on behalf of an invisible, controlling force, the one that Baldwin will later label "criminal." He writes,

It is hard, on the other hand, to blame the policeman, blank, good-natured, thoughtless, and insuperably innocent, for being such a perfect representative of the people he serves. He, too, believes in good intentions and is astounded and offended when they are not taken for the deed. He has never, himself, done anything for which to be hated—which of us has?—and yet he is facing, daily and nightly, people who would gladly see him dead, and he knows it. There is no way for him not to know it: there are few things under heaven more unnerving than the silent, accumulating contempt and hatred of a people. He moves through Harlem, therefore, like an occupying soldier in a bitterly hostile country; which is precisely what, and where, he is, and is the reason he walks in twos and threes. And he is not the only one who knows why he is always in company: the people who are watching him know why, too. Any street meeting, sacred or secular, which he and his colleagues uneasily cover has as its explicit or implicit burden the cruelty and injustice of the white domination. (*Nobody* 62–63)

Baldwin attempts to separate the enforcement officer from the force he represents, but ultimately the human face he attempts to give the police vanishes, for he is speaking in broad generalities: the single policeman "becomes more callous, the population becomes more hostile, the situation grows more tense, and the police force is increased. One day, to everyone's astonishment, someone drops a match in the powder keg and everything blows up" (*Nobody* 63). Baldwin uses the imagery of war (soldiers, powder keg) to indicate the depth of division in his nation, symbolized by the presence of the police in Harlem who are there, in their "insuperable innocence," in the name of keeping the peace. The nation is so divided that it seems more than one nation: Harlem is a "bitterly hostile country." This notion gives Baldwin the title for his third novel.

Another Country develops a theme apparent in Baldwin's early work, especially in *Giovanni's Room*: the dividing line between the public and the private, symbolized by rooms and streets, becomes so sharp in this work that the only logical end point for characters trying to cross and recross the dividing line is alienation. This novel, a bestseller considered prurient by some critics, inchoate by others, and "one of the most powerful novels of our time"[7] by no less a critic than Granville Hicks, has puzzled, pleased, baffled, and intrigued readers for nearly half a century. In an early appreciation, Charles Newman labels it "everybody's existential novel" and claims that "the central burden of the book" is "the frantic attempt to know something of one another."[8] More recent criticism begins with this basic truth and focuses mainly on sexuality, which is certainly a prominent concern in the novel. Emmanuel Nelson has discussed the novel's reception in terms of homophobia, arguing that "the gay content of [Baldwin's] fiction is . . . at least partly responsible for the mixed criticism it has provoked."[9] James A. Dievler combines the motifs of exile and sexuality to argue that Baldwin is, through this novel, "advocating a post-categorical, poststructural concept of sexuality that we might call 'post-sexuality.'"[10] Susan Feldman takes the critical focus on sexuality in a new direction, linking it to psychology: "Baldwin demonstrates that overcoming the categorical barriers that prevent individuals from accepting others' differences only can be achieved by confronting our own buried pasts, our own repressed desires."[11] Feldman's concern is to redress the statements of "literary critics who have criticized *Another Country* for its focus on sexuality and the novel's ostensible failure to explore the racist dynamics of American society."[12] In my reading, such a corrective can be achieved through an examination of the spaces described in the novel and the way they are policed.

Although *Another Country* is devoid of the prison experience, the alienating space of the streets is enforced through a constant police presence, meant to uphold conventional societal mores even in the licentious, bohemian Greenwich Village of the early 1960s. The title *Another Country* has many implications: in a 1961 interview with Studs Terkel, Baldwin says of the title, "It's about this country."[13] In many ways this terse assessment holds true, but there are myriad nuances complicating this simple explanation: for instance, the novel ends with Yves' arrival from France, setting up an implied difference between the nation of Baldwin's exile and the nation of his birth. The American South, from which Leona and Eric hail, is also another country when juxtaposed with the North, and Greenwich Village is another country when seen from Harlem (and vice versa). Finally, though, the novel highlights Baldwin's concern with private and public worlds, and the apartments and streets in Greenwich Village and Harlem illustrate this division. Hybrid spaces like nightclubs demonstrate the volatility of spaces that purport to be both public and private. Bisexuality, interracial sex, and white acceptance of blacks more generally are common in the private spaces of this novel, but these social relationships and attitudes are carefully scrutinized in the public spaces, and this scrutiny is carried out by a ubiquitous police presence.

Baldwin's initial impressions of the Village were formed in 1939, when he first met the painter Beauford Delaney; in the introduction to *The Price of the Ticket* he writes, "racially, the Village was vicious, partly because of the natives, largely because of the tourists, and absolutely because of the cops" (*PT* xi). Rufus, the novel's tragic anti-hero, is aware of this police presence from the very first page of the novel: "The policeman passed him, giving him a look" (*AC* 3). This observation would seem fairly innocuous if the figure of the policeman did not recur a half-dozen times in the following half-dozen pages. Rufus is deep in a pit of suicidal despair, and while it would be too facile to conclude that the police have caused this despair, it is evident that they represent something that has contributed heavily to it. The first policeman merely "gives him a look," but it is this regulatory gaze that has caused him to see himself as the world sees him— through the veil, to borrow Du Bois's metaphor, of law and order. This chaotic protagonist of this chaotic novel[14] rejects every such attempt to control him, and he feels not only regulated, but judged by the police presence that haunts him.

Rufus's inability to love, which corresponds with his emotional scars inflicted by the world's hatred, is also evident throughout this initial description. He notices the emotional vacuity of these late night streets: "Here and there a woman passed, here and there a man; rarely, a couple" (*AC* 4). These people are "whirled away in taxis," presumably toward the comforting spaces of their homes, while "policemen and taxi drivers and others, harder to place" (*AC* 4) remain on the streets. The policemen are difficult for Rufus to "place" because they belong here: they make the streets what they are, a no-man's land of surveillance where a black man's very presence is a cause for suspicion. While strolling through this alienating space, Rufus recalls his first meeting with Leona with whom he is about to "pile into a cab" as though to take refuge, again, from the scrutiny of the police: "The policemen strolled by; carefully, and in fact rather mysteriously conveying their awareness that these particular Negroes, though they were out so late, and mostly drunk, were not to be treated in the usual fashion; and neither were the white people with them" (*AC* 10). It is implied that there is a normal, even official, police treatment of African Americans based on stereotypes: they are potential criminals who are to be carefully controlled and observed. In this setting, in the company of white people and in Harlem, the police avoid their normal treatment of black people, but this behavior is "careful" and "mysterious," which means that it is volatile, or subject to instant change. At any moment they could do what policemen tend to do in Baldwin's work: arrest black people with no due cause or abuse them physically and verbally. After their sexual encounter that night, Leona asks Rufus what his friends are going to think; he responds, "Well, one thing, Leona, they ain't going to call the

law" (*AC* 23). In New York there is no law against interracial relationships, unlike the prohibition of interracial marriage in Virginia, a state in
the region from which Leona has fled, but "the law" could transform the
relationship between them into rape without much trouble. This understanding may account for Rufus's vision of a "lynch mob" during their
first sexual encounter (*AC* 22).

Rufus's memory goes even deeper than this initial meeting with Leona,
though. Her very existence gives way to a lifetime of memories: "For to
remember Leona was also—somehow—to remember . . . the white policemen who had taught him how to hate" (*AC* 6). This vaguely defined
hatred is given more substance on the following page when he is meditating on his sister Ida: "Then he looked out of the window, at the air shaft,
and thought of the whores on Seventh Avenue. He thought of the white
policemen and the money they made on black flesh, the money the whole
world made" (*AC* 7). This may not be the only reason for his "hatred"
of them, but it is initially the only explanation we are given. His feeling
is a complex blend of racial exploitation and frustration at his inability
to protect his sister, or to have any sort of power that might compensate
for the police's abuse of legal power. The viciousness of his initial sexual
encounter with Leona can thus be understood as revenge against white
people, and white policemen in particular. His penis becomes a "weapon"
(*AC* 22) in his imagination, which can be understood through his belief
that the police participate in the exploitation of "black flesh." His affair
with Leona is motivated by the opposite of love—that is, revenge, or the
attempt to gain power over a race that he feels has exploited and systematically humiliated him.

Rufus's unconscious quest is for love and for the related feeling of
security associated with a home, but the ubiquitous police presence makes
it clear to him that the safety of home, like any other notion of safety,
is illusory. In fact, the police actually exist as an obstacle to his reaching
home on the night of his suicide: "Rufus shivered, his hands in his pockets,
looking through the window and wondering what to do. He thought of
walking to Harlem but he was afraid of the police he would encounter in
his passage through the city" (*AC* 41). When Vivaldo tells Rufus that Ida
has reported his absence to the police, Rufus's reaction is physical: "He sat
up. 'The police are looking for me?'" (*AC* 47). He is incapable of imagin-
ing that this circumstance is for his own protection: in his mind the police
represent persecution. Earlier Vivaldo had threatened to report Rufus's
physical abuse of Leona, indicating in no uncertain terms the power the
police have over Rufus:

"You could be killed for this," said Vivaldo. "All she has to do is yell. All *I* have to do is walk down to the corner and get a cop."

"You trying to scare me? Go *get* a cop."

"You must be out of your mind. They'd take one look at the situation and put you *under* the jailhouse." (*AC* 55)

Rufus taunts Vivaldo for having no real power in this situation to protect Leona, but he does silently admit the truth of what Vivaldo says: that if either he or Leona, both white, were to accuse Rufus or even to call attention to him, the police would instantly assess Rufus as guilty and take matters of justice entirely into their own hands (i.e., put Rufus *under* the jailhouse: murder him and hide the body). Initially, Vivaldo is only dimly aware of his own race privilege with regard to the law, but he later empathizes with Rufus's predicament when facing the police: "A policeman passed [Vivaldo and Leona], giving them a look. Vivaldo felt a chill go through Leona's body. Then a chill went through his own. He had never been afraid of policemen before; he had merely despised them. But now he felt the impersonality of the uniform, the emptiness of the streets. He felt what the policeman might say and do if he had been Rufus, walking here with his arm around Leona" (*AC* 59). Soon afterwards he experiences the same kind of paranoid alienation Rufus had felt under the gaze of the police: "[Vivaldo's] awareness of the policeman, prowling somewhere in the darkness near him, made the silence ominous. He felt threatened. He felt totally estranged from the city in which he had been born; this city for which he sometimes felt a kind of stony affection because it was all he knew of home. Yet he had no home here" (*AC* 61). The addition of fear to Vivaldo's instinctive hatred of the police is one first step toward his empathy with his friend, but it is also a crucial moment for Vivaldo's education about the way power works. For both Vivaldo and Rufus, who are aware of their vulnerability on the streets, powerlessness equates with homelessness, and in both cases the scrutiny of the police makes this equation clear.

Whether he empathizes with Rufus or not, whether he rejects the power of the white policeman over the black citizen or not, Vivaldo seems fated to be separated from his friend (and later from Ida), partly because Vivaldo does not fully understand the link between white privilege and legal authority, and partly because Rufus and Ida have been so damaged by this link that they cannot recover enough to sustain loving relationships with white people. Vivaldo takes Leona away to his apartment for her protection and he tells Rufus, "I thought, maybe, I'd stay here with you for awhile—if you don't mind." Rufus responds by interpreting Vivaldo's action in terms of legal authority: "What're you trying to do—be a war-den or something?" (*AC* 67). Without realizing it, Vivaldo has allied him-self with wardens, policemen, and other authoritative representatives from the white world, such as the psychiatrists who commit Leona to a ward and who also express her relationship to Rufus in terms of legality: "The doctors had felt that it would be criminal to release her into the custody of the man who was the principal reason for her breakdown, and who had, moreover, no legal claim on her" (*AC* 71). Vivaldo participates in the mis-take society as a whole has made by infantilizing Rufus and other black men like him. The official laws—the ones that would, through marriage, make Rufus competent to be Leona's legal custodian—are used here to mask the hidden laws: society's racist disapproval of interracial couples.

Similarly, the book's other white liberal protagonist, Cass, tries to teach Rufus that society's conceptions of crime and punishment matter less than the individual's ability to recognize and forgive oneself for one's crimes, essentially developing a conscience: "we all commit our crimes. The thing is not to lie about them—to try to understand what you have done, why you have done it. . . . If you don't forgive yourself you'll never be able to forgive anybody else and you'll go on committing the same crimes forever" (*AC* 79). Rufus acknowledges the truth of this statement, but it is too late: he has deeply internalized the disapproval and raw power of the police force to the degree that he will never be free of its essential judgment of him. In his final conversation with Vivaldo he seems on the verge of forgiving himself, but the police again remind him of his fate: "He laughed. 'It'll soon be Christmas, the year will soon be over—' He broke off, raising his head to look over the cold streets. A policeman, standing under the light on the corner, was phoning in" (*AC* 72). The policeman negates the feeling of friendship and renewal he was grasping for at this point, and Rufus proceeds to the George Washington Bridge, where he jumps to his death.[15]

Rufus is a tragic figure because he, like Richard in *Go Tell It on the Mountain,* is capable of love and friendship despite his propensity toward race-based anger, but he loses this capacity when he finds himself under the gaze of the police. They exist, he feels, to prevent him from developing into a man. Just before his death he conceives of his life as a prison term, also evoking slavery: "a long sentence in chains" (*AC* 85). The remainder of the novel is a consideration of Rufus's legacy as someone who has been destroyed by the power structure represented and upheld by the legal sys-tem, particularly by the police. All of the other characters experience alien-ation, but those who are poor, black, bisexual, or especially a combination (like Rufus was), experience a specific type of alienation that is the direct result of the exercise of legal power.

Rufus's sister Ida in particular inherits his distrust of the police. Soon after his disappearance she expresses to Cass and Richard the futility of reporting it: "[the police] said it happens all the time—colored men running off from their families. They said they'd try to find him. But they don't care. They don't care what happens—to a black man!" Richard reacts to this statement furiously: "'Oh, well, now,'" cried Richard, his face red, "'is that fair? I mean, hell, I'm sure they'll look for him just like they look for any other citizen of this city'" (*AC* 101). For Ida, the police are both unfeeling and discriminatory in the response to their assigned duties; for Richard they are fair-minded and benevolent. Ida insists on the validity of her perspective: "I say they don't care—and they *don't* care" (*AC* 101). If animosity remains between black and white characters by the end of the novel despite all attempts to bridge the divide, the persistent problem begins here: one race believes the law exists to protect, the other believes it exists to persecute.

In fact, policemen seem to target Eric and Vivaldo, the two white characters who are especially earnest about bridging the gap between the races. In this sense the law seems primarily concerned less with safety than with preserving the status quo. Upon Eric's return to New York, as he is reuniting with Vivaldo and meeting Ida for the first time, a hostile policeman again haunts the scene; as Eric approaches the nightclub where Ida is singing he is aware of a "policeman who walked up and down with his lips pursed and his eyes blind with unnameable suspicions and fears" (*AC* 248). As Vivaldo greets Eric and is about to hug him, "the policeman moved directly behind him, glowering, seeming to wait for an occult go-ahead signal" (*AC* 250). This intense scrutiny continues as the two men banter: "The policeman seemed to take a dim, even a murderous view of this, and, ceasing to wait on occult inspiration, peered commandingly into the bar" (*AC* 251). If Eric, Ida, and Vivaldo represent the only hope for improved race relations in the aftermath of Rufus's death, Baldwin's message is clear: the potential for such improvement is severely compromised, if not undermined completely, by the police who exist in this novel to keep society's partitions in place, and thus to prevent progress in black–white relations. Baldwin takes pains to demonstrate how Eric's, Ida's, and Vivaldo's public interaction is monitored by a policeman who is suspicious at best, "murderous" at worst. Later, because of a summertime heat wave, Vivaldo and Ida keep the door to their apartment open, but Vivaldo beats up a young boy who is ogling Ida; when Vivaldo shoves him roughly to the pavement, "The police came shortly afterward, their own combustible imaginations stiffening their ready civic pride. After that, [Ida and Vivaldo] kept the doors not only closed but locked" (*AC* 319). The protection they seek is less from the ogling youth, whom Vivaldo can handle, in his own way, than from the police, whose "combustible imaginations stiffening their ready civic pride" create a volatile kind of power that can thoroughly disrupt the sanctity of the private space. Vivaldo's response is fearful and indicative of a radical withdrawal from society: close and *lock* the doors.

The hopefulness of the younger generation, embodied in Greenwich Village bohemians, is similarly undermined; as they sing folk songs in "unhypocritical voices . . . policemen, in the lamplight, circled around them all" (*AC* 261). Here the police force's ability to contain is highlighted: by circling the crowd, they are defining its size and the space it can inhabit. The police function both to divide and to keep divisions in place. The only force that can hope to combat this division in the novel is love, and that force does not have any power in the public realm of the streets where the police reign. Also, as in Baldwin's earlier works such as "Previous Condition" and *Giovanni's Room,* the police in *Another Country* threaten to invade private rooms and apartments. When Vivaldo and Ida are embattled in a heated argument, Vivaldo is aware of what such an invasion might mean; he says to Ida, "Will you shut up? You're going to have the police down here in a minute" (*AC* 280). He goes on to say, "We're in enough trouble here, as it is" and the narrator explains, "And they were, because the landlord and the neighbors and the cop on the corner disapproved of Ida's presence" (*AC* 280). The link between public opinion and the law is all too clear here: as in "Previous Condition," a landlord or landlady reacts to the disapproval of racist tenants, but the cop on the corner is the one who can use that disapproval to divide this couple and to re-place Ida in Harlem, like Peter in "Previous Condition." This power is closely connected to the policeman's behavior when Eric, Vivaldo, and Ida are meeting for the first time; the difference here is that the interaction between these lovers occurs in a private and supposedly safe space.

Perhaps the fullest expression of the way legal power is unfairly meted out comes in a conversation between Cass and Eric, and it reveals how the safety of Cass's life, related to her husband Richard's perspective that the police are benevolent and fair-minded, has produced a warped perspective that prevents her from understanding the truth of other people's lives. Eric describes how street boys in Paris "hated the cops because the cops like to beat the shit out of them." Cass's silent response reveals her lifelong naïveté about legal power and her unwillingness to question it:

> It was strange how she now felt herself holding back—not from him, but from such a vision of the world. She did not want him to see the world this way because such a vision could not make him happy, and whatever made him unhappy menaced her. She had never had to deal with a policeman in her life, and it had never entered her mind to feel menaced by one. Policemen were neither friends nor enemies; they were part of the landscape, present for the purpose of upholding law and order; and if a policeman—for she had never thought of them as being very bright—seemed to forget his place, it was easy enough to make him remember it. Easy enough if one's own place was more secure than his, and if one represented, or could bring to bear, a power greater than his own. For all policemen were bright enough to know who they were working for, and they were not working, anywhere in the world, for the powerless. (*AC* 290)

This extraordinary analysis of legal power begins with Cass's realization that she has led a sheltered life. This realization sets her apart from the "powerless" of the novel, many of whom she considers friends and lovers. She has not had to face police persecution by virtue of the fact that she is wealthy, white, and heterosexual. Her sympathy for Vivaldo, who grew up poor, for Ida, who is poor and black, and in this case for Eric, who is bisexual, is a limited and impoverished response to social injustice. Here she begins to realize that, far from being at the mercy of the police, she is allied with that group of people who control the police, who are capable of exercising "a power greater" than the one the policeman has. If she understands that the police are "not working, anywhere in the world, for the powerless," then she is beginning to realize that she is among the powerful, though she had never thought of herself this way. Cass is on the verge of understanding interest convergence, or the way race privilege and class privilege work in conjunction with legal power. The fact that she has never understood this idea before diminishes the novel's hopefulness. The novel asks the question: is love a strong enough force to combat the divisiveness represented by the police? If people like Cass are not willing to look directly at the "vision of the world" Eric describes, Baldwin believes, then the odds against love are long.

Cass is poised to learn a lesson about facing reality, though: she wonders aloud with sincere interest, "What . . . *does* one replace a dream with?

I wish I knew," and Ida answers succinctly: "one replaces a dream with reality" (AC 357). Reality, especially the reality of the disenfranchised, is precisely what Cass had refused to see in her conversation with Eric. It is clear that she is beginning to understand the nature of reality, as symbolized again by the police who were once "neither friends nor enemies"; later, when she is with Ida in Harlem, she notices "three white policemen, walking abreast, came up the Avenue. Cass felt, suddenly, exposed, and in danger, and wished she had not come" (AC 352). If to face reality means to experience a little of the fear that the disenfranchised feel, then Cass's story in *Another Country* represents progress. She may not be able to do anything about police intimidation and all that it represents, but her awareness of it will undoubtedly begin to minimize the difference between her own country, speaking metaphorically, and other countries.

After publishing *Another Country,* having established the importance of facing reality, confronting one's fears, and exploring new countries, Baldwin himself realized that he must confront the region where his nation's racial divide was most pronounced, and where it was reaching a crisis point in the early 1960s. Although the American South was part of the complex portrait of humanity in *Another Country* insofar as Leona and Eric had fled it, Baldwin did not fully engage with the nation's embattled region in a fictional work until he wrote *Blues for Mister Charlie.* This 1964 play constitutes not only Baldwin's first fictional rendering of the South that would become so crucial to his vision of America's only hope for the future, but the play also represents the fullest expression to date of Baldwin's engagement with the law in that it dramatizes a trial. Early in this phase of Baldwin's career, he attempts to translate the lessons he has learned about French law to America; in *Blues for Mister Charlie* he attempts to translate the lessons he has learned about the law in New York, as expressed in the essay "Fifth Avenue Uptown: Letter From Harlem" and *Another Country,* to the "other country" of the American South, where, from his perspective, justice was too often in the hands of rogue racists and vigilante lynch mobs. Law enforcement officers, judges, and juries, when not directly involved in this vigilante justice, were at the very least guilty of looking the other way.

Baldwin first traveled to the American South in 1957 to write a series of journalistic essays and, as David Leeming writes, "having seen something of the South for himself, he wondered if nonviolence would be enough."[16] By the time he returned to the South in 1963 he had begun to embrace some of the violent indignation that was affecting many of his black countrymen. Baldwin met civil rights leader Medgar Evers in

January of that explosive year—five months before Evers was assassinated—and the two of them investigated the murder of a young black man who had been the victim of a racially motivated murder, most likely at the hands of a white storekeeper. This biographical context makes it seem as though *Blues for Mister Charlie* was inevitable, but Baldwin's second foray into drama was a reluctant one: as he writes in the published introduction to the text, "[Elia] Kazan asked me at the end of 1958 if I would be interested in working in the Theatre. It was a generous offer, but I did not react with great enthusiasm because I did not then, and don't now, have much respect for what goes on in the American Theatre. I am not convinced that it *is* a Theatre; it seems to me a series, merely, of commercial speculations, stale, repetitious, and timid" (*BMC* 5). And yet, given the subject matter—the play is inspired by the prominent, tragic case of Emmett Till, whose brutal murder and the ensuing trial that acquitted the accused murderers sparked outrage throughout the nation—the theater was the best choice for Baldwin's engagement with this subject. Baldwin brings the audience directly into the courtroom of a nation defined by the contagion of racism ("Plaguetown"), thus showing the audience its complicity in the crimes that have occurred anywhere in the nation, regardless of where the play might be staged, and forcing the audience to participate as witnesses and potential jurors. Richard Posner writes, "Whether historically the trial is modeled on the theater and offers the litigants and society (the audience) the type of catharsis that the theater does, or vice versa, or whether both the trial and the drama have a common origin in religious rituals, few social practices are so readily transferable to a literary setting and so well suited to the literary depiction of conflict as the trial." He goes on to say, "The resemblance between drama and trial may be superficial, making it all the more likely that any borrowing by the first from the second will be metaphoric."[17] The metaphoric value for Baldwin of staging this particular trial is to provoke his audience to action, yet the play is not quite agitprop. *Blues for Mister Charlie* presents both Martin Luther King's nonviolent response to injustice and racism and Malcolm X's willingness to consider violence as a possible response. While Baldwin does not necessarily come down on one side or the other, he reveals the inadequacy of the law to respond to the mounting crisis that would lead to race riots by the end of the decade.

Baldwin's introduction to *Blues* clarifies the play's themes and indicates broader concerns about the law that he will develop in later works. He wryly notes, for instance, that the acquitted "murderer's" brother in the Emmett Till case "who helped him do the deed, is now a deputy sheriff in

Rulesville, Mississippi" (*BMC* 5). (This sheriff is undoubtedly one model for Jesse in Baldwin's story "Going to Meet the Man," which I will discuss in chapter 3.) Baldwin desires to "draw a valid portrait of the murderer," just as he desires to reveal just a glimpse of humanity in Jesse, yet he admits that he feels inadequate to the task: "such people baffle and terrify me and, with one part of my mind at least, I hate them and would be willing to kill them. Yet, with another part of my mind, I am aware that no man is a villain in his own eyes. Something in the man knows—*must* know—that what he is doing is evil; but in order to accept the knowledge the man would have to change" (*BMC* 6). If no man is a villain in his own eyes, the burden of judgment is on others: artists must render villains as humans rather than as archetypes of evil, and audiences or readers, like juries, must be prepared to judge them. American society has historically used two institutions to help clarify the basis for such judgment: the church and the court of law. Baldwin questions the authority of both institutions equally in this play, and while the individual conscience purportedly replaces them, Baldwin does not depict the conscience as a universally noble force. How can it be, when no man is a villain in his own eyes? The law should be an institution that reveals the true villains in society's eyes, but with the acquittal of Lyle Britten, the play demonstrates how thoroughly the law can fail.

The solution for Baldwin is not to despair at this condition, but rather to figure out how to illuminate the problem in such a way that it can be useful to the audience's collective will to improve its society. After the word "crimes," which recurs four times in Baldwin's brief introduction, the most common word is "darkness." Baldwin brings the two words together in one sentence: "The human being, then, in order to protect himself, closes his eyes, compulsively repeats his crimes, and enters a spiritual darkness which no one can describe" (*BMC* 6). He later defines his own role as an artist compelled to describe his world regardless of how difficult it might be to do so: "We are walking in terrible darkness here, and this is one man's attempt to bear witness to the reality and the power of light" (*BMC* 8). He uses the word "crimes" both specifically and generally; on one hand, he is referring to the murder of Emmett Till, which is analogous to the murder of Richard Henry in the play. On the other, he is referring to the crimes all Americans are guilty of in creating the type of society that would create Richard's murderer, Lyle Britten: "For we, the American people, have created him, he is our servant; it is we who put the cattle-prodder in his hands, and we are responsible for the crimes that he commits. It is we who have locked him in the prison of his color" (*BMC* 7). This statement is a fascinating example of the way law acts in Baldwin's work: the phrase "American people" here is used as though it is a nationalistic rather than racialized word, as it was in early essays in which "American" is posited against "Negro," yet in both cases the American people are responsible for a racial identity: the "Negro" of the early essays, a white man caged by "the prison of his color" here. The very notion of race is a kind of prison, just as gender is in the essay about André Gide entitled "The Male Prison." Prison is both a punishment and a force of separation created by the American people who so naively consider themselves innocent. Baldwin turns that innocence definitively into guilt at the end of the same paragraph, transferring the "crimes" from the murderous white racist to all Americans: "These are grave crimes indeed, and we have committed them and continue to commit them in order to make money" (*BMC* 7). The fundamental American notion of individual economic prosperity is implicated in our nation's crimes: while many Americans prosper, some must suffer, and others must directly cause that suffering. Baldwin will not let the audience off the hook here: Lyle Britten may be the murderer, but all Americans have created him, and thus are accomplices to crimes.

This message becomes one of the cornerstones of Baldwin's thinking throughout his career, and it is one reason readers continue to find Baldwin provocative to the point of extreme discomfort, just as they did in his time. *Blues for Mister Charlie* marks a turning point in this sense as Baldwin's audience questioned whether their discomfort came from the ideas and characters Baldwin dramatized or from Baldwin himself. Baldwin's second play was also his first critical failure where there had been until that point nearly universal praise, and he suffered a "near-breakdown" during the play's production.[18] Fern Eckman quotes Baldwin as saying "that the [Actors] Studio [Theatre] and I were at *loggerheads*. Total— *total*—TOTAL opposition."[19] The play has been unevenly received, to put it mildly. In the Baldwin documentary *The Price of the Ticket*, Amiri Baraka credits the play with inspiring the Black Arts Movement—high praise from the leading proponent of that movement who had once distanced himself from Baldwin. On the other hand, Robert Bone, in *The Negro Novel in America,* calls *Blues for Mister Charlie* "one unspeakably bad propaganda piece."[20] David Leeming notes a difference in the initial reception of the play; he writes, "*Blues for Mister Charlie* opened on April 23 to an audience of highly appreciative blacks and sometimes angry and often shocked whites."[21] Calvin C. Hernton agrees, and analyzes this situation in great detail: he argues that this play marks a watershed moment in Baldwin's maturity as an artist and claims, "It was simply too much for the majority of whites to accept or seriously consider."[22] The majority of whites were apparently unwilling to absorb the difficult lessons that Cass and Vivaldo learn in *Another Country*: that race and class privilege are related to legal authority. To be white and wealthy, Baldwin implies, is to be an accomplice, if not a criminal.

The law in *Blues for Mister Charlie* is multilayered. Baldwin depicts the police, who have become a familiar subject in this context, as menacing. One foundational moment in the play's genesis, Baldwin tells us in his introduction, occurs when he and Medgar Evers "had been followed for many miles out of Jackson, Mississippi, not by a lunatic with a gun, but by state troopers. I will never forget that night" (*BMC* 7). Baldwin also examines the power of taking the law into one's own hands—the murderous force of lynch mobs and vigilante justice that plagued the South since Reconstruction and that accounted for the murder of Emmett Till. Finally, the efficacy of the courtroom is brought to bear directly on Baldwin's writing. In a world gone mad with racially motivated revenge, the law should be the ultimate rational force to restore sanity and stability, but if the courts do not uphold justice, they are worthless. Moreover, Baldwin consciously places the courtroom alongside the church in this play as if to show that his lack of belief in one parallels his lack of belief in the other. As he writes in an open letter in 1985, "Every system involves a hierarchy" (*CR* 216), and systems, including the law, therefore foster a climate of oppression.

The police are presented in a very specific context in this play, for it is set in the era leading up to the so-called Freedom Summer of 1964 when Northern white college students traveled to the South with the intention of registering black voters. The police emerged en masse ostensibly to protect the white students and their black counterparts, but these efforts sometimes led to confrontations between student groups and police. In his book *Freedom Ride,* for which Baldwin wrote a brief foreword, James Peck details his many confrontations with police as a longtime activist with the Congress of Racial Equality (CORE); at one point he describes how his group, marching toward a lunch counter demonstration, "was met by a band of white hoodlums armed with bats, sticks, knives, and other weapons. They were followed by the police."[23] The marchers sense violence and reorganize, only to have the police fire tear gas at them and arrest them. The angry young Lorenzo in Baldwin's play expresses skepticism about the police: "And these people trying to kill us, too? And we ain't even got no guns. The cops ain't going to protect us. They call up the people and tell them where we are and say 'Go get them!'" (*BMC* 16). Wary not only of the efficacy of the police but of their very intentions, Lorenzo suggests here and elsewhere that the black community must arm itself against the *posse comitatus* of the white community. If we follow the logic of Lorenzo's indignant anger, the trajectory of the play is bleak, as this type of anger (coupled with the willingness to arm oneself) is what got Richard killed. Yet Baldwin also substantiates this desire to bear arms by allowing other black characters to voice it: Meridian at the end of this play, Black Christopher in *Tell Me How Long the Train's Been Gone,* and Staggerlee in the poem "Staggerlee Wonders" do not shy away from guns as a potential solution to the race problem in the United States.[24]

Police corruption appears to filter down from the top in *Blues for Mister Charlie.* Parnell, the voice of the well-intentioned white liberal in the play, is one of the few characters who can move between Whitetown and Blacktown; he also moves between the law and the people. He is the one who reports to Lyle that he will be arrested, and he gets this information directly from the unnamed Chief of Police, whose integrity is called into question when Lyle asks Parnell if the Chief believes Lyle killed Richard; Parnell responds, "The question of what he believes doesn't enter into it. This case presents several very particular circumstances and these circumstances force him to arrest you. I think we can take it for granted that he wouldn't arrest you if he could think of some way not to. He wouldn't arrest anybody except blind beggars and old colored women if he could think of some way not to—he's bird-brained and chicken hearted and big-assed"(*BMC* 25). At first it seems like Parnell is describing the Chief of Police as the upholder of blind justice: "what he believes doesn't enter into it." But it quickly becomes clear that this officer is cowardly, that he only acts against the extremely powerless, and thus he is guilty not only of upholding the status quo, but of intensifying it. Parnell goes on to make it clear that the Chief's personality and duty are replicated in his underlings: "We pay several eminent, bird-brained, chicken-hearted, big-assed people quite a lot of money to discourage such activity [as murder]. They never do, in fact, discourage it" (*BMC* 25). Law enforcement is seen not only as cowardly but as completely ineffective in curtailing crime.

As in Baldwin's earlier writings, when policemen exercise force in the name of upholding the law or preventing crime, they are likely to actually cause it. Richard becomes bitter partially because of his resentment toward white power in general (which occurs in the form of economic oppression and segregation, both of which are a product of sexual insecurity, in Baldwin's estimation), but also because of his treatment at the hands of white policemen; in an angry rant to his mother he proclaims, "I'm going to remember . . . all them cops. And I'm going to remember all the dope that's flowed through my veins. I'm going to remember everything—the jails I been in and the cops that beat me and how long a time I spent screaming and stinking in my own dirt, trying to break my habit" (*BMC* 36). Although Richard's illegal drug use is at the center of this part of his story, he frames his expression of this drug use in terms of cops and jails. Far from being rehabilitative, this branch of the law appears responsible for Richard's increasing anger, an anger that results in his self-destruction and that could have easily resulted in his murder of Lyle, or of any other white man.

Although the play thematically centers around Lyle's murder of Richard, the event is far from central to the structure of the play: the murder occurs in the opening scene, and Richard only appears afterwards in flashback. The central event of the play is Lyle's trial, and many black characters express profound skepticism from the outset that justice will be served. Juanita voices this skepticism in response to Meridian's naive question about what the courts will do to Lyle: "Convict him. Convict him. You're asking for heaven on earth. After all, they haven't even *arrested* him yet. And, anyway—why should they convict him? Why him? He's no worse than all the others. He's an honorable tribesman and he's defended, with blood, the honor and purity of his tribe!" (*BMC* 19). Juanita's response is not only cynical with response to the law, implying that the law is a tool of oppression in the hands of whites, but she also defines the world of the South in primitive, archetypal terms: the society is composed of Whitetown and Blacktown, after all, and the challenge set up by the play is to move toward a point where at least the relatively conscious blacks and the relatively conscious whites, to use Baldwin's terminology from the end of "Down at the Cross," can move forward into a less hostile future. The law, which should uphold the standards of equality, again seems to be responsible for division here. Juanita, like Ida in *Another Country,* does not trust the justice system, and from what we see elsewhere in the play, she has no cause to. Lorenzo, another black youth, describes the courthouse as the place "where they been dealing death out to us for all these years" (*BMC* 29). Far from protective, the justice system is murderous in the eyes of these young black characters.

Even the white characters in the play acknowledge that the law does not respond the same way to crimes against black and white victims; Parnell says to Lyle, "if the boy [Richard] had been white, it would look very, *very* bad, and your behind would be in the jail house now" (*BMC* 26). Despite this near-acknowledgment that Lyle is guilty, Parnell continues to believe that the law is the right institution to administer justice, and he puts his trust in it. In a conversation with Meridian, Richard's father, Parnell says, "We don't *know* Lyle killed him. And Lyle denies it. . . . We *don't* know—all we can say is that it looks that way. And circumstantial evidence is a tricky thing" (*BMC* 59). Parnell describes one of the difficult realities of the justice system: even when the evidence clearly points to a killer, the process of a trial can redirect such evidence toward one of two specific outcomes, and circumstantial evidence is pliable under such conditions. The audience and Lyle are the only ones who know for certain that Lyle murdered Richard, but the audience must be silent witnesses to the drama. If circumstantial evidence could be allowed, Parnell suggests, then the justice system could be manipulated to wrongfully convict blacks as well as whites; Parnell further explains to Meridian, "We have to operate the way justice *always* has to operate and give him the benefit of the doubt. . . . Don't you see, Meridian, that now you're operating the way white people in this town operate whenever a colored man's on trial?" (*BMC* 60). Although Parnell's perspective is rational and far-seeing, his faith in the justice system is too great, from Baldwin's perspective: for instance, the jury that hears Lyle's case is all white, as Emmett Till's was. This may explain Meridian's response to Parnell's last speech: "When was the last time one of us was on *trial* here, Parnell?" (*BMC* 61). Parnell's belief that everyone should have a fair trial would be easier to accept, in other words, if *all* trials were fair.

Parnell finds himself in a debate with his white friends about whether blacks should be "put" on the jury to try Lyle. He again argues in favor of a fair trial:

> LYLE: How about it, Parnell? You going to find some niggers for them to put on that jury?
>
> PARNELL: It's not up to me. But I might recommend a couple.
>
> GEORGE: And how they going to get to court? You going to protect them?
>
> PARNELL: The police will protect them. Or the State troopers—
>
> GEORGE: That's a good one!
>
> PARNELL: Or Federal marshals.
>
> GEORGE: Look here, you really think there should be niggers on that jury?
>
> PARNELL: Of course I do, and so would you, if you had any sense. For one thing, they're forty-four percent of the population of this town.
>
> ELLIS: But they don't vote. Not most of them.

PARNELL: Well. That's also a matter of interest to the Federal govern-
ment. Why *don't* they vote? They got hands.
ELLIS: You claim Lyle's your buddy—
PARNELL: Lyle *is* my buddy. That's why I want him to have a fair trial.
(*BMC* 79)

This exchange reveals that Parnell is sincere in his belief in a fair trial:
the racial make-up of the jury is one way to ensure it. Yet even his white
friends find him naive, for instance, about the ability of the police to protect the black populace. His naïveté allies him with Cass in *Another Country*. Both believe strongly that one should entrust the legal system to mete
out justice fairly, and in theory they are (hopefully) justified in this belief.
However, in *practice,* Baldwin is arguing, the justice system operates
according to the common biases of the land and is thus flawed in terms of
separating the actual truth from rhetorical effectiveness. This is the reason
Parnell, whose belief in justice and in Lyle's guilt separates him from the
rest of Whitetown, is the witness who actually helps to acquit Lyle: he is
caught by the rhetoric of the State attorney and forced to accept the truth
of Jo Britten's fabricated accusation that Richard physically molested her.
Although an uncorroborated accusation is really no better than circumstantial evidence, it holds more weight in the court of law, especially (in
Baldwin's time) in the case of young black men accused of molesting white
women.

The trial comprises nearly the entire third act of the play. Fern Eckman writes about how Baldwin struggled with this section of the play,
which "had to be pried loose from the straitjacket of legal procedure,"[25]
which was part of his quibble with *Native Son.* He attempted to achieve
this by adding memory scenes that remove the audience from the strictly
naturalistic scenes of the courtroom and that further disrupt the chronol-
ogy of the play. Baldwin's set directions at the opening of Act 3 begin,
"The courtroom is extremely high, domed, a blinding white emphasized
by a dull, somehow ominous gold. The judge's stand is center stage and
at a height" (*BMC* 108). This description connotes not only the hierarchy
and impersonality of the law through the "extremely high" ceilings of the
courtroom and the judge's stand "at a height," but is also symbolic of the
white power that controls the courts: the "blinding white" and "somehow
ominous gold" of the courtroom bring economic power and whiteness
together. The result is distorted vision. The courtroom is perhaps the most
revealing of all public places since anyone called to the stand to testify is
cross-examined in front of an audience. Here the scrutiny and judgment

of the police as seen in *Another Country* is magnified, and any illusion of privacy is exploded. Baldwin adds another layer to his characters' loss of privacy under this type of legal scrutiny through the following dramatic convention: "Each witness, when called, is revealed behind scrim and passes through two or three tableaux before moving down the aisle to the witness stand" (*BMC* 109). Thus the play's audience gains access to an aspect of a character's past that would be seen as irrelevant or immaterial in a court of law, highlighting the difference between courtroom proceedings and art. Baldwin initiates the tension between courtroom evidence and that which is merely evident, a concept he explores in detail in his final book, *The Evidence of Things Not Seen,* discussed in chapter 5.

The audience or reader of Baldwin's play knows that Jo Britten is lying about the day Richard and Lorenzo entered the Brittens' store, for the scene was enacted in Act 2. Jo's version of the story is the one that is examined as evidence, though, because a courtroom case depends upon narrative more than it depends upon objective truth. In his introduction to *Law's Stories,* Paul Gewirtz acknowledges this dimension of narrative and the law: "In short, a trial consists of fragmented narratives and narrative multiplicity. . . . In addition, one side's narrative is constantly being met by the other side's counternarrative (or sidestepping narrative), so that 'reality' is always disassembled into multiple, conflicting, and partly overlapping versions, each version presented as true, each fighting to be declared 'what really happened.'" He goes on to ask a number of "normative questions," such as, "Are the right people getting their stories told, to a sufficient degree and with adequate effectiveness? Do the multiplicities of narratives at trial (and on appeal) undercut the idea of objectivity or the idea that there is such a thing as the truth? Or does this narrative multiplicity suggest only that people are at times fallible or deceptive or at times so indifferent to truth that they may let people literally get away with murder?"[26] Baldwin's play responds to these questions in a complex manner by showing the audience "what really happened" and yet preventing us, through the "fourth wall" convention of drama, from participating in the judicial process. Jo's narrative of rape forms the basis of the trial; presumably Lyle can falsely corroborate it. Richard cannot help to create the counternarrative because he is dead, so the burden rests on Lorenzo. He tries to recount the story faithfully while firmly denying Jo's accusations: "But I know he wasn't trying to rape nobody. Rape!" (*BMC* 123). The state attorney tries to call Lorenzo's character into question, first by invoking Richard's drug habits (*BMC* 122) and implicating Lorenzo by association, then by reminding him that he is under oath (*BMC* 123), then by bringing up Lorenzo's prior arrest record, for "trespassing in the white waiting room of the bus station" (*BMC* 123). The suggestion that Lorenzo is a drug user and has a criminal record is a move to discount the validity of his counternarrative. He falls victim to what Paul Gewirtz describes as a juror's propensity to pass judgment based on what might be considered archetypal stories: "There is some evidence that jurors tend to come to the trial with a set of stock stories in their minds and that they try to fit trial evidence into the shape of one of those stock stories. This suggests that lawyers will have an easier time persuading a jury that their side's story is true if they can shape it to fit some favorable stock story."[27] The stock stories operative in this case all involve contemporary stereotypes of young black men: to wit, they are dangerous, hypersexual, untrustworthy, drug-addicted criminals who prey on vulnerable white women. Framed this way, Lorenzo's testimony is less potent than Jo's, and Richard's behavior is predictable. The jury can easily be led to perceive Lyle as innocent, or, if they believe he committed murder, justified.

Juanita is another witness who could potentially add to the counternarrative that would incriminate Lyle rather than Richard, but she is immediately discounted as another criminal, though she was arrested for the noble causes of protesting and agitating for voters' rights. As she tries to explain the reasons for her arrest, the state attorney cuts her off: "I am not concerned with the reasons for your arrest. How much time, all told, have you spent in jail?" (*BMC* 127–28). The power of the state prosecutor in a legal trial is clear here as Juanita's story is carefully controlled and used to dismiss her credibility. She is forced to admit that she "was not a witness to [the] fight" between Richard and Lyle, which is, technically, extraneous to the case, but which has become central as a result of the state attorney's manipulations of the story. The audience is then given access to a remembered conversation between Juanita and Meridian that is personal in nature, and that has no place in the courtroom. Following this memory, Juanita is reduced to an emotional, impassioned reiteration of Lyle's guilt, and she is promptly dismissed.

Meridian Henry and Parnell are similarly brought to the stand only to have their stories manipulated. Meridian, like Juanita, is finally concerned with the pursuit of manhood: Juanita had claimed of Richard, "we tried to make plans to go, but he said he wasn't going to run no more from white folks—never no more!—but was going to stay and be a man—a *man!*— right here" (*BMC* 131). Meridian becomes frustrated when the state attorney tries to call his character into question by exposing his desire for Juanita; he asks, "How does my celibacy concern you?" and the state

OTHER COUNTRIES, HIDDEN LAWS 71

attorney responds, "Your Honor, will you instruct the witness that he is on the witness stand, not I, and that he must answer the questions put to him!" (*BMC* 136).[28] It is clear that Meridian has no control over his story, and like Juanita, he is left with no hope for justice and can only express his rage against injustice. His only recourse is to assert his manhood and to reveal the potency of white power in this setting in the hopes that his words can influence his community:

> *The questions put to him!* All right. Do you accept this answer? I am a man. A *man!* I tried to help my son become a man. But manhood is a dangerous pursuit, here. And that pursuit undid him because of *your* guns, *your* hoses, *your* dogs, *your* judges, *your* law-makers, *your* folly, *your* pride, *your* cruelty, *your* cowardice, *your* money, *your* chain gangs, and *your* churches! Did you think it would endure forever? That we would pay for *your* ease forever? (*BMC* 136–37)

To return to the title, Meridian is singing the blues for Mister Charlie—the white man—and here he points a finger directly at the white establishment. Their worst aspects (greed and cruelty) are at the center of this screed, but the law is the largest aspect of it (guns, hoses, dogs, judges, law-makers, and chain gangs). Baldwin, through Meridian, is directly and vociferously attacking white power through the institution that the audience is concurrently witnessing in action. Although the younger generation, including Richard, had questioned Meridian for being too willing to accept the status quo, he gains some reputability with this attack and achieves a higher moral ground even as the state continues to question his character; when the attorney asks, sarcastically, "And you are a minister?" he answers, "I think I may be beginning to become one" (*BMC* 139). Like Baldwin, Meridian's identity begins to solidify when he leaves the Christian church and begins to assail other institutions that comprise American power.

Parnell James, the white liberal, meets a sorrier fate in Baldwin's play.[29] His sense of moral superiority to his racist white friends, including Lyle, eventually collapses as he, like the black character witnesses who have preceded him, falls victim to the rhetoric of the courtroom. He at first seems poised through his intellectual acuity to resist rhetorical traps; when the state attorney tries to insinuate again that Richard had been a lascivious drug-user, Parnell replies, "I cannot testify to any of that, sir" (*BMC* 146). As the only figure in the play who has friends in both Blacktown and Whitetown, though, he is in a precarious position with regard to the competing stories of the courtroom. As a character who claims friends on both sides of the trial, Parnell is trapped when he says, "My friends do not lie" (*BMC* 146). The state attorney realizes the trap that Parnell has set for himself; he asks Parnell, "Mrs. Britten has testified that Richard Henry grabbed her and pulled her to him and tried to kiss her. How can those actions be misconstrued?" Parnell weakly admits, "Those actions are— quite explicit" (*BMC* 149). If, as he has claimed, his friends do not lie, he must accept Jo's accusation as true. As a representative of the white liberal mind-set that Baldwin came to denigrate so frequently in this period of his career, Parnell reveals his flaw to be a naive belief in human goodness. Without realizing he is doing so, Parnell is feeding into the overall story that the state attorney is telling. Since Parnell has friends in both racially defined groups, and since he claims that none of them lie, he is poised to betray one group or the other. The jury ultimately concludes either that only Parnell's black friends lie, or that he is not really friends with them.

One of the ways to control the story of a courtroom trial is to repress as inadmissible certain stories. In his essay "Untold Stories in the Law" Robert A. Ferguson writes, "What, in effect, happens when a relevant story is actively repressed in a republic of laws? The simple answer would seem to be that it always returns, but on what terms? Whose terms? In the rugged exchanges of courtroom advocacy, a relevant story that is effectively told belongs to the republic of laws for ready use and further manipulation. Ideologically, it remains available to everyone. But when such a story is actively repressed in a forum that prides itself on its thoroughness and fairness, it belongs to the agent of the repressed."[30] More than anything else, Baldwin's play dramatically demonstrates the suppression of the only story that matters in Lyle's courtroom trial: that is, Lyle's. As with the other characters in Act 3, Lyle is called to the witness stand and prior to his arrival we witness a private memory shown behind the scrim. In Lyle's case, this memory is directly tied to his motive for killing Richard: Lyle reveals his deep sexual anxiety about himself in relation to black men—a topic that becomes prominent in Baldwin's writings of the 1960s—and his general jealousy about black culture: he says to Papa D., "Sure wish I could be more like you all" (*BMC* 151). Yet Baldwin breaks the pattern of moving from private to public in this case, for we never get to hear Lyle's testimony on the witness stand; the set directions read, "*Blackout. As Lyle approaches the witness stand, the lights in the courtroom dim*" (*BMC* 151). Through omitting Lyle's testimony from the play, Baldwin is further indicting the justice system for its arbitrariness and its ability to repress stories. It is clear that Lyle lies about murdering Richard; after the trial, when Meridian asks him point-blank if he killed Richard,

Lyle responds, "They just asked me that in court, didn't they? And they just decided I didn't, didn't they? Well, that's good enough for me and all those white people and so it damn sure better be good enough for you!" (*BMC* 153). Lyle's answer is indirect; moreover, Baldwin removes us from the courtroom trial at a crucial point. We are prevented from seeing Lyle lie under oath, and we have to rely on his synopsis of events now that he is not under oath. Moreover, Parnell regrets his own testimony and admits to Lyle, "I knew that [Jo] was lying and that you had made her lie" (*BMC* 153). There is no doubt but that Baldwin wants us to doubt the efficacy of a system that depends so heavily on competing versions of stories.

Yet as Ferguson says, the story will return, and it will belong to the "agent of the repressed"—in this case, to Baldwin. In other words, the stories that are mistold or manipulated in court can resurface as stories in imaginative literature. The play opens and closes with the "true story"— the objective story—of what happened between Richard and Lyle; the rest of the play adds nuance to this story by problematizing Richard's character and by adding some tiny modicum of humanity to Lyle's, but more importantly, the rest of the play shows how the courtroom—where stories receive their most important judgments—easily distorts stories. Plays, on the other hand, can fulfill their ancient purpose of swaying public opinion and thus effecting real social change. In discovering that the role of the American writer is to "find out what these [hidden] laws and [profound] assumptions are" that really govern society, as he states in "The Discovery of What it Means to Be an American," then art has the potential to be a more powerful and more truthful venue for such discovery than the law is. In order to make this claim, Baldwin had to experiment with literary forms such as the novel and drama even if it displeased his critics. A significant number of Baldwin's readers initially judged *Another Country* and *Blues for Mister Charlie* as aesthetic failures, but looking back on Baldwin's developing understanding of the law's power, these works are better appreciated as aesthetic experiments by an artist attempting to disrupt the status quo and to place art above public policy as a way of exposing the hidden laws that truly govern society.

CHAPTER 3

A Criminal Power

T HE PEAK of Baldwin's notoriety came not during the long period of exile in France that incubated his earliest major works—*Notes of a Native Son, Go Tell It on the Mountain,* and *Giovanni's Room*—but upon his return to his beleaguered country, particularly the southern United States, in the late 1950s and early 1960s. Baldwin became a public figure more than a private writer during this time. His forays into the troubled American South began what might be called his domestic journey, but he also explored some of the nation's other volatile sites, notably college campuses, Harlem, and the headquarters of the Nation of Islam. His experiments with drama and the novel discussed in chapter 2, which had been risky and which did not receive universal praise from critics, had their counterpart in Baldwin's essays and stories of the same period, which were widely praised and are still widely read today. The law, which had metaphorically destroyed the dividing line between public and private in his earlier works, becomes an even more menacing force in this body of work published in the late 1950s and early 1960s. As his thinking about America's legal system matures, Baldwin realizes that the power he has been observing all along is a "criminal power," and his response to it becomes increasingly strident as he begins to explore connections between lawmakers and law enforcement officers.

Baldwin's initial engagement with the law during this period began with the issue of segregation. This engagement marks an expansion of his association between the law and police officers to include the legal decisions that ultimately give the police their authority. The landmark Supreme Court decision of 1954, *Brown vs. Board of Education* (referred to hereafter as *Brown*), paved the way for a number of other decisions that effectively ended the practice of segregation. Yet for Baldwin, the law did not immediately become a benevolent force simply because of this decision and its aftereffects. Baldwin's conclusions regarding the issue of civil rights legislation and its effects anticipate the Critical Race Theorists of the next generation who expressed "deep dissatisfaction with traditional civil rights discourse," according to Kimberlé Crenshaw et al.: "In our view, the 'legislation' of the civil rights movement and its 'integration' into the mainstream commonsense assumptions in the late sixties and early seventies were premised on a tragically narrow and conservative picture of the goals of racial justice and the domains of racial power."[1] Baldwin observed how the power to legislate can even have the opposite effect of its intention: racism and racial discrimination can take more insidious forms when they are driven underground. Baldwin took his first journey to the South in 1957 to gauge the effect of the legislation that had supposedly changed the very nature of black-white relations in the United States. His essays "Faulkner and Desegregation" (1956), "A Fly in Buttermilk" (1958), and "Nobody Knows My Name: A Letter from the South" (1959) paved the way for his most profound and heralded essay, "Down at the Cross" (1962).

In "Faulkner and Desegregation," Baldwin reveals himself to be a native son still brash enough to take on the major figures of American literature (as he had done with Stowe and Wright in his first essay collection, and as he does with Norman Mailer later in this one). He opens the essay with a concise statement of the themes that were coalescing in all of his work at this time: "Any real change implies the breakup of the world as one has always known it, the loss of all that gave one an identity, the end of safety" (*Nobody* 100). This statement could be applied to David in *Giovanni's Room,* to Cass or Vivaldo in *Another Country,* or to Parnell in *Blues for Mister Charlie,* as much as it applies to Faulkner, who comes across in this essay as someone unwilling to accept change, to jeopardize his safety, or to admit that his world has broken up. Baldwin's essay is a response to Faulkner's public comments on segregation, which were brought about by "the pressure of recent events, that is, the Supreme Court decision outlawing segregation" (*Nobody* 101). The Supreme Court's decision isn't responsible for "any real change" in Baldwin's view so much as it is responsible for the pressure that will create that change. The world, in other words, has not been "broken up" by *Brown,* though it has been prepared for such a rupture. According to Baldwin, the real change to be effected is in the "minds and hearts of white Southerners today" (*Nobody* 100). A law cannot effect this kind of change, at least not as radically as it might appear to.

And yet, Baldwin certainly wouldn't have opposed *Brown* simply because of its limited effects. Rather, he wanted to ensure that the focus of the civil rights struggle remained clear. In this essay, the reactionary comments of Faulkner are the enemy. Baldwin implies that the Supreme Court decision was necessary because the South, a nation within (or apart from) a nation, has no intention of changing: "The sad truth is that whatever modifications have been effected in the social structure of the South since the Reconstruction, and any alleviations of the Negro's lot within it, are due to great and incessant pressure, very little of it indeed from within the South" (*Nobody* 101–2). In this formula the Supreme Court acts not only on behalf of the nation in general, but of the North in particular. The pressure to change, according to Baldwin, must be exerted from on high, or from up North.

Baldwin demonstrates the relationship between the North and the South with regard to the law in this quotation: "As far as the Negro's life in the South is concerned, the NAACP is the only organization which has struggled, with admirable single-mindedness and skill, to raise him to the level of a citizen. For this reason alone, and quite apart from the individual heroism of many of its southern members, it cannot be equated, as Faulkner equates it, with the pathological Citizens' Council. One organization is working within the law and the other is working against and outside it" (*Nobody* 102). The NAACP is, of course, a long-standing rights organization based in New York; the "Citizens' Council" is short for the "White Citizens' Council," a group founded in 1954 opposed to integration and based in Mississippi. The WCC was a white supremacist organization, but it did not participate in the vigilante violence associated with the KKK. The NAACP is, according to Baldwin, a law-abiding organization whereas the Citizens' Council works not only "outside" the law, but "against" it. As Faulkner attempts to collapse the distinction between the NAACP and the WCC, Baldwin seeks to reclaim the NAACP's validity by allying it with the law. The NAACP and law together constitute a necessary "pressure" that might ultimately result in a widespread change of attitudes in the South.

Insofar as the law represents progressive or northern attitudes, Baldwin believes, it is a necessary force in effecting change in conservative or southern culture. But the Supreme Court is only one facet of the law, and to the average citizen in his or her everyday life it is perhaps is more symbolic than it is truly powerful. The police in the South represent the more immediately visible power of the law, as Baldwin reminds us toward the end of the essay: "'Things have been getting better,' Faulkner tells us, 'for a long time. Only six Negroes were killed by whites in Mississippi last year, according to police figures.' Faulkner surely knows how little consolation this offers a Negro and he also knows something about 'police figures' in the Deep South" (*Nobody* 106). Those who would believe that the law is a benevolent, rational force, like Parnell in *Blues for Mister Charlie*, must be reminded that the law as elucidated in the high courts is not necessarily consistent with the law on the streets, and police corruption is a consistent, recurrent fact that coexists with the positive, heroic, public face of the police force. The law might be benevolent in general, but it is also a human construction, and susceptible to human flaws. Baldwin's initial alliance in this essay with the law as it is dictated by the Supreme Court is undermined later in the essay by his critique of the law as it is manipulated by the police. In order to understand the impact of the law on American lives, Baldwin suggests, we must scrutinize all of its dimensions. To assume that *Brown* and subsequent desegregation legislation constitute a solution to the nation's racial divide is to view the law too narrowly. Because it is hierarchical like any system, the law is adept at projecting the illusion of change while maintaining the status quo. Baldwin regards it with great skepticism at this point in his career and encourages his readers to look beneath its surface.

Baldwin treats the issues he raises in "Faulkner and Desegregation" in much greater detail in "Nobody Knows My Name." Here again he confronts the relationship between the North and the South, again brings up the WCC and the NAACP, and again indicates the potential for police abuse; toward the essay's conclusion, he writes, "On any night, in that other part of town, a policeman may beat up one Negro too many" (*Nobody* 97). The essay shows a fascinating shift in perspective: Baldwin begins by acknowledging his own prejudices about the South as he flies in. He admits fear as he gazes for the first time on the "Old Country" (*Nobody* 86) and indulges his paranoia about the "rust-red earth of Georgia"[2] which he imagines "had acquired its color from the blood that had dripped down from these trees. My mind was filled with the image of a black man, younger than I, perhaps, or my own age, hanging from a tree, while white men watched him and cut his sex from him with a knife" (*Nobody* 87). His view of the South has clearly been informed by the phantasmagoria of history: his plane has not yet touched down when he experiences this vision.

By admitting his own prejudices, though, Baldwin is attempting to overcome the northern superiority that he is warned about in "A Fly in Buttermilk." His challenge is to avoid seeing the South as another country. As his perspective shifts once he has touched down, he is aware that the divisions between regions are superficial, or that they mask the more meaningful divisions that exist between classes, between the uneducated and the educated, between urban and rural regions, and between races. These divisions are, after all, what segregation was all about and what *Brown* purported to redress. Baldwin expresses how his thinking has changed on this subject: "the South is not the monolithic structure which, from the North, it appears to be, but a most various and divided region. It clings to the myth of its past but it is being inexorably changed, meanwhile, by an entirely unmythical present: its habits and its self-interest are at war. . . . Segregation is unofficial in the North and official in the South, a crucial difference that does nothing, nevertheless, to alleviate the lot of most Northern Negroes" (*Nobody* 93). Having deconstructed his own opposition between North and South, Baldwin brings his microscope closer to examine the inner workings of the conflict.

The nuances of the crisis take the form of legal haggling, in Baldwin's estimation. The Supreme Court decision was a way to catalyze local governmental officials to discover what power they had to interpret the decision and respond to it on their own terms. He writes of the city officials of Charlotte, North Carolina, "The NAACP there had been trying for six years before Black Monday [a derogatory term for the day of the *Brown* decision] to make the city fathers honor the 'separate but equal' statute and do something about the situation in Negro schools. Nothing whatever was done. After Black Monday, Charlotte begged for 'time': and what she did with this time was work out legal stratagems designed to get the least possible integration over the longest possible period" (*Nobody* 92). Baldwin sees the NAACP as one of the best chances to make *Brown* an effective decision as it trickles down to "test cases" tried in local and municipal courts. He even defends some of the white lawyers who are segregated from well-to-do blacks in Atlanta: "Some of the lawyers work with the NAACP and help push test cases through the courts. (If anything, by the way, disproves the charge of 'extremism' which has so often been made against this organization, it is the fantastic care and patience such legal efforts demand)" (*Nobody* 95). The NAACP's legal wrangling, in other words, is necessary to ensure that power is not abused in the hands of the ruling white majority. Even the white mayor of Atlanta, according to Baldwin, "is doing his best to keep [test cases] out of court" (*Nobody* 96).

While politicians and lawyers quibble over legislation, Baldwin argues that it is even more important that individuals examine their consciences: "Any honest examination of the national life proves how far we are from the standard of human freedom with which we began. The recovery of this standard demands of everyone who loves this country a hard look at himself, for the greatest achievements must begin somewhere, and they always begin with the person" (*Nobody* 99).

There is a suspicion lurking at the bottom of all of Baldwin's essays of this era that the benevolence of the law will not change the minds and hearts of citizens regardless of the actions of the police, the mayors, or the Supreme Court. In "Notes for a Hypothetical Novel" (1960) he says, reminiscent of Thoreau, "A country is only as good—I don't care now about the Constitution and the laws, at the moment let us leave these things aside—a country is only as strong as the people who make it up and the country turns into what the people want it to become" (*Nobody* 126). Baldwin's skepticism about the effects of the law (to say nothing of its power) crystallizes here, and he explores this idea obliquely in the essay "A Fly in Buttermilk" which examines the desegregation issue as immediately as possible—by interviewing a young boy who has become the only black student in an otherwise all-white school, as well as interviewing the school's principal. The essay is pessimistic about the future of the country in the aftermath of the Supreme Court decision that has "forced" Southerners "to reexamine a way of life and to speculate, in a personal way, on the general injustice" (*Nobody* 85). Baldwin delves into the heart of the issue at this essay, leaving aside, again, the Constitution and the laws in order to examine the people whom they affect.

One of the reasons Baldwin is such a fascinating critic of the law is that he has experienced and examined its power dynamics on every level, from its penal institutions, to the actions of law enforcement officers on the street, to courtroom trials, to legal decisions. This range of perspectives is perhaps one reason he is able to anticipate the basic tenets of Critical Race Theory decades before it coalesced as an academic discipline. In his most celebrated essay he demonstrates how he can synthesize these perspectives to advance a coherent critique. The impoverished, oppressed young man who developed intense emotional responses to the police and prisons merges with the sophisticated cultural critic whose vantage point was regional, national, and global by turns. *The Fire Next Time* (1963) is a pivotal work in Baldwin's career. It consists of two essays: "My Dungeon Shook: A Letter to my Nephew on the One Hundredth Anniversary of the Emancipation," originally published in *Progressive,* and "Down at the Cross," a lengthy, twenty-thousand word essay that first appeared in *The New Yorker*. Upon the publication of the two essays as *The Fire Next Time*, readers couldn't help but pay attention to Baldwin's passionate intensity which had been building in the later essays collected in *Nobody Knows My Name*. Baldwin's rise to prominence following his first period of exile in Europe was a response to a racially divided nation in desperate need of a spokesperson. He stepped forward to fulfill that role, publishing "Down at the Cross" as a loud wake-up call to his blissfully ignorant countrymen. David Leeming describes it as "his consideration of Western culture from the perspective of the people oppressed by that culture."[3] The essay called attention not only to people like Baldwin, but to Baldwin himself, as it involved elements of personal history, class, religion, and of course race. This widespread attention landed him on the cover of *Time* magazine on May 17, 1963 and garnered him an invitation for a personal audience with Attorney General Robert Kennedy the following week (which resulted in a much-publicized meeting that satisfied neither Kennedy nor Baldwin and his entourage). Moreover, the essay cemented his status as the intellectual leader of the Civil Rights movement, which was entering its most turbulent phase.

"Down at the Cross" integrates experience and observation in one of the most rhetorically powerful essays of the Civil Rights era, culminating in a biblical pronouncement that earned Baldwin the title of "prophet" so frequently used to describe his role in American life. This essay is about the antithetical forces that contribute to the American conundrum: belonging and exclusion, individuals and groups, black and white identity, Christianity and Islam. It is a social critique in the broadest sense, about a specific time period ("this difficult era"), a nation ("an Anglo-Teutonic, antisexual country"), and an individual ("I was utterly drained and exhausted, and released, for the first time, from all my guilty torment") (*FNT* 87, 30, 31). The force that connects these three perspectives and that demonstrates so clearly the power relationship between them is the law as it is defined as well as practiced. Baldwin regards the law as a visible manifestation of power, which, mistreated as it sometimes is, becomes a racially divisive force that systematically destroys the American dreams of unity, freedom, equality, and unmitigated respect for the individual.

Baldwin clearly sensed the urgency of his nation's crisis at this point in history and was called to expand his understanding of what Crenshaw et al. describe as "the vexed bond between law and racial power."[4] *The Fire Next Time* moves from the law's power on the street (represented by the police) to the law's power on the national stage (represented by the

Supreme Court) as a way of demonstrating its pervasiveness in his experience, but also as a way of participating in the reshaping of American democracy through the advancement of a thorough critique. Baldwin's essay asks this question: if the law can supposedly change racial discrimination, then why is the law the very force that seems to harass, subordinate, and torment the victims of such discrimination? To question the law in this way is to reveal a disjunction between law in theory and law in practice, and to show how the disempowered are not necessarily empowered by the legal decisions that supposedly affect the course of history.

In *Whispered Consolations* Jon-Christian Suggs advances some key notions that can be applied to Baldwin; for instance, he writes, a "metaphor for the relationship between American law and African American narrative is that of the palimpsest, in which one text is written over another. . . . African American narratives overinscribe legal texts of the same issues, place, figures, events."[5] Suggs also speaks of a reciprocal relationship between the law and African American narrative that he understands in terms of Henry Louis Gates's concept of "signifying"; he writes, "African American literature exhibits new concerns, other complexities, makes unheard statements in response to the interrogative signifying of the law."[6] If *The Fire Next Time* can be seen as a palimpsest laid over *Brown,* the "new concerns, other complexities, [and] unheard statements" are the very substance of Baldwin's essay. In short, Baldwin's recognition of the power of the law to desegregate is undermined by his realization that the law has not relinquished any of its power in doing so. The law giveth and the law taketh away. The Supreme Court decision that was supposed to integrate American blacks and whites might have represented some social progress, and yet the unheard statement at the core of Baldwin's essay is a plaintive cry: why are the lives of African Americans still regulated primarily by legal power, even to the point of oppression? Moreover, is individual will completely overshadowed by legal power? Referring to Baldwin's final essay *The Evidence of Things Not Seen,* Richard Schur writes, "For Baldwin, legal change without cultural transformation put African Americans at risk because racial barriers still existed, even if the signs announcing segregation had been removed."[7] The same trend can be discerned in "Down at the Cross."

One of the formative documents of Critical Race Theory is an essay by Derrick Bell, "Brown v. Board of Education and the Interest-Convergence Dilemma." Like Baldwin, Bell questions the motives behind *Brown* as well as its long-term effects, albeit from a legal theorist's point of view looking at the decision a quarter-century after it was written. According to Bell,

Brown benefited white policymakers as well as black citizens in need of a better education: "I contend that the decision in *Brown* to break with the Court's long-held position on these issues cannot be understood without some consideration of the decision's value to whites, not simply those concerned about the immorality of racial inequality, but also those whites in policymaking positions able to see the economic and political advances at home and abroad that would follow abandonment of segregation."[8] This is not to take away from the obvious social benefits of the decision so much as to look beyond them, and to see the case as a manifestation of legal power, a benevolent gift from on high that could have only a limited effect on the mind-set of average citizens. Before he discusses *Brown,* Baldwin understands the intersection of legal power and widespread discriminatory attitudes as manifested on the street in the form of the police just as he did in "Faulkner and Desegregation." This direct, experiential contact with the law's power enables Baldwin, in the immediate aftermath of *Brown,* to advance a similar critique to Bell's critique, which derives its authority through legal and historical perspectives.

The dominant note of "Down at the Cross" is not despair over the depraved state of the law in America; as Lawrie Balfour writes, "Does Baldwin's unsettling narrative recommend the abandonment of equality as a political principle? Not at all. In fact, Baldwin's critique is made in the name of the equal humanity of all persons, regardless of race, and of the equal entitlement of all Americans to the basic rights of citizenship."[9] And yet, while "equality" was the ostensible aim of *Brown,* it was certainly not the effect, in Baldwin's eyes. It is difficult to know how to rebel against the law's power other than to commit crimes, often more serious ones than stealing sheets. In "Down at the Cross" crime becomes one of the "gimmicks" that seems to offer a way out of the ghetto, but it is illusory as such. Baldwin observes, "One did not have to be very bright to realize how little one could do to change one's situation" and he recalls how a "cop in the middle of the street muttered as I passed him, 'Why don't you niggers stay uptown where you belong?'" (*FNT* 19). This quotation is evidence of a hard fact of Baldwin's upbringing: law-abiding citizens and criminals of Harlem alike are kept in their place by the law. Ironically, American citizens pride themselves on the freedom of mobility, both literally in the sense that one can live where one chooses and metaphorically in such phrases as "class mobility." Here we see a law enforcement officer attempt to define a place for black people, an attempt which is, of course, the legacy of slavery and, later, of segregation. The police officer's question cannot be separated from his uniform, the symbol of power and often, in Baldwin, the mask of its abuse. At another point in the essay Baldwin describes a young black robber being "carried off to jail" (*FNT* 20), and it is obviously the police who are carrying him. This is another case of law enforcement officers re-placing the black citizen, putting him where, they have decided, he "belongs" (as discussed in chapter 2). Harlem as a whole is, by this association, itself a prison. Baldwin makes this association explicit in his 1971 essay "An Open Letter to my Sister, Angela Davis": "Black people were killing each other every Saturday night out on Lenox Avenue, when I was growing up; and no one explained to them, or to me, that it was *intended* that they should; that they were penned where they were."[10] The question of "belonging" applies not only to segregation in public spaces such as streets and schools, but to less apparent restrictions enforced by property law as well. In his study *Race, Place, and the Law*, David Delaney argues that, in the first half of the twentieth century until a 1948 U.S. Supreme Court decision that invalidated "restrictive covenants" that allowed for racial discrimination in housing, the legal system had been consistently used to determine where black people did, in fact, belong. The end of restrictive covenants, which Delaney describes as "legal techniques for shaping geographies of race and racism," led directly to *Brown*.[11]

Baldwin had experienced first-hand the effects of restrictive covenants throughout his youth, when blacks were "penned" in Harlem despite the fact that it was officially illegal to deny tenancy or property ownership to U.S. citizens based on race since the Civil Rights Act of 1866, as discussed in chapter 1. His awareness of this history is triggered by the policeman's comment. The trajectory of "Down at the Cross" from that moment leads back in time rather than forward into a harmonious future. Moving outside of himself and his community into history, Baldwin discusses the legacy of black servants robbing their white employers.[12] Here he not only redefines crime, but he shows how it can be justified in such a way as to reinforce stereotypes about racial hierarchy: "Negro servants have been smuggling odds and ends out of white homes for generations, and white people have been delighted to have them do it, because it has assuaged a dim guilt and testified to the intrinsic superiority of white people. Even the most doltish and servile Negro could scarcely fail to be impressed by the disparity between his situation and that of the people for whom he worked; Negroes who were neither doltish nor servile did not feel that they were doing anything wrong when they robbed white people" (*FNT* 22). Morality and legality are at odds with one another in this analysis. It is an example of what Karla Holloway describes in *Codes of Conduct:*

"In our contemporary culture, there is too frequent a coupling between altered ethical codes and negative ethnic experiences and stereotyping."[13] The act of robbery, officially a crime, is not considered a sin by either white or black people: the latter "did not feel that they were doing anything wrong" and the former were "delighted." Both races see it as inevitable, but it is another version of the "placement" I describe above: since the rich, white people feel superior, in Baldwin's eyes, a perspective which places them above their thieving servants. The law, in this case, is applied selectively, and is in the control of those in power, reinforcing social hierarchy rather than seeking to erase it. More importantly, though, the law can be interpreted historically, as Baldwin does here: "white people, who had robbed black people of their liberty and who profited by this theft every hour that they lived, had no moral ground on which to stand. They had the judges, the juries, the shotguns, the law—in a word, power. But it was a criminal power, to be feared but not respected, and to be outwitted in any way whatever" (*FNT* 23). The most striking facet of Baldwin's definition here is that power is defined exclusively as legal power, except in the case of firearms: power is "the judges, the juries . . . the law." This power is itself "criminal," though, and therefore does not garner respect. There is "no moral ground" underneath it: it is simply force, which makes sense of the seemingly incongruous word "shotguns" in the middle of Baldwin's definition.

Those in power—wealthy white people who have benefited historically from the legacy of slavery—are thus recast as the criminals of this society. Even more generally, "society" commits a crime by convincing the young Baldwin that he, too, "belongs" in jail, or back in Harlem: "the moral barriers that I had supposed to exist between me and the dangers of a criminal career were so tenuous as to be nearly nonexistent. I certainly could not discover any principled reason for not becoming a criminal, and it is not my poor, God-fearing parents who are to be indicted for the lack but this society" (*FNT* 23). By indicting his society, Baldwin is calling not only for an overhaul of the prejudiced attitudes that contribute to the racial divide, but also for a reexamination of the legal system that invisibly reinforces such attitudes. The racist comment of one police officer expands here to encompass legal power on other levels: the judges, the juries, the shotguns, and the law.

Baldwin's definition of power in terms of the law explains his identification with those who are subjugated by force and his initial interest in the Black Muslims, who represent a viable challenge to the law's power. If the law can take an innocent black man and intimidate him to the point of self-destruction, then it is a powerful force indeed. This real-ization is a kind of rite of initiation for Baldwin in "Down at the Cross" (not unlike his religious conversion) in which he describes "a fear that the child, in challenging the white world's assumptions, was putting himself in the path of destruction. A child cannot, thank Heaven, know how vast and how merciless is the nature of power, with what unbelievable cruelty people treat each other" (*FNT* 27). He realizes that "White people hold the power . . . and the world has innumerable ways of making this differ-ence known and felt and feared" (*FNT* 25–26). The primary source of fear in Baldwin's personal history is the ubiquitous presence in Harlem of the police. The effect of their presence is an invisible barrier that separates the white world from the world where African Americans supposedly belong. "Down at the Cross" in its entirety can thus be read as a meditation on legal power and the barriers it creates.

The first few pages of "Down at the Cross" are saturated with wall-imagery. The essay begins with Baldwin's reflection on his discovery, as a teenager, of "God, His saints and angels, and His blazing Hell" (*FNT* 16). Beyond the obvious and stark distinction between acceptance and pun-ishment, this God is also synonymous with safety, and Baldwin says, "I supposed Him to exist only within the walls of a church—in fact, of *our* church" (*FNT* 16). These walls separate good from evil, and saints from sinners in the mind of the teenaged Baldwin, but for the mature Baldwin these walls are symbolic of the problems of modern society rather than the solutions to its problems. "Safety" in Baldwin's work is always an illusion, or a force that consistently prevents individuals from giving themselves over to love.[14] In a speech entitled "The Artist's Struggle for Integrity" he says, "Art is here to prove, and to help one bear, the fact that all safety is an illusion" (*CR* 42). Even the young Baldwin takes refuge in the church out of fear; he says, "I became . . . afraid of the evil within me and afraid of the evil without" (*FNT* 16). Religion becomes a way to purge the evil within and promise that punishment will come to the evil-doers of the world, if it hasn't already. The walls of the church are meant to protect the saints from the sinners; yet the notion that evil or sin can be purged from the self and the notion that one can ever be in a truly safe place are both self-deceptive, and Baldwin astutely associates the church walls with other institutions that attempt to preserve societal power. The walls of the church in this quotation develop into prison walls later in the essay and throughout Baldwin's career.

Because the walls of the church and of prison are associated with safety and goodness, they are sometimes invisible to those who are most affected by them—those who have been deemed sinners or criminals, often for no other reason than their social status, their sexual orientation, or especially their race. These walls do little more than divide a community. Part of Baldwin's fear of the evil in the world around him is the fate of his friends: "one found them in twos and threes and fours, in a hallway, sharing a jug of wine or a bottle of whiskey, talking, cursing, fighting, sometimes weeping: lost, and unable to say what it was that oppressed them, except that they knew it was 'the man'—the white man. And there seemed to be no way whatever to remove this cloud that stood between them and the sun, between them and love and life and power, between them and whatever it was that they wanted" (*FNT* 19). Here the barrier is some abstract notion of white power that is placed directly in the middle of a black man's life that separates himself from his aspirations. "The man" is also, of course, a euphemism for a police officer, as in Baldwin's most vitriolic short story "Going to Meet the Man," discussed later in this chapter. Baldwin foreshadows the publication of that story in "Down at the Cross" when he writes, "*Whoever debases others is debasing himself.* That is not a mystical statement but a most realistic one, which is proved by the eyes of any Alabama sheriff" (*FNT* 83).

This association with "the man" is foretold in "Down at the Cross" immediately after the quotation in which Baldwin recalls the policeman's comment, "Why don't you niggers stay uptown where you belong?" and relates an incident when he was ten: "two policemen amused themselves with me by frisking me, making comic (and terrifying) speculations concerning my ancestry and probable sexual prowess, and for good measure, leaving me flat on my back in one of Harlem's empty lots" (*FNT* 19–20). This exercise of power becomes an example of "the evil without" from which the young Baldwin must take refuge. His world is a dangerous place, not necessarily because of the criminals who pervade it—"the whores and pimps and racketeers on the Avenue" (*FNT* 16)—but because the law that is supposed to protect him from those criminals reveals itself to be a criminal power. In a dialogue with Nikki Giovanni, Baldwin said, "a cop is a cop. . . . All I know is, he's got a uniform and a gun and I have to relate to him that way."[15] Keneth Kinnamon writes that the incident Baldwin describes in "Down at the Cross" is isolated: "[Baldwin] did suffer harassment from white policemen, including a terrifying incident at the age of ten mentioned in *The Fire Next Time* and treated at length in *Tell Me How Long the Train's Been Gone*. But for the most part white oppression was an abstract force, responsible somehow for the poverty and desperation which surrounded him, the invisible cause of a visible result."[16]

Baldwin, however, describes police harassment as a repeated motif in his life, and anything but abstract; he writes later in the essay, "When a white man faces a black man, especially if the black man is helpless, terrible things are revealed. I know. I have been carried into precinct basements often enough" (*FNT* 53). Referring to a remark by Allen Ginsberg who said, "Don't call the cop a pig, call him a friend. If you call him a friend, he'll act like a friend," Baldwin remarked, "I know more about cops than that" (*RR* 128).

Baldwin's need to seek safety from such a criminal power is a real one, but one that damages his soul, for he realizes later in life, "To defend one-self against a fear is simply to insure that one will, one day, be conquered by it; fears must be faced" (*FNT* 27). To hide from the law would be to acknowledge its intimidating power, and thus to sacrifice one's own power. Without blaming himself, Baldwin realizes the mistake he had made as a youth in supposing that there was a hiding place: "That summer," he says, "all the fears with which I had grown up, and which were now a part of me and controlled my vision of the world, rose up *like a wall* between the world and me, and drove me into the church" (*FNT* 27; emphasis mine). Late in the essay, Baldwin completes the relationship between power, the legal system, and religion when he discusses the desire of the so-called American Negro to gain the sort of power and notoriety black men have in places like Africa: "As [American Negroes] watch black men elsewhere rise, the promise held out, at last, that they may walk the earth with the authority with which white men walk, protected by the power that white men shall have no longer, is enough, and more than enough, to empty pris-ons and pull God down from Heaven" (*FNT* 77). Baldwin's description of the revolt against a white God's power in terms of a prison riot solidifies the connection he sees between religion and the law as institutions that preserve racial hierarchy.

The walls of the early part of the essay are all associated with white power and with punishment, and it follows that the law gradually replaces the church in Baldwin's imagination. In the shorter prefatory essay in *The Fire Next Time,* "My Dungeon Shook," Baldwin makes clear the connec-tion between a false sense of safety and wrongful imprisonment; he writes, "those innocents who believed that your imprisonment made them safe are losing their grasp of reality" (*FNT* 9). He plays with the notions of innocence and crime throughout this brief essay: the "innocents" in this quotation are in fact *guilty,* in Baldwin's mind; they are the perpetrators of the crime of dooming their black brethren to the life of poverty and crime described at the beginning of "Down at the Cross." He writes, "I know what the world has done to my brother and how narrowly he has survived it. And I know, which is much worse, and this is the crime of which I accuse my country and my countrymen, and for which neither I nor time nor history will ever forgive them, that they have destroyed and are destroying hundreds of thousands of lives and do not know it and do not want to know it" (*FNT* 5). He goes on to equate criminality with innocence in the essay's most powerful rhetorical turn: "But it is not permissible that the authors of devastation should also be innocent. It is the innocence which constitutes the crime" (*FNT* 5–6). Here Baldwin redefines the very terms of the legal courtroom—crime and innocence—to prove his point: "innocence" is a close substitute for "ignorance" here, and ignorance, as the saying goes, is no excuse for breaking a law. The crime he speaks of here is a crime against humanity, enabled through a willingness to erase history's impact on the present. This essay is, after all, occasioned by the hundredth anniversary of the Emancipation Proclamation. Baldwin disposes of the notion of "innocence" in a nation that has been historically guilty, but that has never allowed itself to be tried for its crimes. In an atmosphere in which there appear to be victims of history but no acknowledged criminals, Baldwin has no choice but to criminalize the very notion of innocence, just as he has recast safety as a dangerous illusion.

In order for an individual to gain power against such a monolithic institution as the American legal system, he must resort to a new kind of rhetoric. In "Down at the Cross," Baldwin attempts to redefine the concept of "crime" and the meaning of "power" in order to combat the "criminal power" that is held by the representatives of the legal system. "Crime" is synonymous with "sin" in the early section of the essay, when he has run to the church for protection from both of these things. He sees "crime" as something nearly inevitable for the residents of Harlem: it figures into their destiny. He writes, "Crime became real, for example—for the first time—not as *a* possibility but as *the* possibility. One would never defeat one's circumstances by working and saving one's pennies; one would never, by working, acquire that many pennies, and, besides, the social treatment accorded even the most successful Negroes proved that one needed, in order to be free, something more than a bank account. One needed a handle, a lever, a means of inspiring fear. It was absolutely clear that the police would whip you and take you in as long as they could get away with it" (*FNT* 21). Crime here is a way out of the cycle of poverty and despair that trapped Harlem residents in the bleak 1930s. Ironically, the police do not respond to crime in this formulation: they cause it. The police, according to Baldwin, are predisposed to mistreat poor black Americans, so crime becomes a way—the only way—to claim one's identity.

Even though law enforcement officers are only the most visible evidence of the law's power, Baldwin regards them with the invective he generally reserves for church elders; he says, "All policemen have by now, for me, become exactly the same, and my style with them is designed simply to intimidate them before they can intimidate me. No doubt I am guilty of some injustice here, but it is irreducible, since I cannot risk assuming that the humanity of these people is more real to them than their uniforms" (*FNT* 68). The word "injustice" plays on Baldwin's critique of the justice system, which is a much larger power than the police on the street. Baldwin's manipulation of words related to the law (such as justice and guilt) is consistent throughout the essay: his willingness to redefine the words that have been used to define his reality is, in fact, his attempt to secure power for himself. Every society defines crime as an illegal act, and this definition is intended as a line of demarcation indicating a society's moral beliefs. Yet when a society is permeated by widespread immorality, individuals must redefine crimes. For instance, Baldwin, describing his role as a Sunday School teacher, says, "I felt that I was committing a crime in talking about the gentle Jesus, in telling them to reconcile themselves to their misery on earth in order to gain the crown of eternal life" (*FNT* 39). This lesson is a "crime" in the adult Baldwin's eyes because it is not really the handle, lever, or means of inspiring fear that will allow Harlemites to survive on the street; crime itself is. Later in the essay, musing on organized religion, he brings up the term "crime" again in a different context: "whoever wishes to become a truly moral human being . . . must first divorce himself from all the prohibitions, crimes, and hypocrisies of the Christian church" (*FNT* 47). Crimes here are sins against humanity, and thus act as evidence of the hypocrisy of a church that professes love and caritas. Religion in general is a way to make crimes holy; Baldwin later writes, "legend and theology, which are designed to sanctify our fears, crimes, and aspirations, also reveal them for what they are" (*FNT* 70). In making this link, Baldwin seeks to disempower two institutions that have seized control of the definition of American morality: the Christian church and the legal system.

Elijah Muhammad uses the same word when talking about white immorality when he speaks about "the crimes of white people" (*FNT* 65). These "crimes"—not specified as Baldwin conveys Elijah's words—are presumably the racist leftovers of the system of slavery. Baldwin and Elijah Muhammad agree that these are crimes worth examining and trying, but Baldwin chooses to focus more on the second word he seeks to rede-fine: power. In fact, Baldwin becomes interested in the Nation of Islam's speeches not because of their rhetoric, but because their power seems to intimidate the police:

> two things caused me to begin to listen to the speeches, and one was the behavior of the police. After all, I had seen men dragged from their plat-forms on this very corner for saying less virulent things, and I had seen many crowds dispersed by policemen, with clubs or on horseback. But the policemen were doing nothing now. Obviously, this was not because they had become more human but because they were under orders and because they were afraid. And indeed they were, and I was delighted to see it. There they stood, in twos and threes and fours, in their Cub Scout uniforms and with their Cub Scout faces, totally unprepared, as is the way with American he-men, for anything that could not be settled with a club or a fist or a gun. I might have pitied them if I had not found myself in their hands so often and discovered, through ugly experience, what they were like when *they* held the power and what they were like when *you* held the power. (*FNT* 48–49)

Baldwin finds the Black Muslims intriguing and impressive because they have a certain power over the police, who seem suddenly childish (Cub Scout uniforms and faces) in their presence. Although the police still have superior physical strength (symbolized here as clubs, fists, and guns), they now appear afraid and are rendered somewhat impotent in terms of the actual power they have. Still, though, Baldwin realizes the dangerous situation this creates: if the Nation of Islam indeed has power over the police, then there is the potential that the police will act on their fear, over-compensating by using excessive force. The power of intimidation that the Muslims exhibit is really no different from the criminal power of the police. This situation is parallel to what Baldwin concludes about Chris-tianity and the Black Muslim movement, which are essentially similar in terms of their willingness to separate the races and place one above the other; as Baldwin puts it, "The dream, the sentiment is old; only the color is new" (57).

Baldwin ultimately does not endorse the Nation of Islam's solution of gaining the power that has been denied them through revolt because, he believes, there is a higher force than raw power: love. Yet he acknowledges in this essay and elsewhere that it is sometimes difficult to resist the lure of power; he writes, "I knew the tension in me between love and power"

(*FNT* 60). Resisting a facile opposition between these two terms, he seeks to define love as something tough that can, in fact, stand up to the type of power he has been describing throughout the essay: "I use the word 'love' here not merely in the personal sense but as a state of being, or a state of grace—not in the infantile American sense of being made happy but in the tough and universal sense of quest and daring and growth" (*FNT* 95). The love he describes is a commitment to the self-trust and self-knowledge described by American Transcendentalists such as Emerson and Thoreau who believed that the individual conscience was the highest power and the one that all Americans should seek to develop apart from society's institutions; as Baldwin writes, "The person who distrusts himself has no touchstone for reality—for this touchstone can be only oneself" (*FNT* 43). And yet, Baldwin at least raises the question about his individualistic sense of social improvement weighed against the social improvement of the Black Muslims who had managed to teach so many young men to avoid the life of crime Baldwin once saw as a near inevitability. He sees himself as "perpetually attempting to choose the better rather than the worse. But this choice was a choice in terms of a personal, a private better (I was, after all, a writer); what was its relevance in terms of a social worse?" (*FNT* 60–61). As Lawrie Balfour concludes, "Baldwin rejects the sort of up-by-the-bootstraps individualism that is often associated with the term [personal responsibility]."[17]

If Baldwin believes that the solution to America's racial crisis does not take the form of ideological, social, religious, or race-based political commitment such as that required by the Nation of Islam, then one might assume that he would look toward legal avenues for social reform. Deak Nabers argues that Baldwin's essays of the 1960s including "Down at the Cross" marked a "turn from social clarity to historical recognition . . . fueled by a growing skepticism that legislation could meaningfully address America's persistent civil rights problems." He sees Baldwin's writings as part of a larger trend: "in turning from legal and social concerns to historical concerns he participated in a widespread rearticulation of the nature of American racial inequality as the Civil Rights movement scored its major national legislative successes. The trajectory of the Civil Rights movement in the 1960s increasingly took it away from the notion that racial disadvantage in the United States could be effectively addressed by something on the order of a legal strategy."[18] Although there is certainly a good argument to be made that Baldwin turned to "historical recognition," it does not necessarily come at the expense of a belief in the power of legislation, for at the end of "Down at the Cross," Baldwin repeatedly invokes the broadest manifestations of the law's power—Supreme Court decisions of both the past and the present—and he even begins to use the language of the courtroom in his essay.

Nabers is correct insofar as Baldwin is *skeptical* of legal solutions to social problems, and Kieran Dolan uses the word skeptical as well, but says that Baldwin is skeptical "of liberal confidence that *Brown* represented 'a change of heart,' arguing rather that it was born of political pragmatism."[19] Baldwin is wary, as was Dr. Martin Luther King in his "Letter from Birmingham Jail," of the white liberals' calls for patience, and he defends Malcolm X's point that the willingness to fight, physically, for one's rights does not constitute "violence": "Malcolm's statement is *not* answered by references to the triumphs of the N.A.A.C.P., the more particularly since very few liberals have any notion of how long, how costly, and how heartbreaking a task it is to gather the evidence that one can carry into court, or how long such court battles take" (*FNT 59*). Nabers interprets this quotation as follows: "It might seem here as though Baldwin is concerned about the strategic implications of legal responses to segregation. 'Court battles' take too long, and exact too high a cost in human suffering, to count as effective instruments for achieving the social reform America needs. But Baldwin's objection to *Brown* is not simply that it was a very costly way of confronting school segregation; it is also that it was, in an important sense, beside the point of school segregation. . . . If at first Baldwin implies that NAACP-style efforts at reform were inefficient, in terms of both time and human suffering, here he so downplays the force of those efforts as to make them seem virtually irrelevant, irrelevant not merely to the social conditions they might be thought to address but also to the legal results, like *Brown,* they seek to achieve."[20] Nabers bases his conclusion on the following passage from "Down at the Cross":

> White Americans have contented themselves with gestures that are now described as 'tokenism.' For hard example, white Americans congratulate themselves on the 1954 Supreme Court decision outlawing segregation in the schools; they suppose, in spite of the mountain of evidence that has since accumulated to the contrary, that this was proof of a change of heart—or, as they like to say, progress. Perhaps. It all depends on how one reads the word 'progress.' Most of the Negroes I know do not believe that this immense concession would ever have been made if it had not been for the competition of the cold war, and the fact that Africa was clearly liberating herself and therefore had, for political reasons, to be wooed by the descendants of her former masters. Had it

been a matter of love or justice, the 1954 decision would surely have occurred sooner; were it not for the realities of power in this difficult era, it might very well not have occurred yet.

This seems an extremely harsh way of stating the case—ungrateful, as it were—but the evidence that supports this way of stating it is not easily refuted. I myself do not think that it can be refuted at all. (*FNT* 87)

Baldwin's analysis of the Cold War factors surrounding *Brown* anticipates the work of recent CRT scholars such as Mary Dudziak who concludes, "*Brown* was the product of converging domestic and international developments, rather than an inevitable product of legal progress."[21] Geopolitics and the force of history do seem to overwhelm moral reasons (i.e., "love or justice") as the basis for legal reform in Baldwin's formulation and in Nabers's analysis of it. Yet the word "power" here must be connected to the "criminal power" Baldwin speaks of earlier in the essay if we are to make sense of the essay as a coherent whole. The "realities of power in this difficult era" involve *both* geopolitics *and* Supreme Court decisions *as well as* the criminal power of the police and of rich, white people that dominated the early part of the essay. In short, legal power in Baldwin's mind is still in the hands of the oppressors, and even if it is used for good, for "progress," it is still not in the hands of the oppressed. He uses this observation as the basis for his indignation about the very basic premises of legal decisions: "There is absolutely no reason to suppose that white people are better equipped to frame the laws by which I am to be governed than I am. It is entirely unacceptable that I should have no voice in the political affairs of my own country, for I am not a ward of America; I am one of the first Americans to arrive on these shores" (*FNT* 98). The word "ward" is associated with imprisonment, which brings the discussion full circle: Baldwin is denying his status as someone being watched or guarded by the state and asserting his status as someone who has the right "to frame the laws" of his nation. He insists that he should have a "voice," which is precisely the instrument he uses to gain the power that has been used to oppress him. It is also the instrument that he lacked in his prison and trial experience in Paris.

In exercising his voice in order to gain power, it is not surprising that Baldwin adopts the rhetoric of the courtroom in the latter half of the essay. His claim to power is his ability to argue, in writing; in other words, to make a case. He is conscious of the connection between legal argument and rhetorical power from the moment he departs from the table of Elijah

Muhammad and his followers: "And I looked around the table. I certainly had no evidence to give them that would outweigh Elijah's authority or the evidence of their own lives or the reality of the streets outside. . . . All my evidence would be thrown out of court as irrelevant to the main body of the case" (FNT 72). Even this interaction with his Muslim brothers recognizes the importance of legal rhetoric to the shaping of their reality. Baldwin does not feel that he can persuade the Muslims to see things his way. The reason again is power, because for most people, "power is more real than love. And yet power *is* real, and many things, including, very often, love, cannot be achieved without it" (FNT 73). In the conclusion of "Down at the Cross" he overcomes this moment of despair at his inability to persuade anyone who is steeped in any kind of ideology or seduced by power when he reaffirms the ability of "the relatively conscious whites and the relatively conscious blacks, who must, like lovers, insist on, or create, the consciousness of the others" (FNT 105). There is finally affirmation in the essay that love can triumph over power, even legal power, even criminal power.

Toward the end of "Down at the Cross" Baldwin makes explicit the central difficulty of resolving America's racial woes; he says, "there is simply no possibility of a real change in the Negro's situation without the most radical and far-reaching changes in the American political and social structure" (FNT 85). The legal structure is, in theory, the intersection of the American political and social structures, or at the very least the most tangible evidence of those structures. Baldwin was clearly aware of the relationship between the legal and the social/political: the preceding quotation appears in Baldwin's essay directly after a reference to the Dred Scott decision—the 1857 case that concluded that black people were not U.S. citizens—and immediately before a reference to "the 1954 decision"— that is *Brown*—that ended the practice of segregation in public schools. Such examples from history and from Baldwin's lifetime demonstrate how the legal structure of the United States exerts a powerful influence over Baldwin's quest for identity and over his views of his nation's unfulfilled promise of justice for all of its citizens. As he says in a 1963 interview, "there are 20 million Negro people in this country, and you can't put them all in jail."[22] He states the same idea more obliquely in "Down at the Cross": "there is a limit to the number of people any government can put in prison" (FNT 103). The fact that black people make up roughly 12 percent of the U.S. population but over 50 percent of the U.S. prison population suggests that the trend Baldwin noticed fifty years ago—the use of legal power to control racial geography—continues, and indeed has increased. The "criminal power" to incarcerate, to harass, and to legislate decisions that continue to place minorities and other disenfranchised individuals where society believes they belong—in housing projects, in impoverished neighborhoods, and in jail—has certainly not diminished since the publication of Baldwin's essay.

In the period surrounding the publication of *Fire,* Baldwin concentrated on producing short stories, which were collected in 1965 in *Going to Meet the Man.* These stories reveal Baldwin's changing aesthetic as well as the amplification of his responses to the law's power. Baldwin embraced one of the central lessons of "Down at the Cross" in his short fiction, namely, the difficulty and necessity of accepting the other, particularly the criminal other. Arguably the three most successful stories in the collection exemplify this theme: "Sonny's Blues" (1957), "This Morning, This Evening, So Soon" (1960), and "Going to Meet the Man" (1965). The first two cast the "other" as criminals who have served time in prison; the third poses an even greater challenge to the reader's empathy by focusing on the man who might have arrested them. In all three cases, the law represents a dividing line that prevents human relationships from flourishing naturally. *Brown* is briefly evoked in the second story, and the three together argue that its effects are meaningless as long as the law's enforcement mechanisms (prisons and police) retain their criminal and criminalizing powers.

"Sonny's Blues" has become Baldwin's most famous work and has been thoroughly analyzed as such, both for its sharp moral message (the narrator has to learn how to listen to his brother rather than to judge him) and for its keen understanding of the blues, both musically and culturally. Sonny is the epitome of Baldwin's conception of the artist; according to David Leeming, "For Baldwin the artist was a victim and a savior who 'plays' for his very life and for ours."[23] The narrator's difficulty in accepting his brother as a victim/savior stems from his notion of public respectability: the narrator has gotten out of the ghetto by upholding a conventional, bland middle-class life, teaching the emotionally neutral subject of math. Sonny, though, plays jazz music, which the narrator considers a low art form and, much worse, he takes heroin. Yet the story is catalyzed not by Sonny's playing jazz or using heroin, but by his arrest. The public stigma of incarceration fully distances Sonny from the narrator and sets in motion their path toward healing.

It is curious, then, that "Sonny's Blues" carefully sidesteps Sonny's incarceration to the point that the narrator never uses the words "arrest," "prison," or "jail." In fact, he seems to avoid these words on purpose, and he refuses to imagine what Sonny's prison experience must have been like.

In all references to this period of Sonny's life, the narrator uses phrases that refer to nonspecific but still physical sites. Sonny is not arrested, but rather "picked up" (*GM* 103). The police are not even named as the narrator describes the border that is the prison wall: "they'll let him out. And then he'll just start working his way back in again" (*GM* 108). Inmates commonly refer to prison as "inside," but the narrator's purpose in describing Sonny's incarceration this way seems to be related to his avoidance of the subject; he observes his fellow teachers walking through crowds of students "quickly . . . to get those boys out of their sight and off their minds" (*GM* 105) just as he does with his brother. Similarly, in his uncomfortable conversation with Sonny's friend, he admits, "All this was carrying me some place I didn't want to go" (*GM* 107). The physical placement of Sonny in jail is a way for everyone who considers themselves innocent to have him "out of their sight and off their minds," and to enclose him "some place" where they don't want to go: that is, prison.

Sonny perhaps understands his brother's unwillingness to fully see the place that confines him. In his initial letter from prison, Sonny refers to his location nonspecifically as "here" and "down here" (*GM* 109). He speaks of his condition metaphorically: "I feel like a man who's been trying to climb up out of some deep, real deep and funky hole and just saw the sun up there, outside. I got to get outside" (*GM* 109). This description is meant to reveal his emotional state as well as his attempts to recover from heroin use, but it evokes his actual setting: "the hole" is a common term for solitary confinement, and "outside" refers to the space outside the prison walls. After reading the letter, the narrator begins "finally, to wonder about Sonny, about the life that Sonny lived inside" (*GM* 110), again referring to his interior life, but also alluding to his incarceration. As the brothers begin to talk honestly to one another about suffering, about heroin use, and about the emotional power of music, they continue to avoid a discussion of Sonny's arrest and prison experience, which has presumably altered his perspective and which has catalyzed the narrator's awareness of his brother. The narrator refers to Sonny's arrest and incarceration as his "trouble" (*GM* 127) and Sonny himself again refers to his jail cell without naming it as such: "I can't forget—where I've been. I don't mean just the physical place I've been, I mean where I've *been*" (*GM* 134). The story again pushes us away from Sonny's experience in prison in favor of concentrating on his spiritual and emotional crisis; yet here he acknowledges that the physical place of prison has contributed to his perspective.

"Sonny's Blues" is not just a "social problem" story about how black men end up committing crimes and serving time for doing so; to return to

Baldwin's early arguments with Stowe and Wright, it is not "protest literature." Sonny has committed a crime and is "picked up" for it. The narrator does not bemoan this fact and Baldwin does not encourage us to see it
as injustice. Yet prison effectively acts as a metaphor in the story for any of
the forces that can separate individuals, and these forces must be resisted if
a society is to flourish. The story asks the reader to consider difficult questions about interpersonal relationships and responsibility. When Sonny's
friend reads about Sonny's arrest in the paper, he says, "The first thing
I asked myself was if I had anything to do with it. I felt sort of responsible" (*GM* 107). The narrator does not initially feel this way because
he has failed to learn his mother's basic lesson about brotherhood: "You
may not be able to stop nothing from happening. But you got to let him
know you's *there*" (*GM* 119; italics original). When the narrator finally
does begin to act in accordance with this lesson, he begins to develop from
a static, insensitive prig into the role he should have filled all along: the
older brother who is willing to listen. His initial contact with Sonny takes
the form of a letter to his brother in prison. The implications of Baldwin's message can be applied to much of his work during this period: the
social constructs that serve to separate and compartmentalize society—
like prison, like segregation laws, like religious institutions—can be easily
overcome through an understanding that we are all connected and that we
can demonstrate how we are *there* for one another even if we can't prevent
everything bad from happening.

   "This Morning, This Evening, So Soon" presents the same message
to the reader in an even more challenging way, for here the relationship
between the "innocent" narrator and the story's criminal, Boona, isn't
familial (although Boona refers to the narrator as "brother," both in
English and in French). The story's initial conflict involves the narrator's
anxiety over his repatriation to his native America, but the conflict shifts
and develops upon the arrival of Boona, a North African who joins the
narrator and a group of American college students along with Vidal, the
European director of the narrator's recent film. Just before Boona arrives,
the young Americans ask the narrator and Vidal their opinions, from a
European perspective, of the *Brown* decision: "'Then you haven't been
back since Black Monday,' Talley says [to the narrator]. He laughs. 'That's
how it's gone down in Confederate history.' He turns to Vidal. 'What do
people think about it here?'" (*GM* 181). Vidal responds, "It seems extraor-
dinarily infantile behavior, even for Americans" (*GM* 181) and goes on
to say that he doesn't understand Americans. The infantile behavior he
refers to is presumably the tension following the Supreme Court decision

rather than the decision itself, though Vidal never clarifies, and the narrator adds nothing to the conversation. As a black expatriate, he is perhaps not aware of the changes in his home country brought about by the legal end of school segregation. Boona's arrival into the story, then, serves as a reminder of the complexity of the narrator's racial identity and the nagging questions of poverty and criminality that are not addressed by the Supreme Court's decision.

The crucial question at the center of "This Morning, This Evening, So Soon" is, again, not to figure out how to prevent crime so much as it is about understanding what to do with people who have committed a crime. When the young American tourist Pete informs the narrator that Boona has stolen money from his friend Ada, and that the theft has been corroborated by a reliable witness, the narrator tries to explain it away: "I do not know what to say or what to do, and so I temporize with questions. All the time I am wondering if this can be true and what I can do about it if it is. The trouble is, I know that Boona steals, he would probably not be alive if he didn't, but I cannot say so to these children, who probably still imagine that everyone who steals is a thief. But he has never, to my knowledge, stolen from a friend. It seems unlike him. I have always thought of him as being better than that, and smarter than that. And so I cannot believe it, but neither can I doubt it. I do not know anything about Boona's life, these days. This causes me to realize that I do not really know much about Boona" (*GM* 187). The narrator is clearly aligned with the narrator of "Sonny's Blues": both are successful men who are incredulous when their "brother" commits a crime, and both admit that they don't know their brother as well as they should. Yet if the narrator of "Sonny's Blues" is too judgmental, this narrator is perhaps too generous, or insufficiently critical. He also may be deceiving himself, especially when it comes to his point about Boona never stealing from friends. The passage echoes another passage from early in the story when the narrator realizes that his North African friends—whom he also thinks of as "brothers" (*GM* 156)—have stolen from him: "my collection of American sport shirts had vanished—mostly into their wardrobes. They seemed to feel that they had every right to them, since I could only have wrested these things from the world by cunning—it meant nothing to say that I had had no choice in the matter; perhaps I had wrested these things from the world by treason, by refusing to be identified with the misery of my people. Perhaps, indeed, I identified myself with those who were responsible for this misery" (*GM* 157). The word "right" is important here following an oblique discussion of civil rights vis-à-vis *Brown* as it reveals the narrator's guilt and confusion, for his success is itself a kind of crime ("treason"). Just as Baldwin uses history to explain why black servants justifiably steal from white employers in "Down at the Cross," so here does he justify North Africans' stealing from an American, especially one who has "identified himself" with white Americans, presumably through his economic success. It is also possible that he is referring to his marriage to a white European woman. In either case, the narrator expresses a great deal of insecurity about his relationship with Boona and other North Africans, just as Baldwin had expressed mystification about the reality of Africans in his early essay "Encounter on the Seine: Black Meets Brown."

The situation is even more complex here, though, because the story takes place in the immediate aftermath of *Brown* when black people can ill afford any rifts in their racial community. Just as he is uneasy about his relationship with North Africans, the narrator is also insecure about his relationship to America, especially to these young students who represent a certain hope for the future. They, like the narrator, are embarrassed by Boona's actions and want to resolve them quietly and privately, out of the judgmental eye of Vidal who represents the white colonizer to Boona, and powerful, paternalistic old Europe to the Americans. The ethical question of Boona's behavior is a nagging one, though. The narrator is so eager to sweep the mess under the carpet that he takes full responsibility for Boona's actions and offers to pay back the money, but he is not allowed such an easy resolution. Boona publicly denies that he has stolen the money, appealing to him "theatrically" with "tears standing in his eyes," and the narrator doubts his sincerity: "I want to say, I know you steal, I know you have to steal. Perhaps you took the money out of this girl's purse in order to eat tomorrow, in order not to be thrown into the streets tonight, in order to stay out of jail" (*GM* 189). His extreme liberal position begins to break down, though; he goes on, "I also think, if you would steal from her, then of course you would lie to me, neither of us means anything to you; perhaps, in your eyes, we are simply luckier gangsters in a world run by gangsters. But I cannot say any of these things to Boona" (*GM* 190). Society's methods of social control, of crime and punishment, do not seem to apply in this situation. If Boona is stealing so that he doesn't have to go to jail, if the world is indeed "run by gangsters" who embody a criminal power, this petty crime seems justified. This is the only way to explain the narrator's distinction between "a thief" and "someone who steals": he is acknowledging the complexity of the situation and suggesting that jail is not a fitting punishment for someone who steals. The situation tests his loyalties, though: he wants to ally himself with the new generation of black Americans so that he doesn't feel alienated when he returns to an America in which everything has supposedly changed after *Brown*. At the same time, he feels an ancestral race loyalty to Boona, and a kind of pity for him as someone who is stigmatized rather than celebrated in Europe. The situation is difficult and painful, with no satisfying resolution. The narrator, at the very end of the story, steps into an elevator with his son and twice describes it as a "cage" (*GM* 193). He may have kept Boona out of an actual jail only to have placed himself in a metaphorical jail. The illusion of social progress posited by *Brown* may have only served to obscure a vexing reality.

"Going to Meet the Man," Baldwin's most vicious work of fiction, marks a shift from those who are at the mercy of the "criminal power" of the law to those who use that power. Although the reader is encouraged to see how Jesse, the anti-hero of this story, was damaged when his parents brought him to a lynching at the age of eight, Baldwin certainly does not invite sympathy for this character who can only become sexually aroused when he thinks of abusing black people. In "Down at the Cross" Baldwin writes, "A child cannot, thank Heaven, know how vast and how merciless is the nature of power, with what unbelievable cruelty people treat each other" (*FNT* 27). Jesse's childhood experience presses against this observation: in one sickening day, he gains that knowledge. The tragic premise of the story is that Jesse appropriates that power, with all of its attendant cruelty, as an adult. Profoundly unsettled by the behavior of black agitators, he longs for a simpler time when the older generation was in control: "Men much older than he, who had been responsible for law and order much longer than he, were now much quieter than they had been, and the tone of their jokes, in a way that he could not quite put his finger on, had changed. These men were his models, they had been friends to his father, and they had taught him what it meant to be a man" (*GM* 236). These men "responsible for law and order," we learn, constituted a lynch mob. Despite the presence of the National Guard in southern cities, despite *Brown*, despite the efforts of the Southern Christian Leadership Council and the Student Non-violent Coordinating Committee, the memory of lynchings and vigilante justice live on in Jesse's mind as the foundation of "law and order" in the South. The fact that he has become a law enforcement officer who routinely abuses black people is evidence of the "criminal power" that Baldwin fears and hopes to expose.

Jesse realizes that it is getting harder to control black people because of agitators from the North and because, in the words of the police officer from "Down at the Cross," black people have refused to stay "uptown, where they belong." Jesse thinks, "If the niggers had all lived in one place," he and the other white racists could have "set fire to the houses and brought about peace that way" (*GM* 237). He regards himself as a good man, and hopes to see himself and the other would-be vigilantes as "soldiers fighting a war, but their relationship to each other was that of accomplices in a crime" (*GM* 239). Baldwin here indicates that Jesse's authority constitutes a criminal power, and we see him enacting it in his encounter that day with a young black man. He seems unable to control his own actions toward the young man and regards the other officers' treatment of him as inevitable: "Big Jim C. and some of the boys really had to whip that nigger's ass" and "they had to beat him" (*GM* 232). Jesse abuses this man as a way of controlling the entire black community, specifically to stop them from singing protest songs. The narrative perspective shifts; Jesse initially relates the story in first person to his wife—"I put the prod to him" (*GM* 232)—but by the end of the paragraph the perspective has become objective: "he kept prodding the boy, sweat pouring from beneath the helmet he had not yet taken off. The boy rolled around in his own dirt and water and blood and tried to scream again as the prod hit his testicles, but the scream did not come out, only a kind of rattle and a moan. He stopped. He was not supposed to kill the nigger. . . . His foot leapt out, he had not known it was going to, and caught the boy flush on the jaw" (*GM* 233). He has transferred the power he witnessed in his youth of a lynch mob into full-fledged police brutality. There are apparently limitations to his actions that differentiate his behavior from that of his parents' generation—notably, he is not "supposed to kill" the young man—but he is unable to control his actions once he has begun them.

The law supposedly exists to maintain order and control in society. Baldwin's meditations on legal power in the late 1950s and early 1960s, however, reveal its other, sinister dimensions. This "criminal power" knows no limits, for one thing, and as Jesse proves, it can never be extinguished. Moreover, it is motivated more by irrational fear than by the rationality that is supposedly at the core of the law. Finally, its effect is not to maintain order so much as to uphold the separations within society that were supposedly redressed by *Brown*. Beginning with his return to the United States in 1957, Baldwin's period of repatriation ended in extreme frustration and anger, as one can clearly see from the tone and subject matter of "Going to Meet the Man" which, like *Blues For Mister Charlie*, was not universally praised by critics; Joseph Featherstone called the story "inanely simple . . . like . . . the Book of Job in the form of a comic book."[24] This judgment is harsh, but it is clearly a reaction to the fact that

Baldwin's optimism and promise for reconciliation, evident in "Sonny's Blues," erodes in the next two stories I have discussed.

Whether or not they result in inferior works of art, the emotional excesses of "Going to Meet the Man" and *Blues for Mister Charlie* reveal Baldwin's growing feelings of despair at this time. His developing confidence in his ability to combat the criminal power of the law takes a pronounced change in direction from the late 1960s to the early 1970s. Having begun to understand the relationship between the Supreme Court and the law on the streets, Baldwin found himself again focusing on powerlessness and subjugation during this period rather than attacking the institutions that promulgate power. At this time he felt better equipped to deal with the enormous potency of the law's power as an artist in exile rather than as a reporter on the front lines of the battlefield. He was also increasingly paranoid about his own safety in the late 1960s, worried that the violence unleashed by the struggle for Civil Rights would claim him as a victim, as it had already claim Medgar Evers and Malcolm X and as it was about to claim Martin Luther King. He returned to foreign exile in the late 1960s, and returned to an examination of the law in what he saw as its most brutal symbols: prisons and the police.

CHAPTER 4

Return to Exile

"GOING TO MEET THE MAN" was published the year Malcolm X was assassinated. The anger, cynicism, and violence evident in that story had their counterpart in the turbulence that was overtaking the nation, and Baldwin's response was similar to his response to racism in the pre-Civil Rights era: to return to exile, this time in Turkey. Something crucial had changed in the American mood. The "relatively conscious blacks and the relatively conscious whites" from the famous conclusion of "Down at the Cross" were no longer marching arm-in-arm. The gun hidden behind the pulpit in *Blues for Mister Charlie* had surfaced, and was being fired indiscriminately. Confronted with violence, the citizenry seemed eager to put the law's primary power back in the hands of the police, who worked with brute force to incarcerate perceived troublemakers. Baldwin reveals his fear and the realization of "the fire next time" in a 1972 interview in *Transition*: "The fire is upon us. When construction workers in New York can walk, under the eyes of the police, and beat up kids and antiwar demonstrators, helped by the police really, and nobody cares, it's very sinister. Sinister as the Reichstag fire. When the police become lawless, and are allied with the visibly lawless, a society is in trouble. I'm chicken; I don't even want to say what I see."[1] It is astounding for a man described by the interviewer in the same interview as "the greatest Negro writer" alive and by Baldwin himself, humbly, as "the most famous, which is not necessarily the same thing" to admit he is "chicken."[2] This admission occurs not a decade after he appeared on the cover of *Time* following the publication of "Down at the Cross," the apex of his prominence as a public figure.

The legislation of the Civil Rights era coincided with the death of some black leaders (Medgar Evers, Malcolm X, Martin Luther King) and led to the incarceration of their heirs (Eldridge Cleaver, George Jackson, Angela Davis, Bobby Seale, Huey Newton, and a host of others associated with the Black Panther movement). In a 1964 interview Baldwin stated that he was uncomfortable being a "spokesman" for the black race: "I am certainly not a Negro leader . . . it is impossible to be a writer and be a public spokesman, too, because the line which you have to use, really, in polemics, is to my point of view, just a little bit much too simple."[3] His resistance to being considered a leader or spokesman revealed a power vacuum in the black community. In the wake of the assassinations, the Black Panther Party essentially stepped into the role of speaker for the race, and Baldwin was left in the precarious position of both agreeing (largely) with its leaders and distancing himself from the type of platform that would result (he feared) in his death or his incarceration. Baldwin could only agree with the Panthers to a point, similar to his position on the Nation of Islam at the beginning of the 1960s. He had predicted the Panthers' ascendancy, but he certainly was not willing to arm himself, or to risk arrest, in order to demonstrate his solidarity.[4] He was clearly aligned with them on one point, though; in his 1972 discussion with Margaret Mead, he says, "I agree with the Black Panthers' position about black prisoners. I think that one can make the absolutely blanket statement that no black man has ever been tried by a jury of his peers in America. And if that is so, and I know that is so, no black man has ever received a fair trial in this country. Therefore, I'm under no illusions about the reason why many black people are in prison. I'm not saying there are no black criminals. Still, I believe that all black prisoners should be released and then retried according to principles more honorable and more just" (*RR* 67–68). This statement is both hyperbolic ("no black man has ever been tried by a jury of his peers in America") and abstract, for his solution does not define the principles he desires. The statement indicates the resurfacing of Baldwin's fear that he had begun to conquer in the early to mid-1960s—that is, the fear that prisons and police are now associated with "lawlessness," or raw physical power, rather than with any sense of justice.

Although Baldwin believed Civil Rights legislation had only a limited effect on the lives of black people, he ultimately preferred it to the type of activism that might result in police brutality or incarceration. Many of the Panthers spoke from jail; as Bobby Seale wrote in 1970, "To be a revolutionary is to be an Enemy of the state. To be arrested for this struggle is to be a Political Prisoner."[5] Carefully supportive of and yet not fully allied with Seale's cause, Baldwin wrote the introduction to Seale's autobiography in 1978. Angela Davis, whose incarceration became a cause for public outrage in the early 1970s, also received cautious alliance from Baldwin in the form of an open letter published in the *New York Review of Books* in 1971.[6] Most egregiously and most troublesome for Baldwin was the publication of Eldridge Cleaver's bestselling screed about his prison experience, *Soul on Ice,* published in 1968, which contained a lengthy homophobic attack on Baldwin,[7] an attack which Baldwin publicly forgave without much comment, and, uncharacteristically, without retribution: in *No Name in the Street* he writes, "when I did read [*Soul on Ice*], I didn't like what he had to say about me at all. But, eventually—especially as I admired the book, and felt him to be valuable and rare—I thought I could see why he felt impelled to issue what was, in fact, a warning" (*NN* 172). As far as this younger generation of black thinkers and writers were concerned, incarceration was increasingly synonymous with the black experience. The ninth point of the Black Panther Party's official ten-point platform calls for the abolition of prisons: "the ultimate elimination of all wretched, inhuman penal institutions, because the masses of men and women imprisoned inside the United States or by the United States military are the victims of oppressive conditions which are the real cause of their imprisonment."[8] Angela Davis continues to fight for this cause over three decades after her imprisonment, asking the rhetorical question in the title of her 2003 book, *Are Prisons Obsolete?.* Despite her fiery life-long crusade on behalf of the abolition of prisons, the American answer to this question is an emphatic "no." The construction of prisons is in fact a growth industry. Beginning with various "get tough on crime" laws in the early 1970s, the rate of incarceration, especially among black people, has increased dramatically and shows no signs of abating in the twenty-first century. In a 2004 ethnographic study, the authors Murty, Owen, and Vyas succinctly point out that the United States "has the highest rate of incarceration in the industrialized world" and that, in 2000, 47 percent of inmates were black males.[9] The imbalance of black prisoners in the United States penal system did not originate in the mid-1960s, but it has undeniably increased since that time.

Baldwin may have considered himself "chicken" when it came to stating what he saw "when the police become lawless, and are allied with the visibly lawless," but he had to deal with the subject, both in fiction and in nonfiction, if he was to be true to his original goal of being an honest man and a good writer. He also had to legitimate himself as an ally of this younger generation of radical spokespersons even while denying his own role as a spokesperson and writing from an exiled perspective. Thus, in his open letter to his "sister" Angela Davis, Baldwin alludes to his alliance as a brother who has done time: "This may seem an odd, indefensibly impertinent and insensitive thing to say to a sister in prison, battling for her life. . . . I do not say it, after all, from the position of a spectator."[10] He was experiencing some of the fear he felt in a Paris prison before his rise to fame, coupled with his fear of meeting the same fate as the assassinated black leaders or those who died in prison during those turbulent years, notably during the Attica uprising of 1971.

Baldwin's lifelong meditation on the law's power returned to its most primal and visible manifestations during this period. The decade following the publication of "Going to Meet the Man" shows him retreating from a consideration of the effects of *Brown* and other judicial victories and returning to an examination of the law's most brutal exercises of power. His major works of the next decade—*Tell Me How Long the Train's Been Gone* (1968), *One Day When I Was Lost* (1972), *No Name in the Street* (1972), and *If Beale Street Could Talk* (1974) all touch upon or even center around the prison experience, to various degrees. Baldwin's early works revealed prisons to be the distorted mirror image of one's private room—alienating public spaces where the incarcerated subject can be monitored and controlled. In this later phase of Baldwin's career, prisons are much worse: more hell than purgatory, more torture chambers than alienating spaces. The power of the law not only to control but to abuse is magnified in these works, and Baldwin's skepticism over the progress of legislation approved by Congress, including the Civil Rights Act of 1964 and Voting Rights Act of 1965, develops into deep pessimism: the law is as powerful as ever, and the status quo is preserved as a result. Following their wrongful arrests, his protagonist Leo Proudhammer in *Tell Me How Long the Train's Been Gone* and his real-life acquaintance Tony Maynard must rely on the influence of their friends if they are to avoid the desperation Baldwin experienced in Paris. Put back in the hands of the police and prison guards in the turmoil of the late 1960s and early 1970s, the law represents in Baldwin's writings of this time period reactionary force, not reason in the service of social progress. Baldwin believed that the interdependency of American personalities faced no greater test than policing and imprisonment—a fervent attempt to maintain order on one hand and the greatest evidence of Americans' unwillingness to face one another on the other.

A watershed moment in the shift of Baldwin's thinking during this time is the publication of the 1966 essay "A Report from Occupied Territory," originally published in *The Nation* and collected in *The Price of the Ticket* and in the Library of America edition of his essays. It is a penetratingly honest and far from sensationalized account of the so-called "Harlem Six," a half-dozen black men, the oldest of whom was twenty years old at the time of his arrest, who were facing life sentences for murder during a riot inspired by the death of a fifteen-year-old Harlem youth at the hands of a white policeman. The essay uses the case of the Harlem Six as a springboard into a much broader consideration of race and the law. Baldwin gradually moves from a specific date in Harlem at the essay's beginning to "all our Harlems, every single day" by the end (*PT* 423). Along the way, he voices outrage, anger, and fear: he implicitly compares the police "occupation" of Harlem to a kind of genocide, quoting a family member as saying, "Well, they don't need us for work no more. Where are they building the gas ovens?" (*PT* 424). Baldwin's response is to point out that "There is more than one way . . . to get bad niggers off the streets" (*PT* 424). As he details throughout the essay, the main method he is talking about is extreme police brutality.

The degree of police abuse Baldwin describes in "A Report from Occupied Territory" far exceeds any description of it in his work up until this point, and it anticipates his near-obsession with this topic over his works of the next decade. The essay begins as one mild-mannered Harlem salesman named Frank Stafford questions why two policemen are beating up a kid. Baldwin drily notes that this is an "unwise question" and proceeds to recount, in Stafford's voice, how "thirty-five [policemen] came into the room and started beating, punching us in the jaw, in the stomach, in the chest, beating us with a padded club—spit on us, call us niggers, dogs, animals" (*PT* 415–16). All of this occurs without any criminal charges being raised. The beating becomes so severe that Stafford is brought to the hospital and eventually loses an eye. He continues to be targeted as a "cop hater" once he is released, and, Baldwin writes, "You will note that there is not a suggestion of any kind of appeal to justice and no suggestion of any recompense for the grave and gratuitous damage which this man has endured" (*PT* 416). This is the epitome of "criminal power," and it is made possible, according to Baldwin, because there is no accountability on the part of the police force: "the Police Department investigates itself, quite as though it were answerable only to itself." He refers to this condition as the "arrogant autonomy . . . guaranteed to police" (*PT* 423).

This autonomy is one of the forces that separates and divides society.

Harlem becomes less than "another country"—a colony—in this formulation: "Harlem is policed like occupied territory" (*PT* 417). As the descrip-
tions of police beatings intensify over the course of the essay, Baldwin's
analysis of the police presence in black neighborhoods becomes rather
blunt: "Now, what I have said about Harlem is true of Chicago, Detroit,
Washington, Boston, Philadelphia, Los Angeles, and San Francisco—is
true of every northern city with a large Negro population. And the police
are simply the hired enemies of this population. They are present to keep
the Negro in his place and to protect white business interests, and they
have no other function" (*PT* 420). At points, Baldwin attempts to remain
cool in the face of this dangerous situation; he insists, "I am writing a
report, which is also a plea for the recognition of our common humanity"
(*PT* 418). This perspective makes it seem as though Baldwin is appealing to his readers to develop their conscience based on his observations.
Yet he also calls for resistance on the part of black people whose rights
should be recognized as a higher power than the law itself. He recognizes
that the police "know they are hated, [so] they are always afraid. One
cannot possibly arrive at a more surefire formula for cruelty" (*PT* 420).
This observation leads to one of his most profound and rhetorically powerful statements about the law's power: "This is why those pious calls to
'respect the law,' always to be heard from prominent citizens each time the
ghetto explodes, are so obscene. The law is meant to be my servant, and
not my master, still less my torturer and my murderer. To respect the law,
in the context in which the American Negro finds himself, is simply to sur-
render his self-respect" (*PT* 420–421). Following this logic, the law is the
enemy of the self: it is impossible to respect both at the same time.

The defiance in Baldwin's essay is tempered, though: the law may be
meant to be his servant, but there are so many examples in the essay of
its acting as a "master, torturer, and murderer," that he either must submit to it or flee. He is aware of a "portion of the citizenry for whom the
police work and who have the power to control the police" and he realizes
that legislation can be passed to reinforce the "arrogant autonomy" of the
police force, such as New York's "No Knock, Stop and Frisk laws, which
permit a policeman to enter one's home without knocking and to stop anyone on the streets, at all, at any hour, and search him. Harlem believes,
and I certainly agree, that these laws are directed against Negroes" (*PT*
421). What we have come to call racial profiling was clearly systemic
in Baldwin's lifetime. Feeling outraged but powerless and fearful for his
life, Baldwin returned to exile in the mid-1960s and stayed in Turkey and
France for the majority of the next decade.

Baldwin felt a solidarity with the Harlem Six but maintained a cautious distance from them, wary of sharing their fate and aware that he was different from them because of his prominence. Fame, clearly, exacted a cost. After his near-breakdown following the production of *Blues for Mister Charlie,* Baldwin rendered this experience in fiction as a heart attack in *Tell Me How Long the Train's Been Gone.* Leo Proudhammer, an actor, collapses in the novel's opening sentence, and the narrative is a series of flashbacks during his recuperation. As if consciously retreating from his public role as civil rights spokesperson, Baldwin sets much of his tale in the pre-*Brown* era, opening again the wounds he suffered in white-only restaurants, on the streets of racist rural towns, in jails, and in precincts in New York and Paris. Leo's brother Caleb experiences the racial profiling evident in Baldwin's early works, and this experience leads Baldwin to advance an even more forceful indictment of the prison system than he had in earlier works. The difference is that the assassinations and disillusionments of the late 1960s following the promise of the 1950s deprive Baldwin of any hope that the raw power of the law can be altered or overcome. The spokesman disappears, the artist goes back into exile, and the fate of the individual is in the hands of the oppressor.

Tell Me was not well received by critics and has not been the subject of much critical scrutiny since then, with the notable exception of Lynn Orilla Scott's chapter in *James Baldwin's Later Fiction.* Mario Puzo, in *The New York Times Book Review,* called it "a simpleminded, one-dimensional novel with mostly cardboard characters, a polemical rather than narrative tone, weak invention, and poor selection of incident."[11] James Campbell writes, "almost everything that can go wrong with a novel has gone wrong here."[12] Scott attempts to redeem the novel from its harsh criticism and to reevaluate its significance, arguing that "the complete breakdown in understanding between Baldwin and the majority of his critics was, indeed, a sign of the times."[13] There is no denying the novel's unwieldy nature, its centrifugal force emanating from a protagonist so deeply divided that he seems inconsistent in character and random in his attempts to give shape to his life. Leo's responses to the world's injustice range from all-out rage to helplessness. He rejects his brother's religious fundamentalism as well as the artistic bullying of the San-Marquands; he gyrates between belief in long-term monogamy and resignation to bisexual promiscuity; his love for the southern white "princess" Barbara King and for the black nationalist Black Christopher cancel each other out, rather than balance each other out. It can safely be said that the United States was on the verge of madness when *Tell Me* was published in 1967. The nation was as bitterly divided as it had ever been, along the lines of race, gender, political orientation, patriotism, and generational values. Without apologizing for its excesses, *Tell Me* can be appreciated as a chronicle of profoundly confused times from the perspective of a man deeply affected by the confusion. His dredged-up fear of the police and prisons provide a key to understanding how this chronicle falls into the pattern of his career.

Baldwin's rejection of the church and his hatred of policemen, jails, and wardens are the most recognizable traits that link this work to all of his earlier work. He even begins the book with an epigraph from Auden that signals the book's prison motif: "In the prison of his days / Teach the free man how to praise." The quotation is from Auden's famous poem "In Memory of W. B. Yeats," significantly about how the death of a great poet—a private, obscure death on a cold day—affects humanity. The lines of Baldwin's epigraph are from the poem's conclusion, but they echo a line from the poem's first section: "And each in the cell of himself is almost convinced of his freedom." In both of Auden's lines, prison is a metaphor for self-imposed limitations. The artist's role is to liberate the individual, to "teach" him how to transcend such prisons. This optimism about art's potential is countered by the book's essential pessimism when it comes to actual prisons. As an artist, Leo feels used up by the end of the book: he is at the mercy of others in the book's final sentence as he finds himself "standing in the wings again, waiting for my cue" (*TM* 484). Having arrived on death's doorstep, he is miraculously redelivered into the world, yet art does not have the same capacity for transcendence in Baldwin's novel as it has in Auden's poem. Leo's art seems more a job than a calling, and rather than giving him life, it continues to kill him. Love, Baldwin's other saving grace along with art, is similarly draining by the end of the book as Leo perceives that lovers use each other up rather than nurture one another.

It would be reductive to say that the police or prisons are the only factors that lead Leo to this despairing conclusion; yet they are undeniably large factors. Leo's relationships with Barbara and Black Christopher are attempts to regain losses stemming from the end of his most profound relationship in the book: with his brother Caleb. It seems as though it is the church that stands between Caleb and Leo, but the church is, to use Baldwin's terminology from "Down at the Cross," merely Caleb's "gimmick" to lift himself out of despair. The root cause of the rift between these brothers is Caleb's wrongful arrest and the abuse he faces in prison. Leo describes the depth of their relationship in the book's early pages: "We were very good friends. In fact, he was my best friend and for a very long time, my only friend. . . . He was my touchstone, my model, and my only guide" (*TM* 13, 17). We later learn that the brothers also become lovers after Caleb returns from prison. The sexual contact between them is an attempt to heal the emotional wounds Caleb has suffered in prison.

Caleb's removal to prison is, in fact, the central trauma of the book not only for Caleb, but for Leo as well. A central theme of the book is irrecoverable loss; immediately after Leo describes a recurrent nightmare in which he carries a book entitled "*We Must Not Find Him, For He Is Lost,*" he tells the reader,

> When Caleb, my older brother, was taken from me and sent to prison, I watched, from the fire escape of our East Harlem tenement, the walls of an old and massive building, far, far away and set on a hill, and with green vines running up and down the walls, and with windows flashing like signals in the sunlight, I watched that building, I say, with a child's helpless and stricken attention, waiting for my brother to come out of there. I did not know how to get to the building. If I had I would have slept in the shadow of those walls, and I told no one of my vigil or of my certain knowledge that my brother was imprisoned in that place. . . . Alas, he was not there; the building turned out to be City College; my brother was on a prison farm in the Deep South, working in the fields. (*TM* 9–10)

It is deeply ironic that Leo misinterprets a college building as prison, but this misinterpretation reveals the limits of his horizons as well as his sense that threats surround him. All of Harlem is a prison: he describes it as "the prison where" his Barbados-born father "perished" (*TM* 14), and his first home is "the tenement from which Caleb was arrested" (*TM* 17). As his world begins to expand beyond his immediate surroundings, he is aware of "the eyes of white cops, whom I feared, whom I hated with a literally murderous hatred" (*TM* 31). The other white authority figure toward whom he feels a murderous hatred is his landlord (*TM* 16), echoing the association between these two archetypal figures in "Previous Condition." In both cases, Leo feels menaced by white authority figures; he associates his landlord with his own poverty, but the police represent the scrutiny and surveillance that he only dimly understands as power. He is not the only black Harlem resident who feels this fear; when Caleb's friend Arthur leads Leo to Caleb, Leo says, "We walked the length of the block in silence . . . and passed two white cops, who looked at us sharply. Arthur muttered under his breath, 'You white cock-suckers. I wish all of you were dead.' We slowed our pace a little; I had the feeling, I don't know why, that this was because of the cops" (*TM* 50). Leo is becoming aware at this moment that his response to the police is instinctive: fight or flight. The instinct to flee, he learns from Arthur, must be controlled because to run is to admit fear and thus to attract suspicion. Leo takes Arthur's cue and slows his pace in order to avoid persecution, though at the time he is not aware why he is doing it.

This scene foreshadows one that occurs the same night when the two brothers are harassed by the police. Leo is interrupted while narrating the details of a movie to Caleb in order to give a cover story to their parents: "we were hurrying down the long block which led east to our house, when we heard the brakes of a car and were blinded by bright lights and were pushed up against a wall. . . . I had never been so frightened in my life before. . . . A hand patted me all over my body, front and back, every touch humiliating, every touch obscene. Beside me, I heard Caleb catch his breath" (*TM* 57). Leo and Caleb are deliberately disoriented in this first encounter with the police, "blinded by bright lights," hearing only the officers' voices, feeling their hands without seeing their faces. This description is consistent with Foucault's description of the panopticon, a "machine for dissociating the see/being seen dyad: in the peripheric ring, one is totally seen, without ever seeing."[14] Moreover, the police, "white, tight-lipped, and self-important" (*TM* 58), illustrate Foucault's observation that "surveillance is based on a system of permanent registration"[15] by asking the brothers for identification and for an explanation of where they have been and where they are going. There is no indication that Leo and Caleb have done anything suspicious or that there is any justification for harassing them, and Caleb remains cool, saving his anger to mutter under his breath after they have left, "you white cock-sucking dog-shit miserable white mother-fuckers" (*TM* 59). Leo is surprised at Caleb's ability to keep calm throughout the encounter, and he again reveals how this evening has taught him how to act: "I also felt, I don't know how, nor do I really know why, that I couldn't let him feel, even for a moment, that I did not adore him, that I did not respect him, love him and admire him" (*TM* 59). Leo has observed not only that power must be answered with graceful aplomb, but that it must be combated with unconditional love for the fellow powerless. He and Caleb must bond together against such injustice, which they accept as inevitable; Caleb says, "I'm glad this happened. It had to happen one day and I'm glad it happened now. I'm glad it happened while I was with you—of course, I'm glad you were with *me*, too, dig, because if it hadn't been for you, they'd have pulled my ass in and given me a licking just as sure as shit" (*TM* 59). When Leo asks why, Caleb responds, "'Because I'm black' Caleb said. 'That's what for. Because I'm black and they *paid* to beat on black asses. But, with a kid your size, they just *might* get into trouble. So they let us go. *They* knew you weren't nothing but a kid. They knew it. But they didn't care. All black people are shit to them. You remember that. You black like me and they going to hate you as long as you live just because you're black'" (*TM* 60). It is possible that Caleb is referring to all white people here rather than just to policemen, and Leo is confused about this aspect of the lessons he is taught that night. He interprets Caleb's words as "true" and believes that his brother is talking about white people, but associates white power with policemen particularly: "I only saw the policemen, those murderous eyes again, those hands, with a touch like the touch of vermin. Were they people? 'Caleb,' I asked, 'are white people people?'" (*TM* 60). His thoughts immediately turn to the landlord, but he also thinks of his white schoolteacher whom he likes very much,[16] then changes his question: "are all white people the same?" (*TM* 61). Caleb responds, "I never met a good one" (*TM* 61). Leo, who grows to love Barbara and many other white people who work in the theater, is eventually able to reject such racial essentialism and to distinguish between policemen and other white people; but at least initially, the coarsest form of power and abuse is associated with white police, and this association remains in Leo's mind.

One of the reasons these lessons lodge so deeply in Leo's mind is that his father and his mother reinforce them. What Caleb has described in terms of an inevitable if unfortunate awakening in Leo also serves as a connection to his heritage. His father, upon hearing the story of police harassment, grows visibly outraged. He tries to respond practically, first commending Caleb for refraining from talking back to the police, then asking if he at least took their badge number; Caleb responds, "What for? You know a friendly judge? We got money for a lawyer? Somebody they going to *listen* to? You know as well as me they beating on black ass all the time, all the time, man, they get us in that precinct house and make us confess to all kinds of things[17] and sometimes even kill us and don't nobody give a damn. Don't nobody care what happens to a black man. If they didn't need us for work, they'd have killed us all off a long time ago. They did it to the Indians." Their mother agrees: "I wish I could say different, but it's the truth" (*TM* 64). The powerlessness of the Proudhammer family is evident; all they have is their rage and their solidarity in the face of police harassment. Leo remains confused about the difference between all white people and the white police officers who have harassed him, and this confusion is at the core of his more general confusion about his place in the world, even after he becomes a successful actor.

More pointedly, this incident with the police sets in motion the events that will take his beloved brother Caleb away and thus leave a void in his life that will never be filled. He gradually makes clearer the distinctions between white people and white policemen, the latter of whom were the key to the question he raises about "what principle united so peculiarly bloodless a people [i.e., white people]. I suspected that the principle was cruelty, but I was not sure" (*TM* 118). He claims that he and his white peers "fought all the time . . . but I was lucky in that we usually fought fair" (*TM* 119). In other words, their animosity was not agitated by a power imbalance, and in fact he and his classmates "had to band together against the cops—and I had long ago dismissed the cops from all human consideration. But the others, the men and women, young and old, sometimes smiling, sometimes harsh, always distant—if I fell into their hands, would they treat me like the cops?" (*TM* 119). The law's capacity for physical and psychological torment, which Leo has experienced first hand, is, in his mind, a weapon that all white people might have and might use against him if they are indeed motivated by cruelty. This distortion accounts for Leo's cynicism.

The timing of this question within the narrative is significant: immediately after his attempt to work through the difference between white people and white policemen, Leo tells of the fateful day when Caleb is arrested. The circumstances are almost identical to what happens to Richard in *Go Tell It:* "They done robbed a store, whoever they is, and stabbed a man half to death. They say Caleb was with them" (*TM* 122). Leo tries to process the information, but his fear paralyzes him: "My mind had stopped, stuck, screaming, on the faces of white cops" (*TM* 122). Leo runs off frantically to warn Caleb, but the lessons he learned on the night they were harassed by the police have stayed with him: "something cautioned me not to run too fast; something cautioned me to dissemble my distress; something cautioned me to look, to look about me, before I moved" (*TM* 123). These behaviors are not powerful weapons against the police, but they will at least keep Leo relatively invisible. Once he reaches Caleb, though, they both realize that there is nothing to do: "'If I run,' said Caleb, 'I won't get far. And then they'll fix my ass for sure'" (*TM* 124). The three policemen who find Caleb, pointedly white (*TM* 125), are more thuggish and racist than any who have appeared in Baldwin's work until this point. When Dolores, whose house they have entered, asks why they want to see Caleb, one responds, "Listen to the nigger bitch" (*TM* 125). When Caleb asks why they are bringing him to the station, the scene becomes a night-mare; "'You're a very inquisitive bunch of niggers. Here's what for,' and he suddenly grabbed Caleb and smashed the pistol butt against the side of his head. The blood ran down—my brother's blood. I jumped up, howl-ing, from the sofa, trying to get to Caleb, but they knocked me back. . . . I butted one cop in the behind, with all my might I dragged on one of his legs. 'Get that kid out of here,' one of them said, and somebody tried to grab me, but I kicked and bit again. I tumbled headlong down the steps and grabbed the policeman's leg again. I held on, I held on, he dragged me down. . . . Now the cop kicked me, and I tasted blood" (*TM* 126). The violence of this scene is in marked contrast to earlier arrest scenes, such as Baldwin's in "Equal in Paris" or Richard's in *Go Tell It*. Even the officer who asks the young Baldwin in "Down at the Cross," "Why don't you niggers stay uptown where you belong?" seems relatively harmless next to these officers. Their oppressive control has not only shattered the con-fidence of a young black man, as it had done with Baldwin and Richard, but it has divided a family. Caleb's physical removal from Leo's life is only one aspect of this division; immediately after he is taken away, Leo returns to his parents and declares that he hates both of them. The power of the law to divide and disrupt black families becomes an increasingly promi-nent motif in Baldwin's writing from this point on.

The other distinction between Caleb's experience in prison and Bald-win's earlier renditions of this motif is that here the prison experience is described in gruesome detail. This scene has not received adequate critical attention; even Lynn Orilla Scott, who has written the most substantial analysis of Baldwin's later fiction, initially says that Caleb's story "inter-rupts the longer story of Leo's summer at the Actors' Means Workshop," though she later analyzes it in some detail in the context of "the sexual dynamics of racism on the black male body."[18] For the purposes of my study, Caleb's story of incarceration marks a shift in Baldwin's perception of this subject that will pave the way for later works. In earlier fiction, such as *Go Tell It, Giovanni's Room,* and "Sonny's Blues," the incarcer-ated characters are carried away. Regardless of whether or not they return to society, the reader is not given direct access to their experience behind bars. Baldwin describes his own prison experience in "Equal in Paris" in such a way as to show the psychological torment and physical deprivation involved in even the mildest forms of incarceration. In *Tell Me,* though, he chooses to illuminate the prison experience in its most horrifying mani-festation, as a form of raw power abuse and psychosexual torture that damages Caleb forever. Like Sonny and the narrator of "Sonny's Blues," there is initially a communication breakdown between these brothers: "He had been home a week, but he and I had found it hard to talk—he did not want to tell me what his time away had been like. But I knew what it had been like from the way he flinched whenever my breath touched the open wound, from the distance between us, as though he were saying, *Don't come near me. I've got the plague*" (*TM* 202). An abstract, indirect rendering of the prison experience is no longer enough to serve Baldwin's purpose in this novel, though, which is to explore Leo's idea that cruelty might be a stronger force than love, and to contemplate whether psychological and emotional loss are permanent. Caleb's story is evidence of the supremacy of cruelty and the irrecoverable nature of loss. Not even a desperate act of transgression like incest can help to heal Caleb.

The fact that Caleb is taken to a prison "farm"[19] in the "Deep South" suggests more than an incidental relationship between his incarceration and slavery. This connection is a cornerstone of H. Bruce Franklin's study *The Victim as Criminal and Artist,* in which he argues, "Contemporary prison literature returns to the explicitness of the slave narrative. . . . But this literature goes much further than the slave narrative, for it speaks as part of a profoundly more revolutionary age."[20] He dates the beginning of the contemporary era of prison literature in 1965, with the publication of *The Autobiography of Malcolm X,* which was very much in the air when *Tell Me* was published. Joy James, in *The New Abolitionists,* also writes explicitly of this connection: "Prison is the modern day manifestation of the plantation. The antebellum plantation ethos of dehumanization was marked by master–slave relations revolving about sexual terror and domination, beatings, regimentation of bodies, exploited labor, denial of religious and cultural practices, substandard food, health care, and housing, forced migration, isolation in 'lockdown' for punishment and control, denial of birth family and kin" (xxiii). This description closely resembles Caleb's experience; when he finally feels ready to discuss his experience, it initially sounds like an excerpt from a nineteenth-century slave narrative:[21]

The farm I was on, down yonder. They used to beat me. With whips. With rifle butts. It made them feel good to beat us; I can see their faces now. There would always be two or three of them, big mother-fuckers. The ring-leader had red hair, his name was Martin Howell. Big, dumb Irishman, sometimes he used to make the colored guys beat each other. And he'd stand there, watching, with his lips dropping, his lips wet, laughing, until the poor guy dropped to the ground. And he'd say,

That's just so you all won't forget that you is niggers and niggers ain't worth a shit. And he'd make the colored guys say it. He'd say, You ain't worth shit, are you? And they'd say, No, Mr. Howell, we ain't worth shit. The first time I heard it, saw it, I vomited. But he made me say it, too. It took awhile, but I said it, too, he made me say it, too. That hurt me, hurt me more than his whip, more than his rifle butt, more than his fists. (*TM* 232)

Under the system of slavery, supervisors would use similar tactics to the ones Howell uses to dehumanize and divide any spirit of cooperation or community among slaves. Howell parades through the fields on horseback, continually reinforces his racist message through physical force, and turns the black inmates against one another. He also reinforces his power through sexual harassment; after Caleb refuses to acknowledge him, Howell asks, "Nigger, if my balls was on your chin, where would my prick be?" (*TM* 233). Caleb responds by picking up a pitchfork, thus initiating a standoff between the two of them reminiscent of the famous animosity between Covey and Frederick Douglass in the *Narrative of the Life of Frederick Douglass*. Caleb realizes that Howell is attempting to emasculate him: "He made me feel like I was my grandmother in the fields somewhere and this white mother-fucker rides over and decides to throw her down in the fields. Well, shit. You know. I ain't my grandmother. I'm a man" (*TM* 233). His assertion of his own masculine power only gets him to the point of conflict, though, because Howell, entrusted with the power of the law, has greater weapons than a pitchfork. When Caleb and Leo were first harassed by the police, Caleb realized that it was futile to take down their badge number. Similarly, in prison, he understands that he has no recourse to report Howell's abuse: "He was going to break my back. I knew it. He was going to make me kneel down. He was going to make me act out his question. I wasn't going to do it. He knew it. And I knew it. And there we were" (*TM* 234).

The structure of a prison is hierarchical, and its nature is to make the incarcerated feel that freedom is relative. In current parlance, a minimum security prison is better than a supermax. A cell is bad, but "the hole"— solitary confinement—is worse. An outside work detail is preferable to empty time in a cell, even if the work is hard and if the worker is uncompensated. Caleb describes how Howell uses this structure to exercise his power over him: "They had a place there where they put you when they was displeased. It was a kind of cellar. We was already in jail, you understand, but they had a jail inside the jail. But, at least, you know, if they wasn't displeased with you, if you could kiss enough ass, or if they just plain didn't notice you, well, you was in the open air, and, you know, you could talk to your buddies—we was only put there, like they said, for our own good" (*TM* 234). This description illustrates Foucault's assertion that a chief aim of incarceration is to produce "docile bodies": Caleb realizes that he would have an easier time in prison if he weren't defiant, if he submitted to the will of Howell and the other guards. Caleb goes out of his way to explain that Howell was not the only one who wielded power over him, that the white female cook who is his boss for a while is also physically abusive. Moreover, race is not the only factor determining this power dynamic: "sometimes these mother-fuckers was white, baby, and sometimes they was black" (*TM* 237). The point here is that the power of the prison to take away the will of individual prisoners is not in the hands of one person. As the "ring-leader," Howell is merely the most visible figure of power, but not because of his physical power alone. Despite his whips, pistol-butt, and horse, Caleb is assured that he himself can physically overpower Howell. When Caleb attempts to assert himself by counterattacking Howell who has touched him sexually, he realizes how Howell's power is reinforced by the prison structure.

The experience of solitary confinement is finally what undoes Caleb. He describes it as the starkest form of deprivation associated with imprisonment: no window, a door with bars, no plumbing, "stale bread and cold water," and rats (*TM* 237). Caleb loses physical strength and all sense of time. Nevertheless, when Howell returns for the inevitable battle between them, Caleb manages to get the better of him: "I made that mother scream" (*TM* 239). Howell's stated intention is to continue his sexual humiliation of Caleb, but this is only one possible way of reinforcing the sense of hierarchy Caleb has refused to acknowledge. Howell calls in reinforcements; Caleb continues his resistance, but he changes when "one of the black trusties spit[s] on [him]" (*TM* 239). At this point Caleb submits to the race-based self-loathing that Howell has reinforced on all of the other black inmates: "You right, Mr. Howell. I ain't worth shit. And they left me. And I was alone down there for a long time. On bread and water" (*TM* 239). This is the end of Caleb's narrative, and its effect on Leo is to inspire in him a murderous hatred in almost the exact terms Richard uses in *Blues for Mister Charlie*: "Because I could love, I realized I could hate. And I realized that I would feed my hatred, feed it every day and every hour. I would keep it healthy, I would make it strong, and I would find a use for it one day" (*TM* 239). This vow for vengeance has no outlet in Leo's life, though, and he ends up internalizing it, hating himself at times,

Caleb at times, and Barbara and her family at times, but never doing anything productive to combat the law's terrifying and absolute power. Throughout the novel, he remains scared of the police who continue to haunt and scrutinize public life. Rather than revenge, he seeks safety by keeping himself profoundly visible through fame. Caleb's experience does not spur him to action, in other words, but rather reinforces his essential fear. Moreover, it prevents him from being able to follow his life-affirming instinct to love and comfort others.

On the one occasion when Leo attempts to "feed his hatred"—when an elderly white couple regards him suspiciously as he leaves Madeleine's apartment and he responds by reacting in a bizarre and immature way— he is promptly arrested, and his fear is evident. As in his early arrest and when Caleb is in the hole, Leo emphasizes that he is blinded by the police light, and that the police touch him inappropriately: "There they were, of course, in blue, two of them, of course, white, of course. One stood by the car, while the other came up to me, and frisked me. Cops love frisking black boys, they want to find out if what they've heard is true" (TM 251). Despite this initial description in which Leo sounds both angry and bored with this ritual, he immediately reveals his fear: "People become frightened in very different ways—the ways in which they become frightened may sometimes determine how long they live. Here I was, in the country, and on a country road, alone, facing two armed white men who had legal sanction to kill me; and if killing me should prove to be an error, it would not matter very much, it would not, for them, be a serious error" (TM 252). His response is to be neither fearful nor defiant, clearly reacting to Arthur's and Caleb's responses to the police earlier in his life: "They were accustomed to black boys whimpering, or, on the other hand, defiant, and it was easy, in either case, for them to know exactly what to do— to amuse themselves with the whimper or the defiance, and beat the shit out of the boy, and sometimes to beat the boy to death" (TM 252). He determines that he can only combat law enforcement officers by revealing that he understands and has access to higher echelons of the law's power, and he calmly and repeatedly asks the officers why he is being arrested. He does this with the knowledge that he can use the names of the wealthy white people who run the Actors' Means Theater "as a threat" (TM 252). Still, his bravado masks fear not only because of Caleb's experience, but also because of its link to history: "I became faint, and hot and cold with terror. It was in vain that I told myself, Leo, this isn't the South. I knew better than to place any hope in the accidents of North American geography. This was America, America, America, and those people out there, my countrymen, had been tearing me limb from limb, like dogs, for centuries. I would not be the first. In the bloody event, I would not be the last" (*TM* 253). He continues to struggle with these dark fantasies of persecution, trying to maintain his composure enough to keep insisting on his rights; he tells the precinct officer, "I think the law compels you to tell me what the charges are against me. You have no right to hold me without charges. . . . I'm only telling you what my rights are, as a citizen of this country" (*TM* 254). He judges this utterance "a tactical error" (*TM* 254), but it apparently works: he is not booked or charged with anything. In fact, he manages to accuse the officers: "it is *you* who are acting against the law!" (*TM* 257). This pronouncement is consistent with H. Bruce Franklin's claim: "What crime had the African people committed to be imprisoned? Obviously none at all. Hence the Afro-American people quickly arrive at a further conclusion: the real criminals must be those who uphold what is called law and order in America."[22]

Although it might seem like Leo has taken a high-minded approach to combating the law's power and has won, the truth of the matter seems to be less positive. Leo and his friends are able to walk away unharmed and to insult the police officers as "Nazis" as well, but Leo's escape depends entirely on his affiliation with wealthy, powerful white people rather than on his insistence that he has rights. Lola San-Marquand says to the precinct officer, "A word of advice. I will try to put it in extremely simple language so that you can understand it. The people standing before you are more powerful than you. *I* am more powerful than you, and I can break you by making a phone call" (*TM* 261). The lesson Leo learns on this night is not that everyone has equal rights in the eyes of the law, but rather that some people are more powerful, due to wealth and influence, than law enforcement officers, and his recourse is to seek their protection. He admits this to Barbara afterwards: "'[The police] just scared me. . . . They humiliated me. They made me feel like a dog. They tried to turn me into something worse than they are. They had a wonderful time doing it, now they all feel more like men. And I was very lucky. They were afraid to go too far. They were afraid the Workshop might make a stink.' I paused, and I laughed. 'So now I owe my life to Saul and Lola'" (*TM* 266). Even though Leo isn't detained, the social hierarchies of race and class are preserved through this incident. As a poor, black man, Leo cannot hope to be able to assert his rights unless he seeks the protection of rich, white people. There is little comfort in this idea, and no sense of social progress. Leo's "rights" are meaningless when the law is a blunt instrument in the hands of its enforcers.

Leo becomes resigned to his fate, which is ultimately in the hands of others; as he tells an interviewer, "I do not belong to me" (*TM* 324). Through the rest of the novel the police continue to haunt the streets around him—from the restaurant where he works as a struggling young actor to the public rallies he and Christopher participate in once he is famous. He states, of one of these rallies, "The rally was guarded by the police, whom we were, in fact, attacking. They were there to make certain that none of the damage which we asserted was being done to the city's morals would so far transform itself as to become damage to the city's property" (*TM* 108). This sardonic observation suggests that the rallies will not really do much good: the police exist to protect the interests of the wealthy. Leo becomes desensitized to the point that he barely registers incidents of police brutality; he notes, tiredly, "I walked out into the streets again, to find a cop beating up some poor man in the gutter" (*TM* 431).

Leo begins to consider the violent militancy of Black Christopher as the only way to combat such power, but stops short of endorsing it. Christopher represents the spirit and hope of the next generation from which Leo feels distant, perhaps because he has put his faith in the legal leverage of the wealthy and powerful. Christopher informs him, "Leo—you a fat cat now. That's the way a whole lot of people see you, and you can't blame them, how *else* can they see you? . . . all these laws and speeches don't mean shit. They do not mean *shit*. It's the spirit of the [white] people, baby, the *spirit* of the people, they don't want us and they don't like us, and you see that spirit in the face of every cop. Them laws they keep passing, shit, they just like the treaties they signed with the Indians. Nothing but lies, they never even *meant* to keep those treaties, baby, they wanted the land and they got it and now they mean to keep it, even if they have to put every black mother-fucker in this country behind barbed wire, or shoot him down like a dog" (*TM* 479). Both Leo and Caleb had felt as though law enforcement officers had wanted to transform them into dogs. Christopher's metaphor brings back this notion and questions why Leo insists on fighting for civil rights legally. Christopher claims that they need guns, not laws, if they are to prevail. Leo is silent when he hears this, for he remains fearful of the law's power. Christopher's skepticism about the efficacy of "them laws they keep passing"—presumably, given the novel's publication date, the Civil Rights Act of 1964, the Voting Rights Act of 1965, and all of the decisions based upon them—reflects Baldwin's growing skepticism about these laws as well, but Leo does not respond to Christopher's cry for militancy. Fearful of and damaged by the law's power, he prefers to remain visible so that he will not meet the same fate

Caleb met in prison. He has become a "fat cat" because he realizes that wealthy, influential people are to a large degree safe from the law's potential for abuse. He is left with a sense of paranoia about the law, believing strongly that he is "under surveillance" by the police (*TM* 481), and his solution is not to join an underground movement like Christopher's but rather to return to exile and to focus on his artistic career rather than on social change.

Baldwin's feelings of relative powerlessness and skepticism toward social progress in the late 1960s stemmed from his discouragement and disillusionment following the assassinations of black leaders. In 1972 he published *One Day When I Was Lost,* his version of Malcolm X's life based on *The Autobiography of Malcolm X* rendered as a film scenario. The film was never made in Baldwin's lifetime, but Baldwin's script, edited by Arnold Perl, was one of the primary sources for Spike Lee's 1992 film *Malcolm X.*[23] *One Day When I Was Lost* illustrates a number of parallels between Baldwin's life and Malcolm X's: they both underwent a religious conversion, they were both black leaders who fell out of favor with the most radical members of the black community for supposedly sympathizing too much with whites (at least in Baldwin's rendition of Malcolm X's life), and they both feared persecution and even assassination (with obvious foundation, in Malcolm X's case). With regard to the law, *One Day When I Was Lost* brings together a number of themes Baldwin had explored throughout his career: the way prisons foment hatred, the devastating effects of police brutality on the peacefulness of black neighborhoods, and, especially, black desire to achieve some alternative form of power when legal power is denied to them.

The story of Malcolm X's conversion to Islam and his self-education in prison is one of the more famous scenes from his autobiography. *One Day When I Was Lost* depicts Malcolm's imprisonment as a near inevitability: he is a street kid who has a problem with authority, and under the tutelage of "West Indian Archie," he falls into gambling and drugs, among other illegal pursuits. He is aligned with other Baldwin victim-heroes like Sonny in "Sonny's Blues" whose prison experience helps to formulate a crucial insight about social hierarchy as well as spiritual conversion or moral reform. Late in the scenario, Malcolm visits Sidney in jail, a character Baldwin has invented in his dramatic rendition of Malcolm X's life. Sidney, a representative of the younger generation, accuses Malcolm of not understanding the reality of the current situation. Malcolm suggests that there are a number of people, black and white, albeit a small number, who are dedicated to change; Sidney responds, from behind his plexiglass wall,

> Oh, Malcolm, Malcolm, what's come over you? I can take you through
> this prison right now, and show you a *thousand* black men dedicated to
> change! Waiting for someone to help them to change things! For *help*—
> they need *help!* You know who's in these prisons? Niggers and Puerto
> Ricans, niggers and Puerto Ricans. And they in here because ain't no
> other place for them in this fucked-up white man's society—and I'm
> supposed to *love* this man? Shit. (*OD* 262)

Malcolm responds by reminding Sidney that his own perspective was also
altered in prison, and adds his interpretation of oppression not as simply a
black-white hierarchy:

> I know who's in prison—and I know why. I was in prison, too, and I
> remember it, even though I think you think I don't. All I've been try-
> ing to say is that white people in this country are what they are not
> because of the color of their skins—they're what they are because of this
> country—because they live in a racist country. I've been trying to say
> what I'm beginning to see—Christianity and capitalism are the two evils
> which have placed us where we are—in prison. (*OD* 262)

This perspective closely resembles Baldwin's—who, like Malcolm, rejected
Christianity, though not as part of a conversion to Islam. Yet this critical
perspective doesn't matter to the powerless: Malcolm asks Sidney, "How
can I make you believe me again?" and the young man responds, "By getting us out of prison" (*OD* 263). Whether one interprets the force behind
prisons in terms of race, religion, or economic structure, the fact remains
that the subjugated have no power. To be in prison is to be deprived not
only of liberty, but of any means to control one's destiny. This theme has
stayed with Baldwin since the publication of "Equal in Paris."

In fact, the lack of access to legal power is a direct cause leading to
Malcolm's imprisonment in the first place. Having avoided reform school
and graduated as a top student and class president, Malcolm goes to a
young teacher, Mr. Ostrovski, to seek career advice. (Baldwin created the
character of Sidney for dramatic purposes, but Ostrovski is a real person
represented in *The Autobiography of Malcolm X*.) When Ostrovski asks
him what he wants to do, he says, "well, everybody seems to feel that I
have a logical mind—and they seem to think that I talk well and am kind
of presentable—well—the subject which really interests me is—law. . . . I
think I'd like to try to be a lawyer sir" (*OD* 43). Ostrovski immediately
shoots down Malcolm's dreams in no uncertain terms: "Colored people

can't become lawyers, Malcolm. That's all there is to it" (*OD* 44). He even repeats these words in the same speech for emphasis, and they echo in Malcolm's head throughout the book. When he and Shorty walk by the Harvard Law School Forum, Shorty observes, "This is where they turn out all them lawyers—to help keep you and me in jail" (*OD* 47), and Malcolm does not disagree. Having been denied access to the law's power simply because of his skin color, he decides that the law is an oppressive force, not a tool he can get his hands on. After Shorty's observation, Malcolm's hatred immediately starts to germinate: "Malcolm stares at this building. His face is very bitter. Carved on the façade is a Latin maxim meaning 'Equal justice under the law.' Bells begin ringing. They are dismissal bells, resounding now across the campus, as the students, all of them white, pour out of the building. They scarcely see Malcolm and Shorty—they descend on the boys like waves breaking, and pass them with the same indifference—but they leave in their wake a very human resentment and wonder. Malcolm watches these students, with hatred in his eyes" (*OD* 47). The trajectory of the narrative from this moment on sends Malcolm's life into a spiral. Having been summarily denied the ability to act as a practitioner and interpreter of the law, he sees no choice except to break it in every way he can—from illegal drug use, to weapon possession, to pimping. His drive to become literate and his conversion to Islam, both of which take place in prison, break this self-destructive pattern and enable him to become a prominent leader who speaks, pointedly, at the Harvard Law School Forum (*OD* 206).

As was the case with Leo in *Tell Me,* Malcolm's ability to invert the power dynamic that has kept him down throughout his life comes from his gradual recognition that there are higher powers than the police, and also that eloquence and a public declaration of one's rights can be effective weapons against police brutality. This knowledge comes slowly, though. Initially, Malcolm engages with the plainclothes police officers who are tailing him at their level, combatively calling them "dirty, white, low-life motherfuckers" (*OD* 98) and throwing their words back in their faces when they threaten him by saying, "You may not be so lucky next time" (*OD* 99). They continue to monitor him carefully, and one eventually suggests, "I think it's about time you left town, Red" (*OD* 114). This culminating scene of police harassment causes Laura's words to echo in his head, "You a lawyer yet?" (*OD* 115). A hollow realization of his own failure to gain power within the system immediately precedes his sentencing, and he stares at the judge "with murder in his eyes" just as he had stared at the Harvard Law students with hatred in his eyes (*OD* 124). The police, lawyers-in-training, and judges all represent the same thing to him: unchangeable hierarchy.

Malcolm's belligerent behavior does not serve him well in prison. The guards label him "troublemaker" right away (*OD* 129) and, like Caleb in *Tell Me*, he is beaten and forced into solitary confinement. His rage reaches a fever pitch, and while declaring to the guards, "I hate every one of you" he smashes his fist against the prison wall (*OD* 131). His mentor, Luther, turns this self-destructive incident into a lesson: "Red, you got more sense than any cat in this prison—only, you don't use it. You ain't using your brains when you go around busting your fist against stone walls. That's just what the white man wants you to do. Like he wants us to keep fighting each other—because as long as we fighting each other, we ain't fighting *him*. And he wants you to beat your *brains* out, Red, against that stone wall he's built. That's why he built it—for you to beat your brains out against it" (*OD* 135). From the perspective of this wise insider, the power represented by the prison is both a barrier and a weapon, provided that the incarcerated man believes that he must physically attack it as opposed to the forces that created it. Like Malcolm's engagement with the police who are following him, his initial behavior in prison reflects his inability to see beyond the physical and into the more abstract power of the law. At this point, he has only resentment: against Mr. Ostrovski for telling him he cannot become a lawyer, against the white law students who will become lawyers and who fail to see him, against the police who humiliate him, and against the judge who sentences him. Such rage, devoid of any deeper understanding of the law's power, does the opposite of liberating Malcolm: as Luther says, it ensures that Malcolm will "stay locked up all [his] life" (*OD* 130).

The more Malcolm behaves like Caleb from *Tell Me* (pre-conversion, in both cases), the more effective the law is in containing and controlling him. When he begins to associate with powerful figures—that is, when he becomes more like Leo—Malcolm is finally able to combat legal power. His education enables him to write to Elijah Muhammad to thank him for his teachings: "You have made me understand why black men are in prison" (*OD* 155). This knowledge is crucial. When the police beat and incarcerate Brother Hinton, Malcolm arrives and is able to speak on behalf of an angry mob that has gathered on the scene. Though he never becomes a lawyer, Malcolm sounds like one in his interactions with the officer in charge; he says, "You have beaten and imprisoned a certain Minister Hinton, you have him on the premises, we demand to see him, and we have eyewitness proof of the beating" (*OD* 181). The scene is strikingly similar to the scene in *Tell Me* when Leo is arrested and confronts the officer in charge, indicating that he has influence with an authority figure higher than the police. By the end of the encounter, Malcolm has enough courage to order the officer to get Hinton to a hospital and to say to him, "If you spend much more time asking funny questions, you going to find yourself answering some.—You want that pension, don't you? Well, you better get on that phone.—You dog" (*OD* 184). He is finally able to claim a higher moral position than that of the police, and as he becomes a more effective and influential speaker, he is able to exploit this position. Baldwin also exploits it. As Malcolm states in a speech, "The white man is in no moral position to accuse anyone else of hate!" the scenario directions state, "(Cut to: police dogs being used on children. Police on horseback using cattle prods on men, women, and children)" (*OD* 202).[24] Reinforcing Malcolm's description of the police as dogs here, Baldwin associates police with animals, which may connect to the grisly montage in the first part of the scenario in which witnesses to a lynching turn into animals who feed on the corpse, then turn back into people (*OD* 150–51). By rendering the police as subhuman and connecting them through animal imagery to this lynching scene, as he did in "Going to Meet the Man," Baldwin has attempted to invert the hierarchy that would place law enforcement officers above the incarcerated.

Baldwin's rendering of Malcolm X's life recalls both brothers from *Tell Me,* but it also connects to another book he published in 1972, the essay *No Name in the Street.* The brutality and dehumanization of the prison experience is crucial to *One Day When I Was Lost,* but it becomes even more crucial in this essay and in Baldwin's next novel *If Beale Street Could Talk* (discussed in chapter 5). His deeper involvement in prison in these years is based on the incarceration of his friend and sometime bodyguard Tony Maynard, whose fate is connected, in Baldwin's essay, to the fate of the assassinated leaders of the 1960s: Malcolm X, Medgar Evers, and Martin Luther King. Baldwin's sense that he might be the next victim of an assassin's bullet and his concerns with prisoners had both become obsessions at this point of his life. In addition to the Maynard case, he had directed a play by Canadian playwright John Herbert called *Fortune and Men's Eyes* in Turkey that takes place in a prison/reformatory for young men. According to Campbell, "the police tried to ban it" because its homosexual content made it "a threat to public order."[25] Magdalena Zaborowska discusses Baldwin's involvement with the play in detail in her recent study *James Baldwin's Turkish Decade: Erotics of Exile.* She argues that this play was a natural for Baldwin because of his personal and artistic interests at the time: "By having made sexual violence central among the other interlocking systems of oppression—racism, sexism, misogyny, xenophobia—Herbert's *Fortune* privileges male gender and homosexuality and reveals them as embroiled with racism."[26] Baldwin saw prison as a metaphor for the types of struggles that plague the free as well as the incarcerated: "[Baldwin] tried to make the actors understand that the play emphasized the power of experience, that 'life on the inside of the prison was not much different from the life outside.'"[27] One of the most innovative ways Baldwin illustrated this principle on stage was to replace the traditional proscenium curtain with iron bars. According to Zaborowska, "Baldwin's play ends with the deafening sound of the iron bars that separate the stage from the audience being slammed shut, thus sealing the fate of the children imprisoned behind them, 'cut down . . . before our eyes.'"[28] In an interview about the play, Baldwin declared, "Unless the society and the audience feel disturbed by this play, they won't try to correct the situations displayed there," and he attempted to disturb the audience by emphasizing these iron bars: "he would have the actors bang on and shake the heavy iron bars that separated the length of the stage from the audience, or the guard would run his stick over the bars or hit them violently."[29]

The production of *Fortune and Men's Eyes* that Baldwin directed only seemed to whet his appetite for other projects involving prisons. According to Campbell, Baldwin planned to stage a play inside an actual prison, and he was also considering a film project based on *Soledad Brother,* George Jackson's celebrated collection of prison letters written to his brother, the publication of which touched off the riot at Attica.[30] One of Baldwin's lovers during this period was in jail for armed robbery. His letters to Baldwin beg for visits during his furloughs, ask for clothing that he can wear upon his release, and include official letters he has written about the conditions at Walpole prison in Massachusetts, where he was being held.[31] Baldwin's friend, the actor David Moses, co-organized a short-lived program in California prisons called "Artists in Prison," and he enticed Baldwin to send a letter of support for grants and for a quotation to put on the program's masthead. Baldwin complied, and in a letter to Moses dated September 27, 1974, he wrote, "What you are trying to do is to re-create the prisoner's sense of life, of love, to re-affirm the powerful truth of his genuine existence in the human community: to make him know that we have not left him to perish inside the walls." Baldwin was clearly deeply involved with prisoners and the prison experience during this period of his career: Maynard's case was only the beginning.

No Name in the Street was the fullest expression of Baldwin's involvement with the Maynard case, but it was only one expression. As early as January 10, 1968, less than a year after the crime for which Maynard was arrested, Baldwin composed an open letter that expressed his outrage and anticipated his obsession with incarceration that would last the rest of his life. He contemplated an entire book on the Maynard case, to be called *Upon My Soul*. The rough notes for the book, two pages in length, describe that the first part is to be titled "IN" and the second part "OUT," emphasizing the radical, absolute societal divide represented by the prison system. Baldwin saw Maynard's case as representative. Also in rough notes he writes, "Tony has the last word, his voice must control the book, otherwise there can be no book: the world is full of beaten prisoners, and very few of them can speak. Whoever can speak must speak for all the others."[32] Although the book *Upon My Soul* never came to fruition, Baldwin did his best to give Maynard a voice in *No Name in the Street*.

At first glance, *No Name in the Street* is unlikely to be classified as a prison narrative, for it is a wide-ranging essay whose subject is most often described as American race relations in the 1960s. Baldwin examines his own life at length in the first section of the book, "Take Me to the Water." In the second section, "To Be Baptized," he discusses his contacts with the three prominent black leaders who were assassinated in the 1960s: Medgar Evers, Martin Luther King, and Malcolm X. Baldwin also writes about his contacts with other famous African American figures such as Black Panthers founders Bobby Seale, Huey Newton, and Eldridge Cleaver. Taken together, these six men were among the most influential black leaders of their time, despite their different causes, approaches, interpretations, and suggested solutions to the race crisis in the United States. Yet if we back away for a moment from the historical importance of these figures and their contributions to the struggle for equality or their militant pronouncements, we see that all six of them had something else in common: they were all, for varying amounts of time and for various reasons, in prison. Baldwin touches upon their prison experiences briefly (if at all) as he constructs the essay, but the fact that they all spent time in prison leads us to a greater understanding of the central figure of *No Name in the Street*: Tony Maynard, Baldwin's former driver and bodyguard, who was accused and jailed for a murder that he swears "upon [his] soul" (*NN* 104) that he didn't commit.

Yoshinobu Hakutani's "*No Name in the Street*: James Baldwin's Image of the American Sixties," one of the first and longest critical essays on

Baldwin's book, only briefly mentions Tony Maynard. Maynard's case, according to Hakutani, "provides the narrative with a sense of immediacy and attests to Baldwin's personal involvement with contemporary affairs." He goes on to say, "Since Tony Maynard is treated as a victim of the indifference and hatred that exists in society, this episode also becomes a structural thread to other episodes that otherwise appear fragmentary."[33] It is this sense of structure and focus that I would like to consider, for Maynard's case is really at the center of the essay, both thematically and physically (beginning on page 100 of a 197-page text, in the Laurel paperback edition). Zaborowska considers the book's structure as a way of linking Baldwin's "encounter with the South" to the prison-industrial complex: "Read in such a symmetrical manner, the two parts of *No Name in the Street* offer parallel intra- and international contexts for reading the ways in which white males exercise their power through spatial practices of segregation and incarceration of people of color."[34]

Although it is difficult to summarize briefly what Baldwin's rich and complex essay is "about," its most consistent motif is separation: between black America and white America, within black America (as Baldwin's autobiographical segment indicates), between Europe/America and Africa, or between the conditions of imprisonment and freedom. Meditating on the distance between himself and a childhood friend, Baldwin writes, "How can one say that freedom is taken, not given, and that no one is free until all are free? and that the price is high" (*NN* 21). The most obvious and sensational examples of the taking of freedom are the assassinations of Medgar Evers, Martin Luther King, and Malcolm X, but Baldwin consistently turns to the example of Tony Maynard, whose prison experience acts as an intensifying metaphor for the black experience, which amounts to this: "Blacks have never been free in this country, never was it intended that they should be free" (*NN* 177). Such bold statements, Baldwin notes, are not meant to "[advocate] violence" (*NN* 191), but rather "to face certain blunt, human facts" (*NN* 192). The antidote to the disease of separation in American society, according to Baldwin, is the truth.

Baldwin cannot state his thesis this simply because of the complexity of both race relations and imprisonment in the late twentieth century. He describes how a white woman he was involved with once slapped his face in public, causing him to run with the knowledge that he "was a target for police" (*NN* 109). Perhaps recalling the fate of Frank Stafford whose brutal beating led to the Harlem Six incident, he claims that he is "astonished until today that I have both my eyes and most of my teeth and functioning kidneys and my sexual equipment: but small black boys have the advantage of being able to curl themselves into knots, and roll with the kicks and the punches. . . . I was black and visible and helpless and the word was out to 'get' me, and so, soon, I, too, hauled ass. And the prisons of this country are full of boys like the boy I was" (*NN* 108–9). This passive resistance or flight response recalls Leo, who learns that only luck or good connections prevents any black man from being in prison, or from being irrevocably damaged by prison.

In the context of the essay, Tony Maynard's experience carries the weight of being, to some extent, representative. Maynard is still in prison at the end of the narrative despite Baldwin's attempts to plead his case. Moreover, he is innocent[35] in Baldwin's eyes and has been brutally beaten in prison, bearing the scars that Baldwin miraculously escaped years earlier. When Baldwin and his German editor try to visit Maynard, the guard initially tries to prevent them from seeing him. When they insist, Maynard is finally brought before them, "beaten very hard; his cheekbones had disappeared and one of his eyes was crooked; he looked swollen above the neck, and he took down his shirt collar, presently, to show us the swelling on his shoulders. And he was weeping" (*NN* 115). The essay is divided into two major sections with thirty-three subdivisions of varying lengths. Baldwin immediately begins the next subdivision with Maynard's own narrative of the beating in his own voice. The beating occurred after the guard took away Maynard's religious medallion; he says, "I started beating on the door of my cell, trying to make him come back, to listen to me, at least to explain to me *why* I couldn't have it, after he'd promised. And then the door opened and fifteen men walked in and they beat me up—fifteen men!" (*NN* 116). The fragmentary nature of *No Name in the Street* and the multivocal nature of prison narratives come together at this crucial moment in Baldwin's essay. The truth cannot be delivered any other way to a white audience who finds the truth "difficult to swallow." Baldwin's aim is not only for authenticity but also for a complex reality that illuminates the darkest corners of prison and the occasionally bleak despair of black America in the late 1960s.

To construct his narrative effectively, Baldwin must be willing to disrupt conventional narrative devices and to destroy the unity of time and space in addition to the uniformity of plot and voice. Notions of time and place are especially unstable in prison narratives, for one of prison's most devastating psychological effects is to disorient the prisoner's sense of time and place. Bell Chevigny writes, "The state reduces the stuff of time, as it does the captured human, to number. It makes time the prisoner's only possession, while emptying it. . . . Doing time is also doing space, for the temporal distortion is paralleled by tyrannical control of space."[36] Early in his narrative Baldwin writes of the confusion of time and memory, "Time passes and passes. It passes backward and it passes forward and it carries you along, and no one in the whole wide world knows more about time than this: it is carrying you through an element you do not understand into an element you will not remember. Yet, *something* remembers—it can even be said that something avenges: the trap of our century, and the subject now before us" (*NN* 22). Late in the narrative, walking through the streets of San Francisco and meditating on the recent past, Baldwin expresses this disorientation in a way that comments on the structure of *No Name in the Street:*

> I suspect that there really has been some radical alteration in the struc-
> ture, the nature, of time. One may say that there are no clear images;
> everything seems superimposed on, and at war with something else.
> There are no clear vistas: the road that seems to pull one forward into
> the future is also pulling one backward into the past. I felt, anyway,
> kaleidoscopic, fragmented, walking through the streets of San Fran-
> cisco, trying to decipher whatever it was that my own consciousness
> made of all the elements in which I was entangled, and which were all
> tangled up in me. (*NN* 178–79)

The essay is an attempt to represent the alteration of the nature of time that creates this tangle in Baldwin's mind, an alteration that the incarcerated individual experiences as soon as he or she enters prison.

It is important to compare this late passage with the moment that Tony Maynard enters Baldwin's text because the two passages link the confusion in Baldwin's mind to Maynard's prison experience. The essay engages a tug of war between exact dates or moments on one side and vague memories on the other. The moments when Baldwin heard about the assassinations of Evers, Malcolm X, and King, for example, are discernable and precisely dated, but the book begins with a childhood memory about which Baldwin speculates, "I must have been about five, I should think . . . but I may have been younger . . . or I may think I was five because I remember tugging at my mother's skirts once and watching her face while she was telling someone else that she was twenty-seven" (*NN* 3). Other events in Baldwin's life are exactly dated, and his proclamation of Maynard's innocence depends much on exact dates and the slippage of time between the murder and Tony's arrest. Baldwin points out that

a deposition signed by an eyewitness dates the crime "on the morning of
April 3, 1967" which contradicts the fact that "the crime is alleged to
have taken place on the morning of the fourth" (*NN* 110). Baldwin continues to scrutinize the deposition: "This document, to say nothing of the
date of its appearance [October 31, 1967], strikes me as extraordinary. It
appears six days after Hanst's warrant and four days after Judge Weaver's
cable—to say nothing of the fact that this authoritative identification of
the murderer, by means of a photograph, occurs seven months after the
event" (*NN* 111). The way time slips and is manipulated when serializing
evidence in a murder trial reflects a kind of disorientation in Baldwin's
overall narrative, and when he introduces Maynard into his text, he begins
with a vague temporal marker: "sometime during all this" (*NN* 100).
During this section of the essay, which shifts rapidly between voices and
incidents, three of the other subdivisions begin with nonspecific references
to time: "many years ago" (*NN* 106), "a long time ago" (*NN* 107), and
"about four years earlier" (*NN* 109). The contrast between these nonspecific times and the very specific details of the murder and deposition dates
has the effect of compressing and expanding time, or of "radically altering
its structure, its nature."

The description of the world surrounding the prison has a similar
effect, and brings us back to Baldwin's mind-set in San Francisco. Before
Baldwin leads us into Maynard's prison or his life, he describes his own
feelings as he walks to the prison in Hamburg, Germany where Maynard
is imprisoned. Baldwin had to fly from London to get there, and he begins
the Maynard section with these observations: "London was cold, but
damp and grey. Hamburg was frosty and dry as a bone, and blinding with
ice and snow; and the sun, which never came to London, loitered in Hamburg all day long: *über alles.* Germans say that Hamburg is the German
city which most resembles London. It is hard to know, from their tone,
whether they are bragging or complaining, and it did not really remind me
of London, lacking London's impressive sprawl" (*NN* 101). He continues
to contemplate these two cities and as he gets closer to Maynard, he places
the prison in the context of two other great western cities and reveals the
deterioration beneath their stately exteriors: "The prison is part of a complex of intimidating structures, scattered over quite a large area—a little
like the complex on l'Île de la Cité in Paris, or the complex on Center
Street in New York—but it resembles neither of them. It is more medieval
than either, and gives the impression of being far more isolated—though,
as I say, I could walk to it from my exceedingly fashionable hotel. Yet, the
streets were torn up all around it—men at work; I learned to walk from

there because taxis seemed never to come anywhere near it; there was a tramline, but I did not know how to use it, and it also seemed to skirt the prison" (*NN* 102–103). Baldwin takes us deeper and deeper, behind the "great barred door" (*NN* 102, 104) and into the visiting room. To add to the disorientation, "the turnkey smiled at [Baldwin] as he turned the key in the lock," then Maynard "smiled" and "grinned"; Baldwin ends the description by observing, "I saw that [Maynard] hadn't turned his face to the wall" (*NN* 104). All of this smiling provides a ghastly contrast to the cold, sterile, formidable surroundings. While Maynard's smiles and the fact that he faces Baldwin directly are evidence of his hope and his innocence, they also heighten the despair of his beaten, weeping, averted face when Baldwin visits him days later, and the smile of the turnkey becomes especially sinister when we consider that he may have been one of the fifteen guards who beat Maynard.

The fact that Maynard's narrative is so dramatically fragmented— much more so than the rest of the essay—places the burden of connection on the reader. First the reader must connect Maynard's story to Baldwin's and to the global parable that Baldwin tells. Both are built on analogies to prison. Baldwin discusses how his falling in love represented "the key to life. Not merely the key to *my* life, but to life itself" (*NN* 22), and love leaves the individual paradoxically "both free and bound . . . a bondage which liberates you" (*NN* 23). In his sophisticated definition, love is not merely a key that sets one free; it is a key that unifies the opposing forces of bondage and liberation, just as his essay seeks to engage with the distance between outsiders and the inside of prison, or white and black experience. On a global level Baldwin examines France and the United States, countries whose foreign and domestic policies and general cultural arrogance lead to the insurgency of French Algerians, or the Viet Cong, or the Nation of Islam. Because these policies and attitudes promote separation, for example, "One was either French, or Algerian; one could not be both" (*NN* 37). As far as America goes, Baldwin quotes Dostoyevsky: "I don't believe in the wagons that bring bread to humanity. For the wagons that bring bread to humanity, without any moral basis for conduct, may coldly exclude a considerable part of humanity" (*NN* 85). Baldwin sees the seething anger of this part of humanity in the American ghetto, and makes the connection for the reader: "what America is doing within her borders, she is doing around the world" (*NN* 86). The prisoner as the central figure of Baldwin's book is a representative for the millions of those angry and oppressed at the expense of those who seek to gain from the underclass and to keep them in their place. He continues: "it must be remembered—

it cannot be overstated—that those centuries of oppression are also the history of a system of thought, so that both the ex-man who considers himself master and the ex-man who is treated like a mule suffer from a particular species of schizophrenia, in which each contains the other, in which each longs to be the other" (*NN* 87). It is, of course, this "system of thought" that has created the modern prison and stratified modern American society according to race and class. Baldwin sees the complex tragedy of the situation and he prophecies violence. While Baldwin was completing the book, Tony Maynard was transferred to Attica prison. Baldwin realizes the open-ended nature of his inquiry: "this book is not finished—can never be finished, by me. As of this writing, I am waiting to hear the fate of Tony Maynard, whose last address was Attica" (*NN* 196). The 1971 Attica riot had just occurred, leaving forty-two people dead, and Baldwin leaves his readers with a chilling, angry message—a violent amplification of the concluding lines of "Stranger in the Village": "the Western party is over, and the white man's sun has set. Period" (*NN* 197). The crisis could be avoided, Baldwin infers, but not before white readers understand the significance of Tony Maynard's story and make the proper connections both within this story and between it and the other sections of Baldwin's essay.

The anger and defiance at the conclusion of *No Name* sets the stage for Baldwin's final considerations of the criminal power of the law and how best to respond to it, a motif that realizes its fullest expression in *If Beale Street Could Talk*. In the final two decades of his life, Baldwin would move beyond the fear evident in his early writings and the outrage he expressed in the middle of his career, or the combination of fear and outrage he expresses in the works discussed in this chapter. As if to obliterate the vision he had of Tony Maynard, beaten and emasculated in prison, Baldwin imagines a new figure in the person of Fonny Hunt who manages to greet his girlfriend Tish through the glass partition of the visiting room of his prison with his fist in the air. Christopher Bigsby argues that African Americans' "social subordination thus stands as a symbol of society's control over its own anarchic impulses. As a consequence he is offered a role whose significance is not limited to its social utility. Thus, when he resists that caricature the consequent appeals by the dominant society to 'law and order' have metaphysical as well as pragmatic implications. In Baldwin's work the self resists the peripheral role which seems its social fate, and the primary agent in this resistance is the imagination."[37] Baldwin's imagination has the capacity to transform Maynard into Fonny, signaling hope where there had been despair.

Before his deep consideration of prison in a fictional context, though, Baldwin did everything in his power to free his friend. He co-signed an open letter with Ossie Davis, Valerie Maynard, and William Styron, and his own 1968 open letter was frequently quoted in other articles on the Maynard case, which Baldwin painstakingly collected. James A. Wechsler, in *The New York Post* magazine, chronicled the case for years, and it is clear that Maynard's case consumed Baldwin not only because Maynard was a friend, but because it was a grossly magnified version of the same treatment Baldwin had received in Paris. The two men swore they were being wrongfully held; they had no voice; and they had to wait a long time between their arrest and their trial. Baldwin had to wait eight days; Maynard had to wait two and a half years. The witness to such horrors had to speak, and not only to the judge, but to all his countrymen. Baldwin had incorporated Maynard's voice in *No Name in the Street* within his own narrative, but he was not done talking, and in fact, in his final years, his own voice on the subject of the law had never been louder or more insistent.

CHAPTER 5

The Fire Reignited

O NE OF THE common misconceptions of the law as practiced and
shaped in courts is that, because its language is esoteric and even
arcane, it constitutes a kind of sacred text that cannot be altered. The law
is burdened with legal precedent, the citation of which becomes baffling
to the average citizen who assumes that the knowledge lawyers allude to
is something that only they have access to, and that it is handed down
from on high. But as David Kairys points out, "the law is not simply an
armed receptacle for values and priorities determined elsewhere; it is part
of a complex social totality in which it constitutes as well as is constituted,
shapes as well as is shaped."[1] Such a perspective is not easy to come by for
someone as disenfranchised as Baldwin was during his formative years.
The key word in Kairys's analysis for Baldwin might be "armed." There
is a certain force that never escaped his consciousness, a force so dramatically symbolized by jails and police officers that he often had trouble
seeing beyond them to the more abstract manifestations of the law. The
realization that the law is neither monolithic nor impervious to the "shaping" power of citizens like him did not happen quickly, but by the end of
his career he was closer to the perspective of Kairys and other progressive
legal thinkers than he had ever been before.

In the final two decades of his life, Baldwin's concern with the law's
power realized its fullest expression. The major works of this period, critically neglected and seen as extraneous to his main body of work, demonstrate that he eventually overcame his fear of the law's power and learned,

finally, how disenfranchised individuals can effectively struggle to overcome it. In his 1974 novel *If Beale Street Could Talk*, he contemplates the prison experience in greater detail than ever before, seeing it not as destiny but as a force to be resisted calmly, rationally, and patiently; and in *The Evidence of Things Not Seen* he assumes the voice of a lawyer, essentially using the Wayne Williams case as a vehicle for putting his nation on trial for myriad crimes related to racism. In these final works he touches upon all of the themes I have discussed throughout this study. Though he retains a healthy skepticism toward the power of the law, these final works represent a perspective far removed from the terrified boy we encountered in "Equal in Paris." Having recognized the criminal power of the law, Baldwin evolves into a defiant figure willing to take the law on its own terms, and to conquer it with patience and rhetoric.

It is fair to say that Baldwin's involvement with the issue of incarceration was intensely personal during the late 1960s and early 1970s. The massive amount of energy he poured into the Tony Maynard case, the fact that one of his lovers was in prison, and his strained but profound relationships with incarcerated leaders of the Black Panther Party such as Huey Newton, Angela Davis, Bobby Seale, and even Eldridge Cleaver all combined to make the issue of black imprisonment emotional, as described in chapter 4. His impulse to direct a prison-themed play while in Istanbul marked a watershed moment in which he began to treat the subject of incarceration artistically and to make it the thoroughgoing subject of his attention. In his final decade he managed to distance himself emotionally from his subject without taking his eyes off it. In some ways, his final years were parallel to his early expatriation in that he needed to remove himself from his subject before he was able to treat it most effectively in his writing. In terms of the law, this period begins with the publication of *Beale Street* and continues through the publication of his final book, *The Evidence of Things Not Seen*.

A transitional piece between Baldwin's early fear of the law and his ability to rise above it in *Beale Street* and *Evidence* is his 1975 work *The Devil Finds Work*. Part memoir, part reflective essay, and part film criticism, this critically neglected work is a truncated rendition of Baldwin's intellectual journey from a naive, poor Harlem child to a mature thinker capable of knitting together popular culture, history, and religion in a penetrating analysis. The book's three divisions correspond roughly to Baldwin's youth, to his middle years as an expatriate and Civil Rights spokesman, and to his post-1960s incarnation as a protean intellectual, capable of shifting easily between the language of the street, literary analysis, historical discourse, and cultural commentary. We learn from the first section, "Congo Square," that his attitude toward and fear of the police might have been caused by what he had witnessed and experienced early in life, but it was certainly reinforced by what he saw on the silver screen, or what he calls "the American looking-glass" (*DFW* 120).

Baldwin was introduced to the cinema by his teacher, Orilla "Bill" Miller, who led him away from church and family and into the life of the mind. Throughout his career Baldwin cites her as the initial reason he is unable to classify all white people as basically evil, and in a telling paragraph he contrasts her directly to "the cops who had already beaten me up" and "the landlords who called me nigger" (*DFW* 6)—the same types who have haunted his fiction, arm-in-arm, ever since his first story "Previous Condition." Bill, he claims, "was treated like a nigger, especially by the cops" (*DFW* 7), yet at the same time he recalls how she brought a group of black children to a police station where there was supposed to be free ice cream, and stared down the police officers when they initially refused to serve it to black children (*DFW* 26). Her actions here, similar to those of Lola in *Tell Me How Long the Train's Been Gone,* are an indication that police power has its limitations, yet in both cases white women have to defend younger black men. As a result Baldwin feels well connected, but not necessarily powerful. The cultural lessons that are constantly reinforced in his experience make a deeper impression than the bravery of a single white woman does.

Although Baldwin learned much from literature, in his early years he was at least equally influenced by movies. It is not surprising, given the depth of the subject of the law in his fiction, that the movies from his youth that he most vividly recalls have much to do with law and order.[2] One of the first films he mentions is *20,000 Years in Sing Sing;* another is *A Tale of Two Cities,* the most haunting part of which is "Dr. Manette's testimony, written in prison" (*DFW* 21). This film was based on one of the novels he read repeatedly and obsessively as a youth; the other was *Crime and Punishment* (*DFW* 12). Even a film he claims he never saw, *The Prisoner of Shark Island,* awakened his sensibility through its advertisement alone; he writes, "I certainly reacted to the brutal conjunction of the words, *prisoner* and *shark* and *island.* I may have feared becoming a prisoner, or feared that I was one already" (*DFW* 11). The movies he saw, he believed, were "simply a reflection" (*DFW* 22) of his country, and he begins to make connections between current events and their dramatic renditions on the screen, notably the case of the Scottsboro boys (*DFW* 22), whose trial stirred rage, fear, and paranoia in him. He began to read books about incarceration, including Angelo Herndon's *Let Me Live;* he describes Herndon as "a young, black labor organizer in the Deep South, railroaded to prison, who lived long enough, at least, to write a book about it—the George Jackson of the era. No one resembling him, or anyone resembling any of the Scottsboro Boys, nor anyone resembling my father, has yet made an appearance on the American cinema scene" (*DFW* 22). In the cinema of his youth, the reflection of the American looking glass is distorted: black men are criminalized and punished, while "Heroes . . . were white" (*DFW* 21). Occasionally white people are criminals in film, too: Sylvia Sidney, for instance, "facing a cop . . . pulling her black hat back from her forehead: *One of you lousy cops gave me that*" (*DFW* 25). Or Henry Fonda in *You Only Live Once,* who plays a character whose society "will not allow him to live down, or redeem, his criminal past" (*DFW* 28). What is fascinating is how Baldwin alters the racial identity of these two characters who are victims of the law; "Sylvia Sidney was the only American film actress who reminded me of a colored girl, or woman" (*DFW* 24), and "the only actor of the era with whom I identified was Henry Fonda. I was not alone. A black friend of mine, after seeing Henry Fonda in *The Grapes of Wrath,* swore that Fonda had colored blood. You could tell, he said, by the way Fonda walked down the road at the end of the film: *white men don't walk like that!*" (*DFW* 25). Along with Bill Miller off screen, Baldwin respects and admires white film actors who play characters who have been abused by the "lousy cops" or who have been labeled permanently by their criminal records.

The perspective that Baldwin developed in his early years was apparently difficult to shake. The black-and-white worlds he saw reflected on the screen were absolute, and absolutely reinforced by the distinction between cops and criminals. In the middle section of *The Devil Finds Work,* "Who Saw Him Die? I, Said the Fly," Baldwin is able to gain some critical distance on film history, and to comment effectively on how the cinema could be used as a tool to reinforce racial stereotypes even while purporting to subvert them. The persona of the policemen is a primary reason for this paradox. Baldwin singles out *In the Heat of the Night,* the 1967 film in which Sidney Poitier's detective character famously declares, "In Philadelphia, they call me Mister Tibbs!" as a way of proving the following principle: "Blacks know something about black cops, too, even those called Mister, in Philadelphia. They know that their presence on the force doesn't change the force or the judges or the lawyers or the bondmen or the jails. They know the black cop's mother and his father, they may have met the sister, and they know the younger, or the older brother, who may be a bondman, or a junkie, or a student, in Limbo, at Yale. They know how much the black cop has to prove, and how limited are his means of proving it: where I grew up, black cops were yet more terrifying than white ones" (*DFW* 73).[3] Poitier's Virgil Tibbs is thus part of the legal machinery, unable to achieve any real racial progress because of his involvement in the justice system which is, Baldwin implies, broken beyond repair. If there is hope for the future, it cannot be delivered by a white sheriff and a black detective. Baldwin likens their sentimental scene at the end of the film to the Hollywood cliché of the fade-out kiss, which denotes "reconciliation, of all things now becoming possible" (*DFW* 67). The professions of these men, not their races, is what gives the film, according to Baldwin, its "appalling distance from reality" (*DFW* 67), and the message the audience actually receives from the film diverges according to the audience's racial identity: "white Americans have been encouraged to continue dreaming, and black Americans have been alerted to the necessity of waking up" (*DFW* 69).

The second section of Baldwin's book is a chronicle of his own awakening: to the enduring realities of racial prejudice around the globe, to the ability of white Americans to deceive themselves through such devices as cinema, and to the role incarceration plays in all of this. The section builds to his account of being harassed by the FBI during the McCarthy era.[4] Being interrogated about the whereabouts of an acquaintance, Baldwin realizes something about his own reactions to legal harassment: "They frightened me, and they humiliated me—it was like being spat on, or pissed on, or gang-raped—but they made me hate them, too, with a hatred like hot ice, and all I knew, simply, was that, if I could figure out what they wanted, nothing could induce me to give it to them" (*DFW* 108). This epiphany is a formative moment in Baldwin's belief that it is possible to transcend the law's power, and it is responsible for other realizations he expresses elsewhere in this section: "A man can fall in love with a man: incarceration [has] not been able to prevent it, and never will" (*DFW* 82), and, during the McCarthy era, "A disloyal American was anyone who really believed in equal justice under the law. . . . A disloyal American was anyone who believed it his right, and his duty, to . . . visit those in prison" (103). As in the first section of the book, Baldwin has identified with and allied himself with the victims of the criminal justice system. The difference between this work and his earlier work is that he views this identification and alliance in terms of empowerment rather than victimhood.

The Devil Finds Work ends with a brief consideration of the iconic 1970s psychological horror film *The Exorcist,* and perhaps Baldwin's consideration of Hollywood can be regarded as his own exorcism of the cinematic demons that have haunted him. Not surprisingly, he links the concept of the devil (alluded to in the title) to law enforcement officers: "I have seen the devil, by day and by night, and have seen him in you and in me: in the eyes of the cop and the sheriff and the deputy" (*DFW* 145–46). In terms of his disastrous involvement with filmmaking—the abandoned attempt to write the Malcolm X screenplay—he describes it as "my Hollywood sentence" (*DFW* 117) and says, "I would rather be . . . incarcerated . . . than repeat the adventure" (*DFW* 115). Metaphorically, through his analysis, Baldwin experiences an escape from Hollywood's tendency to lock its audiences into a particular way of thinking. He arrives at this realization in his critique of *Lady Sings the Blues,* based on the life of Billie Holliday. The film produces a "pure bullshit Hollywood-American fable" as it simplifies the main character and weakens her: "The off-screen Billie faced down white sheriffs, and laughed at them, to their faces, and faced down white managers, cops, and bartenders. She was much stronger than this film can have any interest in indicating, and, as a victim, infinitely more complex" (*DFW* 133). But just as the legal justice system is not final, permanent, or monolithic in Baldwin's evolving mature perspective, neither is the cinema the final word on reality: "Once the victim's testimony is delivered, however, there is, thereafter, forever, a witness somewhere: which is an irreducible inconvenience for the makers and shakers and accomplices of this world. These run together, in packs, and corroborate each other. They cannot bear the judgment in the eyes of the people whom they intend to hold in bondage forever, and who know more about them than their lovers. This remote, public, and as it were, principled, bondage is the indispensable justification of their own: when the prisoner is free, the jailer faces the void of himself" (*DFW* 134–35). Baldwin's role as a witness thus becomes his identity in the twilight of his career, for the witness is needed to testify for the victim whose stories are too easily framed by "the makers and shakers." There is a familiar prophecy at the end of the essay: "The grapes of wrath are stored in . . . prisons" (*DFW* 147) and elsewhere among the lowly and disenfranchised. Baldwin's new role is to release the grapes of wrath, from the vantage point of a witness who will not be silenced rather than as a powerless victim like those he has seen on screen all his life, or like his younger self, contemplating suicide in a Paris jail.

If *Beale Street Could Talk* is the work that most clearly reveals Baldwin's concerns with the criminal power that results in the imprisonment of black men like himself. Like all of his work after *The Fire Next Time,* it received little more than critical sneers. James Campbell devotes less than a full page to it in his biography, roughly a fourth of the space he devotes to Baldwin's unpublished, short, final play, *The Welcome Table*. Carolyn Sylvander describes the novel as "more impressive for what it attempts than for what it achieves" and faults its "lack of control."[5] Some critics are more generous; Houston Baker describes it as an "interesting and compelling narrative" and Joyce Carol Oates's review of the book in *The New York Times Book Review* is overwhelmingly positive; she describes it as "a quite moving and very traditional celebration of love."[6] Though perhaps the least denigrated of Baldwin's final three novels, *Beale Street* has not enjoyed nearly as much critical attention or readership as any of his first three.

Beale Street represents the pinnacle of the incarceration motif in all of his fiction. It elaborates upon the treatment of this theme in previous work and anticipates the legal discourse of his final book, *The Evidence of Things Not Seen*. David Leeming describes it as "Baldwin's prison parable, a fictionalization of his prison concerns during the 1968–73 period, and the natural illustration and culmination of his long meditation on psychological, emotional, and intellectual imprisonment"[7] (323). Centering around the wrongful imprisonment of Fonny Hunt, *Beale Street* echoes similar narratives throughout Baldwin's career: from "Equal in Paris" and *Go Tell It on the Mountain* through *Tell Me How Long the Train's Been Gone*. Lynn Orilla Scott points to the intersection of *No Name in the Street* and *Beale Street*: "There are some obvious parallels between Maynard's situation and Fonny's plight as well, including the prosecution's weak case based on a critical witness who disappears (in the novel it is the victim who disappears), racist police who target unsubmissive black males, the struggle to maintain body and soul in a brutal prison environment, the high cost of getting a fair trial, and the long wait for justice."[8] The distinct emphasis in *Beale Street* is on the way incarceration affects families.

Judith Scheffler writes of the effects of incarceration on families in terms of three related motifs in prison literature: the Visit Scene, the Phone Call Scene, and the Frustrated Visit; the last of which "illustrates how the pettiness of prison rules can become a sadistic weapon of administrative power."[9] The narrator Tish repeatedly describes her interactions with Fonny through the glass barrier of the prison's visitation room. She succinctly summarizes her emotions in response to this unnatural communication: "I hope that nobody has ever had to look at anybody they love through glass" (*IBS* 4). The irony is, of course, that she has to do so constantly. She and Fonny have a ritual of raising their fists—the Black Power salute—when their visits are over, and this gesture gives them silent hope, but it is no substitute for their sexual intimacy, which Tish describes in detail throughout the novel. As the narrative continues, their parting salute is no longer sufficient, and Fonny asks her for a kiss: "I kissed the glass. He kissed the glass" (*IBS* 120). Their willingness to stay positive helps to preserve them during Fonny's imprisonment, but this attempt at connection is tainted by the very structure of the prison which exists to separate and compartmentalize bodies. She states her dilemma simply: "I couldn't touch him. I wanted so to touch him" (*IBS* 5). The prison may operate metaphorically here and elsewhere in Baldwin's work, but it is also a literal, material means of separating these lovers. By depriving them of even basic physical contact, the prison's ability to dehumanize is clear. And yet Fonny resists dehumanization by focusing on Tish, on the baby, and on his work, and Tish resists the dehumanizing effects that she suffers as the lover of a prisoner. Life and hope triumph; as she says, "the baby was the only real thing in the world, more real than the prison" (*IBS* 5). And yet this triumph is tainted by Frank's suicide, by Daniel's bitterness, and by the ambiguity of Fonny's situation at the end of the novel.

The prison in *Beale Street* can be placed at the far end of a continuum of alienating spaces within the novel. As in *Giovanni's Room,* Fonny's loft is a sanctuary of the most sacred private space, the site of their lovemaking. After initially describing it, Tish observes, "We were to spend a long time in this room: our lives" (*IBS* 66). This assessment is not accurate, though, or it is a romantic notion, for the majority of the narrative is consumed by less private and less safe spaces. Close to the room in terms of privacy and sanctuary is the Spanish restaurant, a semi-private refuge where Tish and Fonny are comfortable, and are accepted, provided for, and protected by the waiters and owners. Tish's home is slightly less safe even though her parents and sister also comfort and provide for her because it is the site of a vicious battle between the Hunt and Rivers families. This battle is fueled by, or perhaps even caused by, Mrs. Hunt's religion, and Tish describes the church she attends as an even more dangerous space, with Mrs. Hunt's high heels sounding "something like pistols" (*IBS* 25). Tish explicitly compares church to prison: "when I first had to go and see [Fonny] in the Tombs, and walked up those steps and into those halls, it was just like walking into church" (*IBS* 29).

Prison is the ultimate alienating space, but it falls along a continuum of such spaces. The novel is, on one level, a narrative of how powerless Tish and Fonny are when it comes to sustaining their lives in the comfortable confines of Fonny's loft, just as the baby in Tish's womb will not stay in its safe space forever. Between the relatively safe zones of the loft, the Spanish restaurant, and the Rivers' home and the alienating spaces of church and prison are the streets, the public spaces monitored and controlled by the police, especially the vengeful, corrupt Officer Bell who is primarily responsible for Fonny's imprisonment. Joyce Carol Oates observes, "Officer Bell's villainy is made possible by a system of oppression closely tied up with the mind-boggling stupidities of the law."[10] These stupidities are related to a deep power structure that Baldwin makes increasingly evident throughout the novel. Initially, Bell seems to have absolute power because his dominion is the public setting of the streets, but he also has the ability to survey or even (with the aid of a search warrant) invade the home. Even in Tish's youth, she perceives that police are the ultimate authoritative figures within the justice system: following the childhood incident when she gouges Fonny's cheek with a nail, her friend Geneva tells her that "the police would come and put [her] in the electric chair" (*IBS* 13). In her naive imagination, police officers have absolute and ultimate authority, the power to kill without legal process. But this is not entirely a childish notion: Tish's sister Ernestine has learned that Officer Bell was responsible for the murder of a young black boy, and she plans to use this information when Fonny goes to trial.

The police presence on the streets connotes a threat rather than what it is supposed to connote: public safety. In the Village, the space surrounding Fonny's sanctuary/loft, the police threaten the intimacy that keeps Fonny and Tish together; Tish writes, "The streets were very crowded now, with youngsters, black and white, and cops. Fonny held his head a little higher, and his grip tightened on my hand. . . . It was just like scenes uptown, in a way, with the older men and women sitting on the stoops; with small children running up and down the block, cars moving slowly through this maelstrom, the cop car parked on the corner, with the two cops in it, other cops swaggering slowly along the sidewalk . . . it was a scene that frightened me" (*IBS* 59). Like Richard in *Go Tell It,* Fonny refuses to be labeled, especially by the police, even as his behavior in the presence of the police is guarded. The surveillance Tish senses in the Village foreshadows the standoff between Fonny and Bell, but it had apparently been initiated long before; as Tish observes, "That same passion which saved Fonny got him into trouble, and put him in jail. For, you see, he had found his center, his own center, inside him: and it showed. He wasn't anybody's nigger. And that's a crime, in this fucking free country. You're suppose to be *somebody's* nigger. And if you're nobody's nigger, you're a bad nigger: and that's what the cops decided when Fonny moved down-town" (*IBS* 41). Blackness along with a will to define the self or to refuse to be "placed," again constitutes a "crime" in this novel. Law enforce-ment officers' attempts to control Fonny and to make him submit to their authority are reminiscent of similar attempts in earlier Baldwin novels (Richard in *Go Tell It,* both Caleb and Leo in *Tell Me*). Fonny's ability to persevere where Richard and Caleb did not, even in prison, stems from his strong sense of self-possession, from his unadulterated love of Tish, from their baby, and from his attitude toward his art, which is pure and uncorrupted by commercial forces (unlike Leo Proudhammer's). Fonny's ability to bear up against the dehumanizing effects of prison is heroic and admirable, but Baldwin does not make it seem facile. Fonny maintains a positive attitude—as Tish puts it, "He hates being in there, but he's trying not to let it break him" (*IBS* 98)—but he could have easily ended up like his friend Daniel, whose prison experience prefigures Fonny's, and who has been damaged emotionally and psychologically by it.

Fonny's label as a "bad nigger" is nearly synonymous with his criminal record. In his study *"Born in a Mighty Bad Land": The Violent Man in African American Folklore and Fiction,* Jerry H. Bryant traces the history of the badman figure from postbellum ballads through the literature of the late twentieth century. Attempting to contextualize the "bad nigger" figure in terms of the law, Bryant writes, "black men were not 'outside the law' in the sense that the white law left them alone; rather, the laws they were most often imprisoned for breaking were laws peculiarly designed for them to break. . . . Jail time was a sign of badness. . . . It indicated a defi-ance of white law and an individual strength in a community where few had the courage to fight back."[11] Prison itself is not only a place to contain society's "bad niggers," but a way to cement their identities as such. The power of incarceration to label and identify is powerful, and Tish real-izes it: "I can't say to anybody in this bus, Look, Fonny is in trouble, he's in jail—can you imagine what anybody on this bus would say to me if they knew, from my mouth, that I love somebody in jail?—and I know he's never committed any crime and he's a beautiful person, please help me get him out. Can you imagine what anybody on this bus would say? What would *you* say?" (*IBS* 9). In narratives of condemnation, a prison-er's identity is determined by others and the prisoner remains powerless to change it. But *Beale Street* is at least partially a narrative of redemption, and Fonny is determined to resist any identity given to him because of his incarceration, just as Tish and her family are determined to do everything in their power to exonerate him.

Fonny's friend Daniel is not so fortunate, or so strong. Like Fonny, he has been arrested for a crime he did not commit, and he is permanently scarred by what he understands to be his ultimate powerlessness; he says, "They were just playing with me, man, because they could. And I'm lucky it was only two years, you dig? Because they can do with you whatever they want. *Whatever they want.* And they dogs, man. I really found out, in the slammer, what Malcolm and them cats was talking about. The white man's *got* to be the devil" (*IBS* 111).[12] This conversation takes place before Fonny's incarceration, and he encourages Daniel to move on, replaying a recurrent debate in Baldwin's fiction between bitterness, despair, or racial hatred on one side and forgiveness, hope, or racial cooperation on the other. Although there is no easy way to summarize the debate or to determine that Baldwin felt consistently about it throughout his career, Daniel's mindset is meant to be a caution to the reader, not a model. It allies him in this novel with Frank, Fonny's father, whose bitterness about white oppression affects his ability to love and eventually leads to his suicide. In earlier works, the same attitude is evident in Richard from *Blues for Mister Charlie,* Rufus from *Another Country,* and Malcolm X himself in *One Day When I Was Lost,* all of whom die young. Yet Daniel's feelings are valid: Fonny does not judge him so much as he tries to help him. The keys, again, to Fonny's perseverance are his secure identity, his art, his love for Tish, and the promise for the future represented by his unborn child.

From Baldwin's point of view, another factor that enables Fonny to see beyond the literal power of the prison is an understanding that the law does not end there. The law's true power is not only concrete cells, iron bars, and billy clubs. Having overcome his fear of the police initiated in Harlem and Paris during his youth, Baldwin is able to recognize the flexibility and inner workings of the law in practice. Although he does not necessarily gain respect for lawyers or for the justice system, he does reach a more expansive understanding of trial law and how the testimonies of corrupt police officers like Bell and of intimidated witnesses like the rape victim Victoria do not necessarily determine the outcome of a trial. Following the same logic Baldwin uses in *No Name in the Street* and anticipating the logic he will use in *The Evidence of Things Not Seen,* Tish begins to think like a trial lawyer. In reconstructing the crime, she comes to the following realization: "Orchard Street is damn near in the East River and Bank Street is practically in the Hudson. It is not possible to run from Orchard to Bank, particularly not with the police behind you. Yet, Bell *swears* that he saw Fonny 'run from the scene of the crime.' This is possible only if Bell were off duty, for his 'beat' is on the West Side, not the East. Yet, Bell could arrest Fonny out of the house on Bank Street. It is then up to the accused to prove, and pay for proving, the irregularity and improbability of this sequence of events" (*IBS* 127). Tish does not get the opportunity to reconstruct the evening of the rape in a court trial, for the prosecution, as she says, has "fucked itself out of its principal witness" (*IBS* 200) and the trial is deferred indefinitely; yet she does realize the importance of being able to think in these terms, and she is painfully aware of the cost of hiring someone to do so.

The lawyer Hayward is a pragmatic character who is both sympathetic to the plight of his clients and aware of the realities of the power structure, not unlike Parnell in *Blues for Mister Charlie*. Tish describes him as "nice enough" but she immediately admits, "I certainly wouldn't be comfortable with a lawyer" (*IBS* 97). Yet she finds his honesty refreshing; on one hand he makes cynical pronouncements about the efficacy of the law, such as, "The truth of a case doesn't matter. What matters is—who wins" (*IBS* 101). On the other hand, Hayward reassures Tish that he *believes* in the truth and that it is worth fighting for; he says, "If I didn't believe in Fonny's innocence, I would never have taken this case. I know something about Officer Bell, who is a racist and a liar—I have told him that to his face, so you can feel perfectly free to quote me, to anyone, at any time you wish—and I know something about the D.A. in charge of this case, who is worse" (*IBS* 101). Hayward believes that the D.A. and the police are collaborating to determine the outcome of the case. Yet his knowledge of the inner workings of the justice system combined with his willingness to combat its abuses through any means necessary project some hope that the system can be defeated, and that the societal hierarchies it upholds can eventually erode as a result.

He cannot act alone, though, and the process requires money and time, neither of which is plentiful in the Rivers and Hunt households. Tish's mother Sharon and her sister Ernestine take primary roles in working outside of their prescribed roles and helping Hayward to combat the abuses of the justice system on its own terms. Sharon's essential optimism is what keeps Tish from falling into despair, and also from resorting to prostitution to pay Fonny's legal debts; Sharon reminds her daughter, "I know a lot of our loved ones, a lot of our men, have died in prison: but not *all* of them. You remember that" (*IBS* 121). Long before she travels to Puerto Rico to confront Victoria directly and to appeal to her good nature, Sharon describes to Mrs. Hunt how she has been using the same tactics the D.A. has been using to influence the trial: "I have been running myself *sick,* all up and down the Bronx, trying to get the very best legal advice I can *find*—from some of the people I used to work for, you know—one of them is a city *council*man and he knows just *everybody* and he can *pull* some strings—people just *got* to listen to him, you know" (*IBS* 69). Such connections, she realizes, amount to legal influence, and Ernestine has been accumulating information about Officer Bell through her work that might be useful in the trial. These two women operate on the margins of what is strictly legal, but such behavior is necessary and perhaps effective when it comes to defending Fonny's innocence. Fonny's and Tish's fathers take this logic even further: both resort to theft (*IBS* 139) to pay Fonny's legal bills. Tish believes, "Each of these men would gladly go to jail, blow away a pig, or blow up a city, to save their progeny from the jaws of this democratic hell" (*IBS* 139). Tish herself steals from her employer, and assumes that all of this crime is justifiable because it is, along with Hayward's legal knowledge and Sharon's personal appeal to Victoria to change her testimony, the only way to combat the criminal power that has placed Fonny in jail for a crime he did not commit.

The conclusion of the novel is deliberately ambiguous: either the trial has been deferred and Fonny is still in jail, or he is out on bail and with Tish and the baby; Tish says, "Fonny is working on the wood, on the stone, whistling, smiling. And, from far away, but coming nearer, the baby cries and cries and cries and cries and cries and cries and cries and cries, cries like it means to wake the dead" (*IBS* 213). Michelle Phillips writes: "By ending the novel with the relentless cries of Fonny and Tish's newborn child, Baldwin leaves Fonny's prison narrative unresolved. Whether the child's cries imply anguish and the continuing struggle toward freedom or whether they serve to connect the birth of the child with the rebirth of Fonny, thereby suggesting his imminent release, is left undetermined."[13] Leeming sees the conclusion less ambiguously: "the bail is raised and Fonny returns home."[14] Craig Werner hedges: "The successfully freed (although not completely free) Fonny and the messianic-apocalyptic baby combine at the end."[15] Lynn Orilla Scott suggests that the last paragraph of the novel "may refer to a dream rather than to a point in the future after Fonny's release from jail" and adds, "We really don't know whether Fonny gets out of jail."[16] Sylvander describes the end as "not clear," but "given the heroism of the family, we know it will all turn out all right, whatever all right is" (87). Regardless of which interpretation the reader chooses, the ending is affirmative despite all of the crying, for Fonny inhabits a space, either real or imagined, that has brought him together with his art and with his loved ones. The alienating space of the prison is not explicitly part of the setting, and thus has been defeated. It has taken an enormous amount of faith, sacrifice, hard work, and money on the part of both families to arrive at this place, but that is the substance of Baldwin's faith in the future.

Baldwin's concerns with the prison experience were giving way to his understanding of legal power in the context of trial law in *Beale Street,* yet he was still concerned with the lives of prisoners and he published two essays in a prison magazine called *Inside/Out,* later called *Time Capsule,* in the early 1980s, recently reprinted in *The Cross of Redemption.* The editor of the original pieces was Baldwin's friend Marc Crawford, and though most of the content was written by actual prisoners, professional writers and critics like Baldwin and H. Bruce Franklin also appeared here. The first essay Baldwin published, simply titled "A Letter to Prisoners" and published in 1982, considers the solidarity between artists and prisoners: "the artist, insofar as the State is compelled to consider this inconvenient creature at all, is nothing more—and, also, nothing less—than a potential prisoner" (*CR* 213). There is plenty of despair in the essay, which speaks of the corruption and unnaturalness of the power human beings wield over one another, and which complains about the economic expenses, not to mention the costs to humanity, of maintaining prisons. Yet there is also some hope. Having allied the artist with the prisoner, Baldwin arrives at this conclusion: "knowing perfectly well how little can be done, one discovers how to do some things" (*CR* 213). Baldwin celebrates "a real recognition of, and respect for the other and for the condition of the other. The other is no longer other and is, indeed as the song puts it, closer than a brother—the other is oneself" (*CR* 213).

This radical empathy effectively eradicates the distance between those in prison and those who are free. Baldwin's attempt to merge the other with the self in the context of incarceration illuminates one of his central points throughout his career: that prison is nothing more than the concrete manifestation of any number of social forces that conspire to separate and compartmentalize society. He offers comfort to his imprisoned readers, whom he addresses as "Brethren" in the final paragraph: "We are, in ourselves, much older than any witness to Carthage or Pompeii and, having been through auction, flood and fire, to say nothing of the spectacular excavation of our names, are not destined for the rubble" (*CR* 214). The word "auction" and the allusion to the "excavation of our names" indicate that Baldwin assumes his audience to be not only incarcerated, but black. Neither race nor the condition of incarceration determines one's destiny, though; the final note is of perseverance, and Baldwin's encouragement is based on writing itself. Alluding to the Bible, he reminds his readers that "in the beginning, was the Word," and the illustration above his essay in the original publication shows a black prisoner with the word "FREE" where his prison identification number should be, a cigarette in one hand and a pencil in the other. An armed prison guard can be seen in the background, behind a chain link fence, scrutinizing the prisoner. The cigarette is visible to the guard, but the pencil is hidden, though clearly visible to us.[17] The Word that Baldwin refers to has two meanings: a supreme being, but also language itself. The way for prisoners to free themselves is to write.

The second essay published in *Time Capsule,* "This Far and No Further," published in 1983, is even more substantial and more defiant in terms of the power of prisoners and those who are criminalized to rise up against those who oppress them. Baldwin sees the situation historically and globally: "Every State, without exception, co-opts, corrupts, or destroys all those within its proclaimed jurisdiction—and sometimes, as in the present century beyond it—capable of saying 'No'" (*CR* 131–32). This "No" leads to the defiance of the title, which might be uttered by an accomplice, a prostitute, or the children of the State's victims. Baldwin argues again that "the State creates the Criminal, of every conceivable type and stripe, because the State cannot operate without the Criminal" (*CR* 132). In this paragraph he defines the criminal power of the state in such terms that individuals are not in control of their fate: their only choice, faced with the coercion of legal and governmental agencies, is to become "a Criminal accomplice or: a prisoner" (*CR* 132). Baldwin continues to draw important distinctions between criminals and prisoners, rendering them as well as the State and Society in archetypal terms, using capital letters to indicate this rhetorical device:

> If the State creates the Criminal and uses him, until—for reasons of State—it becomes necessary that he be, with extreme prejudice, terminated, it simply throws the Prisoner into Society's lap. This has the effect of reassuring Society that Society is being protected, while at the same time, causing him to hate the Prisoner (far more than he hates the Criminal) because the Prisoner—so he is told, every hour on the hour—is costing him an awful lot of money. (*CR* 132)

Baldwin relies on economics to continue to distinguish the Prisoner from the Criminal: the former is someone who got caught, the latter might be someone who never will, and in that case the latter is likely to be wealthy—a "white collar" criminal. He contends, "rare and spectacular it is that the Prisoner has been dragged from the seats of power." He uses Spanish dictator Franco as an example who was "never hauled before the moral Western tribunal on any charge" (*CR* 133). Baldwin feels the pressure to be drawn into the machinery that would keep society functioning. He retells an anecdote of flying thousands of miles to visit a friend in prison, presumably Tony Maynard when he was held in Germany, only to meet resistance from the warden. Baldwin was told to try to convince his incarcerated friend to cooperate with the prison by doing prison work at prison wages, rather than resisting such work and demanding to join a union. Baldwin concludes, "I do not pretend, in any way whatever, to be able to assess the price the person who is the prisoner pays: but I know that prisons do not rehabilitate because it is not their purpose and it is not in their power. One is not rehabilitated by learning to cooperate with the structure designed to debase the person into the Prisoner" (*CR* 134). Refusing to accept the rehabilitative role of prisons and penitentiaries, Baldwin puts the burden of society's problems not on prisoners, but on those who depend upon them: "The incarceration of the Prisoner reveals nothing about the Prisoner, but reveals volumes concerning those who hold the keys" (*CR* 134). The response is, again, an alliance between artists and prisoners and a combined defiance from both groups: "the Artist and the Prisoner must fight very hard against debasement and isolation. It is the responsibility of the Artist perpetually to question the zealous State and the narcoticized Society" (*CR* 134). This redefinition of the artist's role sets up Baldwin's final book-length essay, *The Evidence of Things Not Seen*.

Having immersed himself in the prison experience in *If Beale Street Could Talk*, Baldwin spent virtually no time in this setting in his final novel, *Just Above My Head*. In fact, Baldwin's longest novel has less to do with the law in any sense of the word than any of his others do. Still, it is a novel that straddles the struggle for civil rights, and Baldwin's familiar archetypes are evident here, just not as prominent. Hall Montana, the narrator, depicts a world characterized by individual and familial strife. As Baldwin says in an interview, "There are virtually no white [characters] in this novel,"[18] which puts his final novel in proximity with his first. The workings of white legal power and the white threat to black self-definition are thus muted in the novel, but they are clear. From the beginning, Hall is "ridiculously aware of the Sunday policemen, scattered sparsely over the landscape. I do not look at them. But I know that they see me. I know that they never expected to, never intended to, and are smoldering with the need to be revenged for this violation. *Up yours, mac, and I hope it puts a hurting on you:* but I do not usually feel this way" (*JA* 33). For a narrator of a Baldwin novel, Hall is surprisingly devoid of venom toward authority; at one point he admits, "I worried about cops and billy clubs" (*JA* 130), but he keeps this worry largely buried. In fact, when he is in a crowd welcoming his brother Arthur home from the army, he is able to intimidate the police rather than the other way around: "I looked at the cop, he looked at me: something in my look made him look around him, and look away" (*JA* 283). The intimidating gaze of the law enforcement officer is inverted here: Baldwin's narrator is the one with the power to intimidate. The law is not a very serious force in this book; when Hall talks to Arthur about his underage drinking, he phrases it, "So you been breaking the law already?" and Arthur replies, "Just a little light lawbreaking. Nothing extravagant" (*JA* 287).

Although the police and the prison experience do not achieve the threatening heights they scale in his earlier fiction, Baldwin uses this novel to revisit the impact of desegregation. In a debate between Paul, Florence, Peanut, Arthur, and Hall, Baldwin advances the idea that the laws ending segregation were not really passed out of any advanced moral position, but rather out of convenience, and black people did not need such laws to survive, to raise their children, and to love each other; Florence recalls, "I remember when you had to change trains in Washington and go to the Jim Crow car—when you wouldn't be allowed in the dining room until all the white folks was through. Well, of course, you don't want to eat with fools like that—but all that's changed. It don't mean I want to eat with white people. It just makes life a little easier—might make my children's lives a little easier" (*JA* 292). Peanut disagrees and voices his anger: "These people got the *gall* to claim to be giving us something they didn't never have the right to take away" (*JA* 292). The power of desegregation laws is under scrutiny here: whether or not they are beneficial, the question, according to Peanut, is a hypothetical one about history rather than the future. Paul and Florence, members of the older generation, try to instruct Peanut to refocus his position, and their son Arthur agrees: "Well, anyway . . . it ought to make things better in the schools" (*JA* 292). Peanut snorts at this, but Paul uses this opportunity to teach him something and to express, in essence, the idea of interest convergence central to Critical Race Theory:

> "Listen. You all are young. Like it or not, we here now and we can't go
> nowhere else. I was a kind of half-assed Garveyite when I was young—
> you would have been, too, had you been young when I was. . . . All I'm

saying is, you going to have to do what we've always done, ain't nothing new—take what you have, and make what you want."

He looked around the table, but especially at me.

"We didn't wait for white people to have a change of heart, or change their laws, or anything, in order to be responsible for each other, to love our women, or raise our children. You better not wait, either. They ain't going to change their laws for us—it just ain't in them. They change their laws when their laws make *them* uncomfortable, or when they think they can see some kind of advantage for *them*—we ain't, really, got nothing to do with it." (*JA* 293)

The two perspectives expressed here align with the younger Baldwin when he was witnessing desegregation laws in the 1950s and with the older Baldwin looking back on the effects of that era from the vantage of the 1970s. The law is not something that black people feel they have control over, in either case; the question is whether or not they feel the law has control over them. Florence elaborates: "You've got to depend on yourself. . . . The only reason we talking now is because it looks like they've decided to desegregate this and desegregate that. I hope they do. It might make life a little easier for you and little better for them. But we're not really talking about *them*: we talking about *us*. Whatever they do, honey, you still got your life to live. I'm glad you don't have to ride in no Jim Crow car, like me and your daddy had to do. But, Jim Crow car or no Jim Crow car, we still had to raise you—it was a good thing they changed the law, but we couldn't wait for that!" (*JA* 293). This position, clearly one to be listened to and respected, demonstrates a newfound empowerment in Baldwin's writing: the law is neither to be feared nor respected. Love is, finally, stronger.

This is not to say, though, that the law does not remain a force of intimidation. Immediately after the above conversation, Paul tells the story of how Julia Miller's father raped and beat her within an inch of her life; he recounts, "Somebody wanted to call the police, but I said, 'No, let me call the ambulance'" (*JA* 295). The police are thought not only to be inefficacious in this matter, but actually a threat; when Paul sees the apartment, he describes it as "a slaughterhouse, partly from whatever had gone on there that morning, and partly from the cops—they had turned out the joint, looking for anything but especially for dope" (*JA* 297). Far from protecting or healing the victim, the police are seen as responsible for perpetuating racial stereotypes and for using violence to do so. Even a black policeman is unsympathetic to the young victim; he says, "'If this chick's still breathing, she's lucky—must be they just didn't have no room up top for her yet'" (*JA* 297). Once the police do manage to find Joel, one of the most contemptible villains in Baldwin's *oeuvre,* they cannot "hold him" (*JA* 299) for lack of eyewitnesses and for lack of the testimony of Julia, who is initially unable to talk. Given the corruption and manipulation of eyewitnesses in *If Beale Street Could Talk,* this circumstance is bitterly ironic.

Baldwin's shift in emphasis from fear of the police toward an understanding of the workings of trials is especially clear in his final book, a work of nonfiction that struck many readers as an unlikely conclusion to his powerful and prodigious body of work. *The Evidence of Things Not Seen* is, stylistically, light-years away from the early essays and stories that earned Baldwin his fame and respect in the 1950s and early 1960s. A common response to Baldwin's career is that his powers failed him after the publication in 1963 of *The Fire Next Time.* For instance, Horace Porter writes, "[Baldwin] moves from the promethean figure, the man who stole the fire of 'Notes of a Native Son,' the powerful writer of *The Fire Next Time,* to the embittered and self-indulgent nay-sayer of *No Name in the Street* and *Evidence of Things Not Seen.*"[19] According to this response, *Evidence* was just another example of Baldwin out of his depth, and many readers dismissed it as inchoate, unfocused, and impenetrable. Even the most generous readers must admit is a confusing work. Yet the Baldwin scholar who attends to Baldwin's entire career might be more likely to see *Evidence* as the last in a long line of works that are increasingly complex not because Baldwin had spent his powers, but because the world he was writing about was increasingly complex. Moreover, the subject of *Evidence* was really nothing new for Baldwin, even if his voice had changed. In marked distinction to the sermon-inflected tone of *The Fire Next Time,* *Evidence* is framed, at times, by historical research, by a density of facts, and by legal rhetoric. In their 1994 preface to the paperback edition of *Evidence* Derrick Bell and Janet Dewart Bell write, "James Baldwin was not a lawyer" (*E* viii), which is of course true. Yet never in his life did Baldwin sound more like a lawyer than in this essay: from an in-depth discussion of the history of fingerprint and fiber evidence to a police-blotter list of the murdered children, Baldwin points to exhibit A and exhibit B as though he *were* a lawyer.

Despite this shift in voice in *The Evidence of Things Not Seen,* Baldwin is doing what he has always done, in fictional and nonfictional works: that is, uniting the personal, the historical, and the national. Baldwin regards the law as the very substance of white power, which systematically destroys the American dreams of unity, freedom, equality, and unmitigated respect for the individual. His complex definitions of equality and freedom in *Evidence* are inseparable from his complex definition of power. Unlike many of Baldwin's imprisoned characters, Wayne Williams is like Sonny in "Sonny's Blues" in that they actually did commit the crimes of which they are accused; but in these cases Baldwin dismisses the reality of the crime and its punishment in favor of its implications.

The Evidence of Things Not Seen has been taken seriously and put into the contexts of democratic theory and the law in recent work by Lawrie Balfour and Richard Schur. Baldwin's essay is a shadowy presence in a recent essay in PMLA by Eric Gary Anderson, "Black Atlanta: An Eco-social Approach to Narratives of the Atlanta Child Murders," though many of the assumptions of Anderson's argument are evident in Baldwin's essay, including "the ecological as well as the social implications of crimes against blacks in the South, including the urban South."[20] Anderson's argument develops an observation made by Amiri Baraka (then Leroi Jones) in *Blues People* that contends that, for African Americans, "the southern and the criminal have been and will always continue to be linked."[21] Although this idea can be traced from Baldwin's writings beginning with "Nobody Knows My Name" through "Going to Meet the Man" and into *Evidence,* he certainly doesn't confine his critique to the South in this book. His ideas apply to national crimes and beyond, linking America to South Africa, which was undergoing its revolution before the world's eyes when Baldwin published his book.

Richard Schur has provided the most thorough criticism yet of *Evidence* in the context of the law; he writes,

> If previous generations of African American storytellers emphasized the injustice of *substantive* law, such as property and criminal law, Baldwin and [Toni] Morrison focus on the injustice of legal *processes* for eliciting testimony and recognizing the credibility of that testimony. This shift speaks to a generational shift in emphasis or tone from civil-rights-era tactics for legal reform (changing the substance of the law) to post-civil-rights-era concerns about the unconscious racism of legal discourse (the faulty process of law).[22]

What interests me is how Baldwin was once defined as a member of the "previous generations" Schur describes. In other words, the generational shift Schur ably identifies also marks a shift in Baldwin. Critics who complained that Baldwin was merely rehashing old ideas in his later works completely miss the point that he was trying, in all earnestness, to change with the times as well as to change the times. If he tried to reach out to a younger readership by narrating *Beale Street* from a 19-year-old's perspective, in *Evidence* he was clearly trying to speak from a position of authority as someone who had lived through history, survived to tell the tale, and could offer wisdom based on his experience as well as his interpretation of events. In terms of the law, this shift takes the form of appropriating legal rhetoric to fight the law itself.

In *Evidence* Baldwin carefully but narrowly sidesteps the precarious position of the public defender who must stand up for the monsters of society—the role of Boris Max in *Native Son*. To accomplish this delicate balancing act, Baldwin must convince the reader that convicted murderer Wayne Williams is not on trial in this book; the American legal system is. In *No Name in the Street* Baldwin writes, "I do claim that the law, as it operates, is guilty, and that the prisoners, therefore, are all unjustly imprisoned." He goes on to say, "if one really wishes to know how justice is administered in a country, one does not question the policemen, the lawyers, the judges, or the protected members of the middle class. One goes to the unprotected—those, precisely, who need the law's protection most!—and listens to their testimony. Ask any Mexican, any Puerto Rican, and black man, and poor person—ask the wretched how they fare in the halls of justice, and then you will know, not whether or not the country is just, but whether or not it has any love for justice, or any concept of it" (*NN* 148–49). This observation serves as the foundation for Baldwin's extended meditation on race, power, class, and geopolitics in *Evidence*.

From the title on, Baldwin focuses on "evidence" not as the truth, as he says throughout his career, but as that which is merely evident. Evidence becomes something to be interpreted, for Baldwin, and is linked in the title to the crucial concept of invisibility. As Schur writes, "For Baldwin, this failure [of courts] to realize the goal of the civil rights movement followed from law's myopic vision of social life. Courts, judges, and juries could 'see' only what their life experiences had conditioned them to see."[23] Late in the essay Baldwin discusses the role of the writer in similar terms: "a writer is never listening to what is being said, he is never listening to what he is being told. He is listening to what is *not* being said, he is listening to what he is *not* being told" (*E* 95). The role of the writer can be augmented: once he has discerned these "things not seen" or heard, he is then to *tell* someone else what has not been said or told, which is precisely the role Baldwin takes throughout the essay, no matter what the subject is. Of course, the subject varies widely: Wayne Williams and the Atlanta child murders are an occasion for Baldwin to meditate on the desperate, multi-layered situation of oppression in contemporary America.

Far from being intimidated by the police here, Baldwin barely acknowledges them. He has set his sights higher—on the entire justice system that accords police officers their power. He states, with cool detachment, that "the role of the White cop is a necessary American invention" (E xvi), entertaining the possibility that the policeman is nothing more than an actor ("role") or an artificial construction, like a robot ("invention"). In Paris he, as prisoner, had been reduced to a rag doll; this description is perhaps his retaliation for such dehumanization, but he has had to pay a price for this understanding. His journey from victim to intellectual analyst has been a long one, but he now has command of history, of technology, and of legal discourse in a way he never did before. All of this can be marshaled forth as he performs his cultural analysis of Reagan's America. The very first thing he does is to raise the possibility that even juries and judges selected supposedly at random might be tainted by the humanness of this process: "everyone appeared to suspect that this particular computer had had its own reasons for selecting this particular judge" (E 1). He goes on to say, "Each of us knows, though we do not like this knowledge, that a courtroom is a visceral Roman circus. No one involved in this contest is, or can be, impartial" (E 1). So much for legal objectivity. Baldwin uses expansive pronouns in these pronouncements: everyone, each of us, no one. The clear implication is that the law, as a democratic institution, is subject not only to the strengths of a population, but to its weaknesses as well. Thus, a society plagued by prejudice cannot help but produce a prejudiced legal and judicial system.

Baldwin reveals his perspective using the same terms: "It is one thing to be part of the audience at the courtroom Roman circus, and quite another matter to be in the ring. The audience is there to distract or justify itself with questions of right or wrong. The gladiators know only that one of them must win. They are not suspending judgment. They are *creating* judgment: ours" (E 2). The pronouns are again crucial here: there is an audience and "gladiators," or players. There is a "they" and an "us." Baldwin has, of course, been "in the ring" in Paris, and is thus aware of the cruel laughter of the audience and the humiliation of the person on trial. He is now also aware of the other gladiators: the police, the lawyers, and the judges. He gives all of them due consideration as human beings in *The Evidence of Things Not Seen*, for, if "no one involved in this contest can be impartial," it is important to be aware of the personalities involved and the prejudices they bear. Baldwin also seeks to give us a portrait of the primary player in the ring, the accused murderer Wayne Williams, who does not come across as an admirable character in any sense: Baldwin describes him as "authoritative and puny . . . demanding and remote" but also adds that these characteristics are magnified because we are studying Williams "on the witness stand" (*E* 19). Baldwin is opening up a particularly repugnant can of worms in trying to look deeper into a case involving the murder of twenty-eight children, for the reader's visceral reactions are likely to interfere with his or her ability to follow Baldwin's intellectual moves around the case. Baldwin seeks to clarify his purpose roughly halfway into the essay: "The accused may be guilty, for all I know, but I fail to see his guilt as proven. Others may see American progress in economic, racial, and social affairs—I do not. I pray to be proven wrong, but I see the opposite, with murderous implications, and not only in North America" (*E* 56). It is too easy to scapegoat Wayne Williams, Baldwin believes, and to see the case of the Atlanta child murders as closed, just as it is too easy to assume that there has been "American progress in economic, racial, and social affairs." Baldwin's primary goal is to complicate any conclusions that are too easy, or too conclusive. He does not believe in open-and-shut cases.

Assuming the voice and rhetorical stance of a lawyer, Baldwin repeatedly shows the difference between accusation and assumption, more specifically, between the crimes Wayne Williams was tried for and the crimes he is assumed to have committed:

> The Black man who has been tried for two murders and—for the moment—condemned as the mass murderer of Black children is an odd creature: but so would you or I be, sitting on the witness stand, under such an aura. He is not, literally or legally, *accused* of being a mass murderer: but he is the only suspect, and he is *assumed* to be a mass murderer.
>
> Once under suspicion, and so dreadful a suspicion, everything the person does is intolerably suspect—beginning, perhaps, with his intolerable assumption that he has any right to be born. It is much, much simpler, after all, and more considerate, for the accused to agree, at once, to be guilty. (*E* 9)

Baldwin believes that there is a world of difference between the accusation actually leveled at Williams—for two murders, and those not technically of "children," as he insists—and the assumption that the jury and the public in general are led to believe—that Williams is guilty of murdering all twenty-eight of the missing children who together comprise the Atlanta Child Murders. He makes much of the fact that the prosecution is trying to establish a pattern, and that Williams's conviction is sufficient to prove that there was a pattern, that the conviction will put an end to the murders or disappearances, and that Atlanta, the "city too busy to hate," can return to its prosperity, which (according to popular belief) has everything to do with hard work and nothing to do with race. Armed with the latest technology and attorneys who can construct a convincing story that frames Williams, the prosecution has the power to "solve" the case and to bring much-needed closure to an anxious public.

Perhaps this closure is one of the functions of the legal system, but Baldwin smells something rotten at the core of the Williams case, namely, the smugness of a system that is based on the relentless pursuit of the truth and yet resorts to a kind of three-card monte game to convince the public that it is safe from a monster such as Williams. The truth of the case, according to Baldwin, goes much deeper than what is told in a courtroom and summarized in newspapers. At times he is quite literal about the shortcomings of this trial: "If [Williams] is *not* being tried for twenty-eight murders, it can only be, after all, for lack of evidence. How, then, does it happen—legally—that a man charged with *two* murders can be tried for twenty-eight?" (*E* 12). At other times, his analysis is expansive to the point that the Williams trial is beside the point: the essay becomes much more about the historical failings of Western democracies, about the anemic culture of America that is at the mercy of corporations and their advertisers, and about religious hypocrisy. The Williams case is an opportunity to meditate on all these subjects, and many more.

The courtroom trial, and Baldwin's courtroom language,[24] serve a much broader purpose than just to indict the American justice system in practice. The ultimate point of Baldwin's argument has to do with power: murder trials, race, international trade, the history of slavery, and all of the other myriad sub-topics of *Evidence* are about power. In the following passage, he moves from a specific critique of judicial practice to a broad critique of power: "This species of circumstantial evidence (the 'fiber' evidence, to be considered) is, itself, unprecedented in the legal history of the United States. Not only is it unprecedented: it is, also, *scientific.* This can be taken to mean that the layman (in this case, the jury), who may or may not be able to understand it, will certainly not be able to understand it well enough to be able to challenge or refute it. And it must be added, too, however one may wish to avoid this, or deny it, that the history and the situation of Black people in this country amounts to an indictment of

America's legal and moral history" (*E* 12–13). Baldwin insists throughout the essay that we make such difficult connections: here the tool of power is understanding. If juries do not fully understand the science behind fiber evidence or fingerprinting, their judgment can be manipulated by those who do (broadly, the state; more narrowly, lawyers). If Americans in general don't understand the realities of minority groups because these experiences are either unseen or not seen, the entire legal system reveals itself to be similarly flawed.

Baldwin's point has largely to do with perception, and with a certain simplistic way of thinking that is anathema to what he believes as the hope for the American future. As Richard Schur writes, "Baldwin announces a new terrain for the fight for freedom and equality: the realm of perception. As described by Baldwin, perception operates prior to rationality and impedes impartial judgment. Our preconceived notions 'tyrannize' our logical faculties."[25] Critiquing the American way of thinking and the American legal system at the same time, Baldwin writes, "there is nothing that won't, under pressure, establish a 'pattern,' and, once one begins looking for a 'pattern,' this 'pattern' will prove anything you want it to prove" (*E* 15). This pressure either originates from or is exacerbated by the criminal power of the law; he goes on to say that, if he were forced to explain his presence on a certain bridge, as Williams did, "I might have had many reasons, all of them, from my own point of view, guilty, or private: these two words being, very often, alas, synonyms among us. I also know that I might not have wished to explain anything at all to the cops. I was certainly like that when I was young and I am not so very different now" (*E* 16). It is striking here that "guilt," a word that precipitates conviction in a court of law, is equated with "privacy," one of America's most cherished ideals, and yet one that is routinely threatened in Baldwin's works. In the stark light and under the magnifying glass of courtroom scrutiny, the truth can somehow be distorted rather than illuminated. This motif has been consistent throughout his career. The witnesses to crimes in *Go Tell It,* in *Tell Me,* and in *Beale Street* all claim to have seen something that did not exist: a black man committing a crime. In this case, where we are presented with a black man who has committed a crime, Baldwin provides the opposite of claiming to have seen something that does not exist: hence, his title.

Much of the evidence he provides is historical. The reality of the African American experience is directly related to legal status. He reminds his reader, "Our first sight of America was this marketplace and our legal existence, here, begins with the signature on the bill of sale" (*E* 29).[26] In this sentence he is attempting to deflate any exuberance that might have arisen over American prosperity, or the prosperity of such nations as South Africa which, in the 1980s, provided a clear example of the principle that a nation's wealth has always been "extorted out of the flesh of their Black slaves" (*E* 29). For Baldwin, this situation is not merely historical, and it relates to the definition of citizenship in this democracy: "Blacks have never been, and are not now, really considered to be citizens here. Blacks exist, in the American imagination, and in relation to American institutions, in reference to the slave codes: the first legal recognition of our presence remains the most compelling. This is why each generation has been forced to insist, at mounting pressure—and higher cost—on 'civil' rights: a revealing demand, indeed, from a citizen!" (*E* 31). The word "pressure" is again at the heart of Baldwin's critique, and this pressure certainly does not exonerate Wayne Williams, but it may go a long way toward explaining him. The pressure comes from "American institutions" revealed in constitutional law, and this is the criminal power that should also be put on trial.

The pressure is exerted by the wealthy, presumably to protect property. Baldwin reserves part of his critique for those who believe that the presence of blacks in a neighborhood lowers property values, and that "white flight" has nothing to do with this devaluation. He arrives at a definition of wealth, like legal influence, in terms of power: "Wealth is the power to influence or to change the city's zoning laws, or the insurance rates or the actuarial tables they apply to Blacks or the textbook industry or the father-to-son labor unions or the composition of the grand juries and the boards of education. Wealth is the power to make one's needs felt and to force a response to those needs" (*E* 38). This is a scrupulous critique that connects the legal system to other institutions and that debunks the myth of "the magic of the marketplace" as something that is separate from such institutions. In Reagan-era America, with the divide between wealthy and poor becoming increasingly sharper, such an observation was necessary, and was likely to provoke Baldwin's readers regardless of race.

The terror of the poor young man who had been thrown in jail, reduced to a "rag doll," and who nearly killed himself because his friend stole a sheet, has changed and matured considerably. Throughout his career he replays this terror, examines it from many angles, and gives it due consideration, but eventually moves on. The law, he concludes, is not terrifying. The feeling of powerlessness in the face of it is. In order to conquer that feeling, Baldwin relies on his experience, his intellect, his artistry, and the legends of his people. Forty years after he nearly died defeated in a Paris hotel, he died defiant, above the law's power rather than at its mercy.

From Death Row to the Beer Summit

VIRTUALLY the same year Baldwin wrote "Equal in Paris," W. E. B. Du Bois wrote a pair of essays called "The Trial" and "The Acquittal" in which he details his own experience with the American judicial system, albeit in the more politicized context of the HUAC hearings. Du Bois begins these essays with the same feeling of intimidation Baldwin felt; he writes, "I have faced during my life many unpleasant experiences: the growl of a mob; the personal threat of murder; the scowling distaste of an audience. But nothing has so cowed me as that day, November 8, 1951, when I took my seat in a Washington courtroom as an indicted criminal. I was not a criminal. I had broken no law, consciously or unwittingly. . . . Juries are selected in devious ways and by secret manipulation. Most Negroes are sent to jail by persons who hate or despise them."[1] As perhaps the preeminent African American man of letters at the time, a literary lion with a PhD from Harvard, Du Bois was in a very different position from the young Baldwin, yet the power of the legal system to intimidate reduces both to the same state and places them in a position where the only recourse they have to resist their fate is to write about it afterwards, if they live to tell the tale. Du Bois recognizes that the justice system is flawed because of "the lack of attention on the part of the respectable public to the procedures of court trials." The general public, he feels, "keep[s] as far from courts as possible and let[s] flagrant and cruel injustice escape without remark or attention."[2] Secure in his position following the trial, Du Bois writes "The Trial" and "The Acquittal" as a way of enlightening his audience. The 25-year-old Baldwin, barely cognizant of the implications of his wrongful imprisonment and fragile enough to have been driven to the brink of suicide, spent virtually the rest of his career working to get to Du Bois's perspective and elaborating on it considerably as he became increasingly aware of all of the dimensions of the law's power and its implications for African Americans fighting not only for civil rights, but for survival, self-respect, a stable identity, and a power greater than that of the law.

I write this conclusion during the presidency of Barack Obama, the first African American president—a circumstance that was unimaginable in Baldwin's lifetime just a few decades ago. The other day a student asked me if I thought Baldwin's attitude toward race relations would be different if he were alive today, and I have no doubt that she was thinking of President Obama when she asked the question. Baldwin would have applauded Obama's ascendancy; and yet, it is clear that he would not have become complacent as a result of Obama's election. The success of prominent figures in a historically disenfranchised group can in fact obscure the realities of the vast majority of that group. Baldwin would be the first to point out that Obama's election does not mean we have moved into a harmonious, brave new future in which we can all just get along, to paraphrase Rodney King. Baldwin would merely have to open the doors of any jail or prison in the country to make his point.

And yet, of course, very few people open the doors to prisons. In America, perhaps even more so now than in Baldwin's lifetime, reality doesn't exist for most Americans until it happens to a celebrity. It took the arrest of the most prominent African American scholar in the country, Henry Louis Gates, Jr., to bring the issue of racism and wrongful arrest into the American consciousness.

In fact, Gates's arrest might have been confined to a local and/or academic-interest story if President Obama had not made public, unguarded comments about the situation. Gates was arrested on July 16, 2009 upon returning to his Cambridge, Massachusetts home after a research trip to China. A neighbor called the police to report that two black men (Gates and his driver) were lurking around the home, which Gates had rented for the semester. After being initially questioned and asked for identification, Gates reacted to the officers on call, yelling repeatedly, "Is this how you treat a black man in America?"[3] The confrontation between them escalated and Gates was arrested for disorderly conduct. Before he had gathered sufficient information about the circumstances of the arrest, President Obama described the behavior of the Cambridge, Massachusetts police department as "stupid." After learning that the arresting officer had acted in accordance with his department's policy, Obama apologized, and allegations began to flow through the media indicating that Gates had perhaps antagonized the officer. The three men met privately (joined by Vice President Biden) at the White House in what became known as "the beer summit," an attempt to tamp down any racial conflagration that threatened to spread from this unfortunate event.

It is not my intention to take sides on this issue, nor to speculate about what was said at the so-called "beer summit," or what more might have been said if the summit had not occurred. I do want to point out that two very prominent black men, the intellectual heirs to Baldwin, reacted hastily and emotionally to Gates's arrest that night. The actual circumstances of the arrest are less important to my analysis than what both Obama and Gates initially felt. Black men, in short, know that what happened to Baldwin in Paris *could* happen to them. Laws may change in response to the culture that they govern or acutely observe, but cultures don't change because the law says they should. Even the most powerful members of a relatively powerless group feel this.

In an article comparing Obama to Baldwin, Irish novelist Colm Tóibín observes, "Baldwin made it clear that the black experience in America could not be described using merely political terms; it could not be dealt with as a set of demands that could simply be satisfied by legislation."[4] This is a valid observation about Baldwin and the law, and yet as I hope I have demonstrated here, it only begins to tell the story of Baldwin's position regarding the law. Legislation was certainly not everything to Baldwin, but it was undoubtedly something, and its connection to law enforcement and to court trials weighed heavily on his imagination. His interrogation of the law certainly evolved, but it remained in a state of flux. Ultimately, Baldwin scrutinized the law with the type of skepticism with which he regarded anything or anyone that attempted to define him. To be labeled a "criminal," as Baldwin felt he was in Paris, was a challenge to turn that label against those in power, to in fact call it a criminal power, and to make that claim stick. Baldwin's ability to rise above the law, to regard it as something he had control over as opposed to something that controlled him, derived from what he knew to be his most valuable abilities: to write and to speak. Barack Obama and Henry Louis Gates have also demonstrated their prodigious gifts in these areas. Yet were Baldwin alive in the twenty-first century, his concern would certainly be for those who have not found their voice, or whose voices echo around the prison cells that they regard as their fate—not necessarily the Bigger Thomases whose lack of self-knowledge causes them to be used as political pawns and racial symbols, but the Sonnys, the Fonnys, the Richards from his own fictions whose very humanity seems at the mercy of the justice system and of the society that has created it and replicated it in so many subtle ways.

At the James Baldwin Conference at Queen Mary University in 2007, Tóibín presented a thoroughly researched overview of Baldwin's neglected nonfiction, the bits and scraps of uncollected work that provide valuable insight into the ever-expanding portrait of Baldwin the writer. Toward the end of his talk he praised Baldwin's prescience as a social critic, but indicated that Baldwin had been naive about incarceration, citing as evidence Baldwin's observation from a 1963 interview (discussed in chapter 3) that "there are 20 million Negro people in this country, and you can't put them all in jail."[5] Tóibín felt that Baldwin had failed to see the depth of this crisis as it has evolved in the past half-century. I debated briefly with him about this point, and I continue to feel strongly that Baldwin understood the social implications of what I have described in detail throughout this study: that the law can be unjust, and that revolutions are one effective way to combat such injustice.

Tóibín graciously conceded my point; and yet, something about his words continues to nag me. As Derrick and Janet Dewart Bell point out in their introduction to *Evidence,* the crisis of black incarceration was to get much worse even between Baldwin's death in 1987 and their introduction in 1994: "As a direct result of the closing off of access to legal employment, 80 to 85 percent of black men in urban areas will be caught up in the criminal 'justice' system, most on drug-related charges, before they reach their thirtieth birthday—if they are lucky enough to live that long. The number of black men in prison now exceeds 800,000, the largest number of any country in the world. That number is expected to reach one million before the year 2000" (*E* x). According to H. Bruce Franklin, since 1975, the year after the publication of *Beale Street,* until 2008, the number of inmates in jails and prisons in the United States has grown from 360,000 to over 2.4 million, "almost twenty-five percent of all the prisoners in the world. During these thirty-three years, this country has constructed on average one new prison every week."[6] Tóibín's point, as I now see it, was not necessarily that Baldwin was completely naive about incarceration, but rather that he could not have foreseen the meteoric rate of incarceration, disproportionately for young black men, that has occurred since his death in 1987.

I'm not sure anyone could have. Even in the midst of this mind-numbing rise in incarceration, one is hard pressed to comprehend it. What Baldwin can continue to teach us, though, is that it is imperative for anyone who is largely oblivious to the power of the law to listen to the stories of the individuals who collectively comprise these statistics. The numbers that Franklin and many others present are so staggering to the reader that the response may be simply to shudder, or to fail to fathom what the numbers mean. Baldwin's life work forces our comprehension by demonstrating the gradual transformation of one brilliant if fragile man who nearly died in obscurity in a Paris prison as his career was just beginning into one who could speak confidently about the nuances of legal power in both imaginative and nonfictional contexts.

We tend to think of revolutions as violent, even bloody. In the context of the law over the past half-century, "revolution" connotes the Black Power movement, the Attica uprising of 1971, or the so-called Rodney King riots of 1992. These recognizable moments of violent resistance are one way to rage against the injustice of a system that unfairly imprisons black men, but the trajectory of Baldwin's life suggests that there are other ways. Through a lifetime of working to understand the implications of his demeaning experience in a Paris jail and all of the manifestations of legal power that radiate outward from that event, Baldwin's life can be seen as a revolution of a less violent kind, a revolution of thinking that would transform those who are intimidated to the point of suicidal despair into mature, complex, wide-ranging thinkers about the subject of legal power. Baldwin's career is instructive not as the final word about how to cope with racism in legal contexts, but rather as a reflection of the value of emotional and intellectual struggle when such racism presents itself. Baldwin's response to the law's injustice was increasingly intellectual and decreasingly emotional. *If Beale Street Could Talk* is a turning point: the rage that turns one character (Fonny's father) suicidal has its counterpart in the hopefulness of the next generation, and despite all of the frustrations and perhaps even failure that occur along the way, the efforts of Tish's mother and sister to fight the law through legal and even illegal means are noble.

Nearly a decade into the twenty-first century, the law's power has grown. The USA PATRIOT Act—a sweeping tome of legislation passed by Congress in the aftermath of the 2001 terror attacks—has proven just how easily the United States government can override the legal rights of its citizens, and even foreigners, in the name of national safety. Images of tortured inmates at the Abu Ghraib prison during the U.S. occupation of Iraq are vivid examples of the nation's flouting of basic rights in the contemporary world. Arizona's anti-immigration legislation of 2010 was recently deemed unconstitutional, but only after it had been enacted long enough to remind people of color that they had to prove their very citizenship with documentation upon request. California's "three strikes" legislation has had the effect of punishing petty criminals who do not have access to influential lawyers as though they had committed much more serious crimes. In one of his last published works, "Staggerlee Wonders," the most substantial poem in the collection *Jimmy's Blues,* Baldwin's speaker sardonically comments on the state of contemporary America: "Up to our ass in niggers / on Death Row" (*JB* 10). Ripping hard into the naïveté and complacency of 1980s America, Baldwin's Staggerlee, a legendary badman figure who terrified everyone, including judges and policeman, because of his vengeful nature, uses Baldwin's rhetoric to reverse the terms of criminality. White, Western civilization, according to Staggerlee, is based on a corrupt history, a series of broken treaties. He wonders, "perhaps they imagine / that their crimes are not crimes?" (*JB* 13). He envisions "the single eye of God" staring critically at America and yearns for a primal, cleansing response to the corruption of history: "creation yearns to re-create a time / when we were able to recognize a crime" (*JB* 18). As the poem builds to its prophetic conclusion, Staggerlee, like his fellow "niggers" who "are calculating," resolves to distance himself from his nation because they have different definitions of criminality: "we don't need you, / are sick of being a fantasy to feed you, / and of being the principal accomplice to your crime: / for, it is *your* crime, now" (*JB* 22). The criminal power he identified in "Down at the Cross" is fully an accusation here, and the accused must reckon with the charge.

Baldwin has often been identified with two related terms: prophet and witness. Both terms connote vision, the first in a mystical or religious sense, and the second, it could be argued, in a legal sense. Both are apt terms. And yet, writing to Angela Davis in prison he takes pains to claim that his role is not merely to see: "I do not [speak] from the position of a spectator."[7] He was also at times on the front lines of the struggle, reporting from occupied territory, in the title of his 1966 essay. At other times he was both the seeing subject and the seen subject, the "eye" and the "I." Baldwin had the capacity to be inside and outside at the same time, to explore surface and depth, to feel and to describe feelings. The facets of his identity that have made it difficult for critics and literary historians to unify his career are ultimately less important than this unique gift: to be an artist, to experience, then to articulate that experience. Yet artists, even those in perpetual exile, do not exist apart from their societies. Baldwin's experience was shaped according to specific changes in the way legal power was distributed, manipulated, and enforced during his lifetime. This power was undeniably distributed unevenly from the point of view of someone who grew up poor, bisexual, and black. As other critics explore other such forces, we will continue to gain appreciation for this gifted, varied, and complex writer.

NOTES

Introduction

1. David Leeming, *James Baldwin* (New York: Alfred A. Knopf, 1994), 72.

2. He also worked on a teleplay describing the incident with Sol Stein; also titled "Equal in Paris," it was never produced, but Stein recently published it in his book *Native Sons* (New York: One World/Ballantine, 2005).

3. H. Bruce Franklin, *The Victim as Criminal and Artist* (New York: Oxford University Press, 1978), xxii.

4. James Boyle, ed., *Critical Legal Studies* (New York: New York University Press, 1992), xiv.

5. Robert W. Gordon, "Critical Legal Studies." *Readings in the Philosophy of Law,* 3rd ed., eds. John Arthur and William H. Shaw (Upper Saddle River, NJ: Prentice Hall, 2001), 198.

6. Gordon, 198–200. See also David Kairys's introduction to *The Politics of Law: A Progressive Critique,* rev. ed. (New York, Pantheon, 1990), 1–9.

7. Kairys, 5.

8. Peter Gabel and Paul Harris, "Building Power and Breaking Images: Critical Legal Theory and the Practice of Law," *Review of Law and Social Change* 11 (1982–1983): 370.

9. Barry R. Schaller, *A Vision of American Law* (Westport, CT: Praeger, 1997), 5.

10. Gabel and Harris, 371.

11. Cornel West, foreword to *Critical Race Theory: The Key Writings that Formed the Movement,* ed. Kimberlé Crenshaw et al. (New York: The New Press, 1995), xi.

12. Crenshaw et al., xiv.

13. See West, xi and Crenshaw et al., xxv.

14. Patricia J. Williams, *Alchemy of Race and Rights* (Cambridge, MA: Harvard University Press, 1992), 149.

15. Williams, 152.

16. Crenshaw et al., xiii.

17. Gabel and Harris, 371.

18. Gabel and Harris, 372.

19. Gabel and Harris, 373–74.

20. Jon-Christian Suggs, *Whispered Consolations: Law and Narrative in African American* Life (Ann Arbor: University of Michigan Press, 2000), 8.

21. Suggs, 16.

22. Suggs, 311.

23. Gregg D. Crane, *Race, Citizenship, and Law in American Literature* (Cambridge: Cambridge University Press, 2002).

24. Robert M. Cover, "Nomos and Narrative," *Harvard Law Review* 97.1 (Nov. 1983): 45.

25. Richard A. Posner, ed., *Law and Literature,* rev. and enlarged ed. (Cambridge, MA and London: Cambridge University Press, 1988), 22.

26. Fern Marja Eckman, *The Furious Passage of James Baldwin* (London: Michael Joseph, 1966).

27. W. J. Weatherby, *James Baldwin: Artist on Fire* (New York: Donald I. Fine, 1989), xiii.

28. Herb Boyd, *Baldwin's Harlem: A Biography of James Baldwin* (New York: Atria, 2008).

29. James Campbell, *Talking at the Gates* (New York: Viking, 1991). Leeming 72.

30. Trudier Harris, *Black Women in the Fiction of James Baldwin* (Knoxville: University of Tennessee Press, 1985); Trudier Harris, *New Essays on Go Tell It on the Mountain* (New York: Cambridge University Press, 1999); Lynn Orilla Scott, *James Baldwin's Later Fiction: Witness to the Journey* (East Lansing: Michigan State University Press, 2002); Magdalena Zaborowska, *James Baldwin's Turkish Decade: The Erotics of Exile* (Durham and London: Duke University Press, 2009).

31. Fred L. Standley and Nancy V. Burt, eds., *Critical Essays on James Baldwin* (Boston: G. K. Hall and Co., 1988), 95.

32. Robert A. Bone, *The Negro Novel in America* (New Haven: Yale University Press, 1965), 215.

33. Fred L. Standley and Louis H. Pratt, eds., *Conversations with James Baldwin* (Jackson and London: University Press of Mississippi, 1989), 284.

34. Horace Porter, *Stealing the Fire: the Art and Protest of James Baldwin* (Middletown, CT: Wesleyan University Press, 1989), 12.

35. Campbell, 203.

36. Standley and Burt, 155.

37. Standley and Burt, 166.

38. Standley and Burt, 94.

39. Lovalerie King and Lynn Orilla Scott, *James Baldwin and Toni Morrison: Comparative Critical and Theoretical Essays* (New York: Palgrave Macmillan, 2006).

40. Dwight McBride, ed., *James Baldwin Now* (New York: New York University Press, 1999); D. Quentin Miller, ed., *Re-Viewing James Baldwin: Things Not Seen* (Philadelphia: Temple University Press, 2000).

41. Carolyn Wedin Sylvander, *James Baldwin* (New York: Frederick Ungar, 1980), 18.

42. Peter Caster, *Prisons, Race, and Masculinity in Twentieth-Century U.S. Literature and Film* (Columbus: The Ohio State University Press, 2008), 22.

Chapter 1

1. Michael Hames-Garcia, *Fugitive Thought: Prison Movements, Race, and the Meaning of Justice* (Minneapolis and London: University of Minnesota Press, 2004), 19.

2. Ian Haney-López, *White by Law: The Legal Construction of Race* (New York and London: New York University Press, 1996), 1.

3. Haney-López, 8.

4. Haney-López, 10.

5. Ariela Gross, *What Blood Won't Tell: A History of Race in America* (Cambridge, MA and London, Harvard University Press, 2008), 8.

6. Gross, 8.

7. Haney-López, 10.

8. The phrase "driving while black" has become common, and it was the title of at least four books published in the first decade of the twenty-first century. See especially Kenneth Meeks, *Driving While Black* (New York: Broadway Books, 2000).

9. Malcolm X did not necessarily romanticize prison itself, though. He admits that he "wasn't framed. I went to prison for what I did," but he also says, "I firmly believe that it was the Christian society, as you call it, the Judaic-Christian society, that created all of the factors that send so many so-called Negroes to prison. And when these fellows go to prison there is nothing in the system designed to rehabilitate them. There's nothing in the system designed to reform them. All it does is—it's a breeding ground for a more professional type of criminal, especially among Negroes." Kenneth B. Clark, *King, Malcolm, Baldwin: Three Interviews* (Middletown, CT: Wesleyan University Press, 1985), 38. Malcolm X, with Alex Haley, *The Autobiography of Malcolm X* (1965, New York: One World / Ballantine Books, 1999).

10. It is important to note that King's prison experiences involved racially segregated jails, even a decade after the *Brown vs. Board of Education* decision; when Kenneth Clark asks him in a 1963 interview, "Have you ever been in an integrated jail? In the South?" King responds, "No, that's one experience I haven't had yet." The irony that jails were among the last public institutions in the United States to be integrated is self-evident. Clark puts the same question to Malcolm X in the same year about a northern prison; Malcolm responds, "It was an integrated prison at the prison level, but the administrators were all white" (Clark, 22–23, 36).

11. Martin Luther King, "Letter From Birmingham Jail" in *Why We Can't Wait* (New York: Signet, 1963), 72.

12. Franklin, 147, 148.

13. Franklin, 133.

14. Leeming, 24, 16.

15. Campbell, 25.

16. Campbell, 60.

17. Campbell, 90–91.

18. Cornel West, *Race Matters* (Boston: Beacon Press, 1993), 14.

19. Michel Foucault, *Discipline and Punish*, trans. Alan Sheridan (New York: Vintage, 1995), 197.

20. Caster, 13, 16.

21. Suggs, 26.

22. Crane, 58.

23. In a 1980 speech he said, "I was dealing with cops before I was seven years old" (*CR* 126).

24. David Delaney, *Race, Place, and the Law* (Austin: University of Texas Press, 1998) 181.

25. Delaney, 150.

26. Standley and Burt, 96.

27. Miller, 77.

28. Foucault, 143.

29. Foucault, 237.

Chapter 2

1   See also Scott Malcolmson, *One Drop of Blood* (New York: Farrar, Strauss, Giroux, 2000).

2. See Haney-López, 117–18.

3. Haney-López, 119.

4. Leeming, 133.

5. Foucault, 141.

6. Foucault, 149–56 and 162–69.

7. Standley and Burt, 149.

8. Keneth Kinnamon, *James Baldwin: A Collection of Critical Essays* (Englewood Cliffs, NJ: Prentice-Hall, 1974), 60.

9. Emmanuel Nelson, "Critical Deviance: Homophobia and the Reception of James Baldwin's Fiction," *Journal of American Culture* 14.3 (1991): 91.

10. McBride, 163.

11. Miller, 90.

12. Miller, 88.

13. Standley and Pratt, 23.

14. *Another Country,* though a best-seller, has been denounced by critics and reviewers as unwieldy. George E. Kent, for example, writing in *CLA Journal,* assessed the novel this way: "*Another Country* . . . is a serious and ambitious attempt, a fact which should be recognized despite the fact that to make it a serious novel of the first rank would demand severe cutting and some intensive re-writing" (Kinnamon, 25). Robert Bone calls it "a failure on a grand scale" (Kinnamon, 41).

15. Perhaps not coincidentally, Baldwin's own moment of suicidal despair in prison occurred, like Rufus's, just before Christmas.

16. Leeming, 145.

17. Posner, 22, 23.

18. Leeming, 234.

19. Eckman, 225.

20. Bone, 216.

21. Leeming, 238.

22. Kinnamon, 110.

23. James Peck, *Freedom Ride* (New York: Simon and Schuster, 1962), 78.

24. See also D. Quentin Miller, "Playing a Mean Guitar: The Legacy of Staggerlee in Baldwin and Morrison," in *James Baldwin and Toni Morrison: Comparative Critical and Theoretical Essays,* ed. Lovalerie King and Lynn Orilla Scott (New York: Palgrave MacMillan, 2006), 121–48.

25. Eckman, 218.

26. Peter Brooks and Paul Gewirtz, eds., *Law's Stories: Narrative and Rhetoric in the Law* (New Haven and London: Yale University Press, 1996), 8–9.

27. Brooks and Gewirtz, 9.

28. This exchange directly recalls an exchange between the state's coroner and the lawyer Boris Max in Wright's *Native Son* (1940, New York, Harper Perennial, 1991), 320–24.

29. For a discussion of Baldwin's critique of white liberals, see Rebecca Aanerud's essay "Now More than Ever: James Baldwin and the Critique of White Liberalism," in McBride, 56–74.

30. Brooks and Gewirtz, 96.

Chapter 3

1. Kimberlé Crenshaw et al., *Critical Race Theory: The Key Writings that Formed the Movement* (New York: The New Press, 1995), xiv, xvi.

2. Baldwin uses similar imagery to describe the South in the opening scene of *Another Country*: "[Rufus] remembered, suddenly, his days in boot camp in the South and felt again the shoe of a white officer against his mouth. He was in his white uniform, on the ground, against the *red, dusty clay*. Some of his colored buddies were holding him, were shouting in his ear, helping him to rise. The white officer, with a curse, had vanished, had gone forever beyond the reach of vengeance. His face was full of clay and tears and blood; he spat *red blood into the red dust*." (*AC* 12–13; emphasis mine).

3. Leeming, 211.

4. Crenshaw et al., xiii.

5. Suggs, 11.

6. Suggs, 11.

7. King and Scott, 206.

8. Derrick A. Bell, Jr., "Brown v. Board of Education and the Interest-Convergence Dilemma," *Harvard Law Review* 93 (1979–1980): 524.

9. Lawrie Balfour, *The Evidence of Things Not Said: James Baldwin and the Promise of American Democracy* (Ithaca and London: Cornell University Press, 2001), 125.

10. James Baldwin, "An Open Letter to My Sister, Angela Davis," *If They Come in the Morning: Voices of Resistance,* ed. Angela Davis (New York: The Third Press, 1971), 15.

11. Delaney, 181.

12. See also Lovalerie King, *Race, Theft, and Ethics: Property Matters in African American Literature* (Baton Rouge: Louisiana State University Press, 2007).

13. Karla Holloway, *Codes of Conduct* (New Brunswick, NJ: Rutgers University Press, 1995), 175–76.

14. See especially *Giovanni's Room*.

15. James Baldwin and Nikki Giovanni, *A Dialogue* (New York: Laurel, 1973), 30–31.

16. Kinnamon, 3.

17. Balfour, 131.

18. Deak Nabers, "Past Using: James Baldwin and Civil Rights Law in the 1960s," *The Yale Journal of Criticism* 18.2 (2005): 221.

19. Kieran Dolin, *A Critical Introduction to Law and Literature* (Cambridge: Cambridge University Press, 2007), 191.

20. Nabers, 227, 228.

21. Mary Dudziak, "*Brown* as a Cold War Case," *Journal of American History* 91.1 (June, 2004): 40.

22. Standley and Pratt, 41.

23. Leeming, 136.

24. Standley and Burt, 154.

Chapter 4

1. James Baldwin, interview by John Hall, *Transition* 41 (1972): 22–23.

2. Interview with Hall, 24.

3. James Baldwin, interview by Francois Bondy, *Transition* 12 (1964): 13.

4. See also Campbell, 217–22.

5. G. Louis Heath, ed., *The Black Panther Leaders Speak* (Metuchen, NJ: The Scarecrow Press, Inc., 1976), 23.

6. Baldwin also wrote an open letter in defense of Stokely Carmichael, but he didn't manage to get it published. He did, however, read it in a public forum on February 23, 1968 (Campbell, 222).

7. For an analysis of Cleaver's attack on Baldwin, see William Spurlin's essay "Culture, Rhetoric, and Queer Identity" in McBride, 103–19.

8. In 1966, this was originally the eighth point of the platform, worded this way: "We believe that all black people should be released from the many jails and prisons because they have not received a fair and impartial trial." Philip S. Foner, ed., *The Black Panthers Speak* (New York: Da Capo, 1995), 3.

9. Komanduri S. Murty, Angela M. Owens, and Ashwin G. Vyas, *Voices from Prison: An Ethnographic Study of Black Male Prisoners* (Dallas: University Press of America, 2004), 15.

10. Davis, 14.

11. Standley and Burt, 155.

12. Campbell, 226.

13. Scott, 21.

14. Foucault, 202.

15. Foucault, 196.

16. This scene has an apparent biographical model in Orilla "Bill" Miller, the midwestern schoolteacher who helped greatly to broaden Baldwin's cultural horizons. W. J. Wetherby quotes Baldwin as saying of Miller, "It is certainly because of her . . . that I never really managed to hate white people. . . . Bill Miller was not at all like the cops who had already beaten me up, she was not like the landlords who called me nigger" (17). Baldwin's most sustained description of Bill Miller can be found in *The Devil Finds Work*, discussed in chapter 5.

17. Baldwin makes a similar point about coerced confessions in "A Report from Occupied Territory": "A crime, as we know, is solved with someone arrested and convicted. It is not indispensable, but it is useful, to have a confession. If one is carried back and forth from the precinct to the hospital long enough one is likely to confess to anything" (*PT* 422). He echoes and develops this idea in *The Evidence of Things Not Seen*.

18. Scott, 38, 59.

19. Prison farms, still occasionally in use today, were common in the southern states

beginning in the mid-nineteenth century. Their method of punishment/rehabilitation involves hard agricultural labor. The landmark case *Gates v. Collier* (1972) scrutinized the infamous Parchman Farm and ruled that its practices constituted cruel and unusual punishment. This case is considered one of the foundational pieces of civil rights legislation.

20. Franklin, 247.

21. Scott also notes that this episode "reads like a neoslave narrative, an iconography of American black male subjugation" (Scott, 59).

22. Franklin, 246.

23. Due to a legal dispute, Baldwin is not acknowledged in the film's credits, and Perl is listed as the screenwriter.

24. Spike Lee updates this imagery at the beginning of his film *Malcolm X* by using actual footage of the infamous police beating of Rodney King that sparked riots in Los Angeles in 1991.

25. Campbell, 234.

26. Zaborowska, 154.

27. Zaborowska, 175.

28. Zaborowska, 178.

29. Zaborowska, 188–89, 179–80.

30. Campbell, 236, 241.

31. I have withheld the name of Baldwin's lover to protect his privacy.

32. Unpublished; David Leeming has given me access to Baldwin's files, including the rough notes for *Upon My Soul*.

33. Standley and Burt, 287.

34. Zaborowska, 239.

35. Maynard's case was eventually dismissed after years of legal wrangling.

36. Bell Gale Chevigny, ed. *Doing Time: 25 Years of Prison Writing* (New York: Arcade Publishing, 1999) 25.

37. Standley and Burt, 96.

Chapter 5

1. Kairys, 6.

2. In Baldwin's illustrated children's book, *Little Man, Little Man* (co-authored with Yoran Cazac), his main character TJ also sees his own experience mediated through the cops-and-robbers dramas he has seen on television or in the movies; he describes his street this way: "This street long. It real long. It a little like the street in the movies or the TV when the cop cars come from that end of the street and then they come from the other end of the street and the man they come to get he in one of the houses or he on the fire-escape or he on the roof and he see they come for him and he see the cop cars at that end and he see the cop cars at the other end. And then he don't know what to do. He can't go nowhere. And he sweating" (15). This passage, which continues for another page, uses police representations on screen as a vehicle for describing TJ's neighborhood, but the anxiety of the persecuted criminal and the ubiquity of the police are telling.

3. Baldwin again tees off on black policemen in *The Evidence of Things Not Seen*: "Black policemen were another matter. We used to say, "If you *must* call a policeman"— for we hardly ever did—"for God's sake, try to make sure it's a *White* one." A Black

policeman could completely demolish you. He knew far more about you than a White policeman could and you were without defenses before this Black brother in uniform whose entire reason for breathing seemed to be his hope to offer proof that, though he was Black, he was not Black like you" (66). Here a sense of racial community is obliterated by the presence of the law or, rather, Black participation in the law's enforcement.

4. See also James Campbell, *Syncopations: Beats, New Yorkers, and Writers in the Dark* (Berkeley: University of California Press, 2008).

5. Sylvander, 83, 87.

6. Standley and Burt, 74, 159.

7. Leeming, 323.

8. Scott, 66–67.

9. Judith Scheffler, "Imprisoned Mothers and Sisters: Dealing with Loss through Writing and Solidarity," *Prose and Cons: Essays on Prison Literature in the United States,* ed., D. Quentin Miller (Jefferson, NC: McFarland, 2005), 116.

10. Standley and Burt, 160.

11. Jerry H. Bryant, *"Born in a Mighty Bad Land": The Violent Man in African American Folklore and Fiction* (Bloomington: Indiana University Press, 2003), 24.

12. As Oates says, Daniel's story stresses "that the most devastating weapon of the oppressor is that of psychological terror. Physical punishment, even death, may at times be preferable to an existence in which men are denied their manhood and any genuine prospects of controlling their own lives" (Standley and Burt, 160).

13. Michelle H. Phillips, "Revising Revision: Methodologies of Love, Desire, and Resistance in *Beloved* and *If Beale Street Could Talk*," in King and Scott, 63–81, 77.

14. Leeming, 324.

15. Standley and Burt, 90.

16. Scott, 88.

17. James Baldwin, "A Letter to Prisoners," *Inside/Out,* 3.1 (Summer 1982): 1.

18. Standley and Pratt, 191.

19. Porter, 160.

20. Eric Gary Anderson, "Black Atlanta: An Ecosocial Approach to Narratives of the Atlanta Child Murders," *PMLA* 122.1 (January 2007): 194.

21. Anderson, 206.

22. Richard Schur, "Unseen or Unspeakable? Racial Evidence in Baldwin's and Morrison's Nonfiction," in *James Baldwin and Toni Morrison: Comparative Critical and Theoretical Essays,* ed. Lovalerie King and Lynn Orilla Scott (New York: Palgrave MacMillan, 2006), 206.

23. Schur, 207.

24. Schur describes Baldwin's courtroom rhetoric as "a move that might appear strange—given his literary, not legal background," but argues that his "detailed evaluation of the court's decisions about evidence . . . form a necessary part of his kaleidoscopic critique of legal discourse that judicial assumptions and experience taint law's objectivity and infuse it with the subjective experience of white people" (Schur, 210).

25. Schur, 209.

26. Baldwin had used almost exactly the same language in "Stranger in the Village" three decades earlier: "any American Negro wishing to go back so far will find his journey through time abruptly arrested by the signature on the bill of sale which served as the entrance paper for his ancestor" (*NNS* 169).

Conclusion

1. W. E. B. Du Bois, *Writings*, ed. Nathan Huggins (New York: Library of America, 1986), 1071.

2. Du Bois, 1075, 1076.

3. Krissah Thompson, "Scholar Says Arrest Will Lead Him to Explore Race in Criminal Justice," *The Washington Post*, July 22, 2009.

4. Colm Tóibín, "James Baldwin and Barack Obama," *The New York Review of Books* 55, no. 16 (23 October 2008): 38–41.

5. Standley and Pratt, 41.

6. H. Bruce Franklin, "Can the Penitentiary Teach the Academy How To Read?" *PMLA* 123.3 (May 2008): 643.

7. Davis, 14.

WORKS CITED

Aanerud, Rebecca. "Now More than Ever: James Baldwin and the Critique of White Liberalism." In *James Baldwin Now*, edited by Dwight McBride. New York: New York University Press, 1999, 56–74.

Als, Hilton. "The Enemy Within." *The New Yorker.* 16 February 1998, 72–80.

Anderson, Eric Gary. "Black Atlanta: An Ecosocial Approach to Narratives of the Atlanta Child Murders." *PMLA* 122.1 (January 2007): 194–209.

Arthur, John and William H. Shaw, eds. *Readings in the Philosophy of Law.* 2nd ed. Upper Saddle River, NJ: Prentice Hall, 2001.

Baldwin, James. *Another Country.* 1962. New York: Vintage, 1993.

———. *The Amen Corner.* New York: Laurel, 1968.

———. *Blues for Mister Charlie.* 1964. New York: Vintage, 1995.

———. *The Cross of Redemption: Uncollected Writings.* Edited by Randall Kenan. New York: Pantheon, 2010.

———. *The Devil Finds Work.* New York: Laurel, 1976.

———. *The Evidence of Things Not Seen.* 1985. New York: Henry Holt, 1995.

———. *The Fire Next Time.* 1963. New York: Vintage, 1993.

———. *Giovanni's Room.* New York: Laurel, 1956.

———. *Going to Meet the Man.* 1965. New York: Vintage, 1995.

———. *Go Tell It on the Mountain.* New York: Laurel, 1953.

———. *If Beale Street Could Talk.* New York: Laurel, 1974.

———. *Jimmy's Blues.* New York: St. Martin's 1985.

———. *Just Above My Head.* New York: Laurel, 1979.

———. "A Letter to Prisoners." In *Inside/Out,* 3.1 (Summer 1982).

———. *Little Man, Little Man.* New York: Dial, 1976.

———. *Nobody Knows My Name: More Notes of a Native Son.* New York: Laurel, 1961.

———. *No Name in the Street.* New York: Laurel, 1972.

———. *Notes of a Native Son.* 1955. Boston: Beacon Press, 1984.

———. *Nothing Personal* (photographs by Richard Avedon). New York: Atheneum, 1964.

———. *One Day When I Was Lost.* 1972. New York: Vintage, 2007.

———."An Open Letter to My Sister, Angela Davis." In *If They Come in the Morning: Voices of Resistance,* edited by Angela Davis. New York: The Third Press, 1971.

———. *The Price of the Ticket: Collected Nonfiction 1948–1985.* New York: St. Martin's, 1985.

———. *Tell Me How Long the Train's Been Gone.* 1968. New York: Vintage, 1998.

Baldwin, James, and Nikki Giovanni. *A Dialogue.* New York: Laurel, 1973.

Baldwin, James, and Margaret Mead. *A Rap on Race.* Philadelphia: Lippincott, 1971.

Baldwin, James, and Sol Stein. *Native Sons.* New York: One World / Ballantine, 2005.

Balfour, Lawrie. *The Evidence of Things Not Said: James Baldwin and the Promise of American Democracy.* Ithaca and London: Cornell University Press, 2001.

Bell, Derrick A., Jr. "Brown v. Board of Education and the Interest-Convergence Dilemma." *Harvard Law Review* 93 (1979–1980): 518–33.

Bigsby, C. W. E. "The Divided Mind of James Baldwin." In *Critical Essays on James Baldwin,* eds. Fred L. Standley and Nancy V. Burt. Boston: G. K. Hall and Co., 1988. 94–111.

Bondy, François. "James Baldwin, as Interviewed by Francois Bondy." *Transition* 12 (1964): 12–19.

Bone, Robert A. *The Negro Novel in America.* New Haven: Yale University Press, 1965.

Boyd, Herb. *Baldwin's Harlem: A Biography of James Baldwin.* New York: Atria, 2008.

Boyle, James, ed. *Critical Legal Studies.* New York: New York University Press, 1992.

Brooks, Peter, and Paul Gewirtz, eds. *Law's Stories: Narrative and Rhetoric in the Law.* New Haven and London: Yale University Press, 1996.

Bryant, Jerry H. *"Born in a Mighty Bad Land": The Violent Man in African American Folklore and Fiction.* Bloomington: Indiana University Press, 2003.

Campbell, James. *Syncopations: Beats, New Yorkers, and Writers in the Dark.* Berkeley: University of California Press, 2008

———. *Talking at the Gates.* New York: Viking, 1991.

Caster, Peter. *Prisons, Race, and Masculinity in Twentieth-Century U.S. Literature and Film.* Columbus: The Ohio State University Press, 2008.

Chevigny, Bell Gale, ed. *Doing Time: 25 Years of Prison Writing.* New York: Arcade Publishing, 1999.

Clark, Kenneth B. *King, Malcolm, Baldwin: Three Interviews* (Middletown, CT: Wesleyan University Press, 1985.

Cover, Robert M. "Nomos and Narrative." *Harvard Law Review* 97.1 (Nov. 1983): 4–68.

Crane, Gregg D. *Race, Citizenship, and Law in American Literature.* Cambridge: Cambridge University Press, 2002.

Crenshaw, Kimberlé, et al., eds. *Critical Race Theory: The Key Writings that Formed the Movement.* New York: The New Press, 1995.

Delaney, David. *Race, Place, and the Law.* Austin: University of Texas Press, 1998.

Dolin, Kieran. *A Critical Introduction to Law and Literature.* Cambridge: Cambridge University Press, 2007.

Du Bois, W. E. B. *Writings.* Edited by Nathan Huggins. New York: Library of America, 1986.

Dudziak, Mary. "*Brown* as a Cold War Case." *Journal of American History* 91.1 (June 2004): 32–42.

Eckman, Fern Marja. *The Furious Passage of James Baldwin.* London: Michael Joseph, 1966.

Ferguson, Robert A. "Untold Stories in the Law." In *Law's Stories,* edited by Peter Brooks and Paul Gewirtz. New Haven and London: Yale University Press, 1996, 84–98.

Field, Douglas, ed. *A Historical Guide to James Baldwin.* New York: Oxford University Press, 2009.

Foner, Philip S., ed. *The Black Panthers Speak.* 1970. New York: Da Capo, 1995.

Foucault, Michel. *Discipline and Punish.* 1977. Translated by Alan Sheridan. New York: Vintage, 1995.

Franklin, H. Bruce. "Can the Penitentiary Teach the Academy How To Read?" *PMLA* 123.3 (May 2008): 643–50.

———, ed. *The Victim as Criminal and Artist.* New York: Oxford University Press, 1978.

Gabel, Peter, and Paul Harris. "Building Power and Breaking Images: Critical Legal Theory and the Practice of Law." *Review of Law and Social Change* 11 (1982–1983): 369–411.

Gates, Henry Louis, Jr. *Loose Canons: Notes on the Culture Wars.* New York: Oxford University Press, 1992.

Gordon, Robert W. "Critical Legal Studies." In *Readings in the Philosophy of Law.* 2nd ed., edited by John Arthur and William H. Shaw. Upper Saddle River, NJ: Prentice Hall, 2001, 196–205.

Gross, Ariela J. *What Blood Won't Tell: A History of Race in America.* Cambridge, MA and London: Harvard University Press, 2008.

Hall, John. "James Baldwin: A Transition Interview." *Transition* 41 (1972): 20–24.

Hames-Garcia, Michael. *Fugitive Thought: Prison Movements, Race, and the Meaning of Justice.* Minneapolis and London: University of Minnesota Press, 2004.

Haney-López, Ian. *White by Law: The Legal Construction of Race.* New York and London: New York University Press, 1996.

Harris, Trudier. *Black Women in the Fiction of James Baldwin.* Knoxville: University of Tennessee Press, 1985.

———. *New Essays on* Go Tell It on the Mountain. New York: Cambridge University Press, 1999.

Heath, G. Louis, ed. *The Black Panther Leaders Speak.* Metuchen, NJ: The Scarecrow Press, Inc., 1976.

Holloway, Karla. *Codes of Conduct.* New Brunswick, NJ: Rutgers University Press, 1995.

James, Joy. *The New Abolitionists: (Neo) Slave Narratives and Contemporary Prison Writings.* Albany: State University of New York Press, 2005.

Kairys, David, ed. *The Politics of Law: A Progressive Critique.* Rev. ed. New York: Pantheon, 1990.

Kent, George E. "Baldwin and the Problem of Being." In *James Baldwin: A Collection of Critical Essays,* edited by Kenneth Kinnamon. Englewood Cliffs, NJ: Prentice-Hall, 1974, 16–27.

King, Lovalerie. *Race, Theft, and Ethics: Property Matters in African American Literature.* Baton Rouge: Louisiana State University Press, 2007.

King, Lovalerie, and Lynn Orilla Scott, eds. *James Baldwin and Toni Morrison: Comparative Critical and Theoretical Essays.* New York: Palgrave Macmillan, 2006.

King, Martin Luther. *Why We Can't Wait.* New York: Signet, 1963.

Kinnamon, Keneth. *James Baldwin: A Collection of Critical Essays.* Englewood Cliffs, NJ: Prentice-Hall, 1974.

Leeming, David. *James Baldwin.* New York: Knopf, 1994.

Malcolmson, Scott. *One Drop of Blood.* New York: Farrar, Strauss, Giroux, 2000.

McBride, Dwight, ed. *James Baldwin Now.* New York: New York University Press, 1999.

Meeks, Kenneth. *Driving While Black.* New York: Broadway Books, 2000.

Miller, D. Quentin. "Playing a Mean Guitar: The Legacy of Staggerlee in Baldwin and Morrison." In *James Baldwin and Toni Morrison: Comparative Critical and Theoretical Essays,* edited by Lovalerie King and Lynn Orilla Scott. New York: Palgrave MacMillan, 2006, 121–48.

———, ed. *Prose and Cons: Essays on Prison Literature in the United States.* Jefferson, NC: McFarland, 2005

———, ed. *Re-Viewing James Baldwin: Things Not Seen.* Philadelphia: Temple University Press, 2000.

Murty, Komanduri S., Angela M. Owens, and Ashwin G. Vyas. *Voices from Prison: An Ethnographic Study of Black Male Prisoners.* Dallas: University Press of America, 2004.

Nabers, Deak. "Past Using: James Baldwin and Civil Rights Law in the 1960s." *The Yale Journal of Criticism* 18.2 (2005): 221–42.

Nelson, Emmanuel. "Critical Deviance: Homophobia and the Reception of James Baldwin's Fiction." *Journal of American Culture* 14, no. 3 (1991): 91–96.

Oates, Joyce Carol. "A Quite Moving and Very Traditional Celebration of Love." In *Critical Essays on James Baldwin,* edited by Fred L. Standley and Nancy V. Burt. Boston: G. K. Hall and Co., 1988, 158–61.

Peck, James. *Freedom Ride.* New York: Simon and Schuster, 1962.

Phillips, Michelle H. "Revising Revision: Methodologies of Love, Desire, and Resistance in *Beloved* and *If Beale Street Could Talk.*" In *James Baldwin and Toni Morrison: Comparative Critical and Theoretical Essays,* edited by Lovalerie King and Lynn Orilla Scott. New York: Palgrave Macmillan, 2006, 63–82.

Porter, Horace. *Stealing the Fire: The Art and Protest of James Baldwin.* Middletown, CT: Wesleyan University Press, 1989.

Posner, Richard A., ed. *Law and Literature.* Rev. and enlarged ed. Cambridge, MA and London: Harvard University Press, 1988.

Schaller, Barry R. *A Vision of American Law.* Westport, CT: Praeger, 1997.

Scheffler, Judith. "Imprisoned Mothers and Sisters: Dealing with Loss through Writing and Solidarity." In *Prose and Cons: Essays on Prison Literature in the United States,* edited by D. Quentin Miller. Jefferson, NC: McFarland, 2005, 111–28.

Schur, Richard. "Unseen or Unspeakable? Racial Evidence in Baldwin's and Morrison's Nonfiction." In *James Baldwin and Toni Morrison: Comparative Critical and Theoretical Essays,* edited by Lovalerie King and Lynn Orilla Scott. New York: Palgrave MacMillan, 2006, 205–22.

Scott, Lynn Orilla. *James Baldwin's Later Fiction: Witness to the Journey.* East Lansing: Michigan State University Press, 2002.

Spurlin, William. "Culture, Rhetoric, and Queer Identity." In *James Baldwin Now,* edited by Dwight McBride. New York: New York University Press, 1999, 103–21.

Standley, Fred L., and Nancy V. Burt. *Critical Essays on James Baldwin.* Boston: G. K. Hall and Co., 1988.

Standley, Fred L., and Louis H. Pratt. *Conversations with James Baldwin.* Jackson and London: University Press of Mississippi, 1989.

Suggs, Jon-Christian. *Whispered Consolations: Law and Narrative in African American Life.* Ann Arbor: University of Michigan Press, 2000.

Sylvander, Carolyn Wedin. *James Baldwin*. New York: Frederick Ungar, 1980.

Thompson, Krissah. "Scholar Says Arrest Will Lead Him to Explore Race in Criminal Justice." *The Washington Post*, 22 July 2009, sec. A.

Tóibín, Colm. "James Baldwin and Barack Obama." *The New York Review of Books* 55, no. 16 (23 October 2008): 38–41.

Weatherby, W. J. *James Baldwin: Artist on Fire*. New York: Donald I. Fine, 1989.

West, Cornel. "Foreword." In *Critical Race Theory: The Key Writings that Formed the Movement,* edited by Kimberle Crenshaw et. al. New York: The New Press, 1995.

———. *Race Matters*. Boston: Beacon Press, 1993.

Williams, Patricia J. *Alchemy of Race and Rights*. Cambridge, MA: Harvard University Press, 1992.

Wright, Richard. *Native Son*. 1940. New York: Harper Perennial, 1991.

X, Malcolm, and Alex Haley. *The Autobiography of Malcolm X*. 1964. New York: One World, 1999.

Zaborowska, Magdalena J. *James Baldwin's Turkish Decade: Erotics of Exile*. Durham and London: Duke University Press, 2009.

INDEX

CPSIA information can be obtained
at www.ICGtesting.com
Printed in the USA
BVHW030204190320
575384BV00001B/16